DATE DUE

NOV 27 1998	
MAR 1 5 2000	
JUN - 6 2001	
OCT 18 2001	
MAR 2 0 2002	
MAR 1 1 2003	
JAN 1 9 2005	
MAR 1 2 2007	

The Library Store   #47-0106

They Also Served

Military Biographies of Uncommon Americans

Scott Baron

MIE PUBLISHING

MIE Publishing
PO Box 17118
Spartanburg, SC 29301
(800) 937-2133
E-mail: MIEPUB@aol.com
http://www.militaryusa.com

Library of Congress Cataloging-in-Publication Data:

Baron, Scott
They also served: military biographies of uncommon Americans /Scott Baron,
    p. cm.
    Includes bibliographical references and index.
    ISBN 1-877639-37-0
    1. Military biography. 2. United States—Biography. I. Title.
U52.B37   1998
355'. 0092 ' 273—dc21   97-32343
                                                         CIP

DISCLAIMER:
Every effort has been made to make this book as accurate as possible. A variety of sources were used when researching information, including actual military records when available. Therefore, the information contained in this book should be used as an additional reference and not as a final source.

Dedication

This book is dedicated to my mother, Annebelle Baron, who always told me I could do anything,

and

...to my wife, Marisela Angel Baron, who believes I'm capable of anything...and lives in constant anticipation.

I'll love you both forever.

Acknowledgments

To paraphrase the current First Lady, it takes a village to write a book. The author, therefore, gratefully acknowledges the assistance, knowledge, expertise, support and patience of the following people, without whose help this book would not have been possible.

To the Boys (Eric, Heath, Mitchell and Anthony); Bill and Susan Bazlin, Bazlin Library, Soquel, CA; Storm and Beth Moody; good neighbors and computer wizards; Kevin Reem, Reemvision (the next Spielberg); Ward Garing, author and padrino; Don Eddy of Monterey Publishing for review and encouragement; Dave's Computers, Santa Cruz, CA; Morgan Fey, who always comes through; George Toy, historian and amigo supremo; John Maraldo, Master of the Law; Beverly Lyall, archivist, Nimitz Library, Annapolis; the reference librarians and staff at Watsonville Public Library; Eric Voelz, archivist, National Personnel Records Center; Jack A. Green, historian, Naval History Institute, Washington DC; Kelly Charef, Very Important Secretary; Lt. Col. Harry Cliff (USAF, Ret.), former WWII POW.

A special tip of the hat to my editor, Tom Ninkovich, who has taught me so much in so little time.

And especially, gratitude to my publishers Debra Knox and Lt. Col. Richard S. Johnson (USA, Ret.) of Military Information Enterprises whose encouragement, patience and expert advice has made this project both an education and a joy.

Foreword

The American soldier has never let his country down—and never will.

Scott Baron has made that case admirably. He has pointed out that the citizen soldier has always answered the call to arms where the situation demanded. Young men and women who never thought that they would man the ramparts of our nation rose to the occasion.

I speak from my experience in commanding young Americans in three wars. Thus, I know that those who answered their country's call and went to battle are justifiably proud.

—General William C. Westmoreland

Table of Contents

Section 1

Politics, Government, and the Law

The Presidents

Of the 41 men elected President to date, 24 have served in the military. Surprisingly, or maybe not so, all served during times the nation was at war. Of those 24, the first 17 served in the Army. Six of the seven most recent served in the Navy. No President has served in the Marines or Air Force.

Ten Presidents (Washington, Jackson, Wm. Henry Harrison, Taylor, Pierce, Grant, Hayes, Garfield, Benjamin Harrison, and Eisenhower) have been generals in the U.S. Army. None have been admirals. One, Andrew Johnson, was a general of volunteers in his state's militia. Seventeen Presidents have had no military service and are not listed here.

Several generals have run for President. The nominated but unsuccessful candidates include Winfield Scott, George McClellan, Benjamin Franklin Butler, John Charles Fremont, Winfield Scott Hancock, and Douglas MacArthur.

Five Presidents have served in more than one war. Andrew Jackson served in four (Revolutionary War, Creek War, War of 1812 and the Seminole War). W. H. Harrison served in three (Northwest Territory War, Shawnee Wars, and the War of 1812). Zachary Taylor served in four (War of 1812, Seminole War, Black Hawk War, and the War with Mexico), Ulysses S. Grant served in the Mexican War and the Civil War, and Dwight Eisenhower served in both World Wars.

Four Presidents (Monroe, Pierce, Hayes, and Kennedy) were wounded in action. Two Presidents (McKinley and Hayes) served together in the same regiment (23rd Ohio) during the Civil War.

Chester Arthur (1830–86), term of office: 1881–85

In 1861 Arthur was in charge of outfitting the New York State militia, then went on to serve as New York State's quartermaster general.

George H. Bush (1924–   ), term of office: 1989–93

Bush enlisted in the U.S. Navy on June 12, 1942, at the age of 18. He was commissioned an ensign and pilot and served aboard the USS *San Jacinto* flying Grumman Avenger bombers with the 3rd and 5th Fleets.

George H. Bush

On September 2, 1944, Bush was assigned to take out a radio station located in the Bonin Islands. In the course of the action, Bush's plane, *Barbara*, was hit with enemy fire, forcing him to splash down offshore from Chichi Jima, a Japanese-held island near the more well-known Iwo Jima. He floated in his inflatable raft, armed only with a .38 revolver. Bush, aware of the fate of airmen captured by the Japanese (often summary execution), was prepared to fight to the end. Luckily he was rescued by a submarine after only three hours. A genuine hero, Bush was awarded the Distinguished Flying Cross and three Air Medals. He was discharged in September 1945 with the rank of lieutenant (j.g.)

James Earl Carter (1924–   ), term of office: 1977–81

Carter entered the Naval Academy at age 19 in 1943 with the dream of eventually becoming Chief of Naval Operations. Upon his graduation three years later in 1946, he was commissioned an ensign and served as an officer of the line. He served as an electronics officer aboard battleships.

In 1948 he began submarine training, and in 1951 was assigned to help develop nuclear submarines under the direction of Admiral Rickover. Carter served as engineering officer on the USS *Seawolf* (SSN-575), the second nuclear submarine.

James Earl Carter

With the death of his father in 1953, Lt. Commander Carter resigned from the navy to take over the family business. Carter was the first and only Annapolis graduate to become President.

Grover Cleveland (1837–1908), terms of office: 1885–89 and 1893–97

With two brothers serving in the army, and being responsible for the support of his mother and two sisters, Cleveland avoided military service by paying a substitute $150 as permitted by the terms of the Conscription Act of 1863. It wasn't an issue in his first presidential contest, as his opponent also purchased a substitute.

Dwight Eisenhower (1890–1969), terms of office: 1953–61

Ike entered West Point in 1911 and graduated 61 in a class of 164 in 1915. As a second lieutenant, he was posted to Ft. Sam Houston, Texas, where he met, and later married, Mamie Geneva Doud. Because of his talent for administration, he served in staff rather than combat duties during WWI.

He graduated first in a class of 275 from the Command and General Staff School in 1926, and went on to the War College. He was promoted to colonel in March 1941, then brigadier general in September of the same year. Recognized by General Marshall, the Army Chief of Staff, he served as the Commanding General of American Forces in Europe, and then was appointed as Supreme Commander of Allied Forces in 1943.

He supervised the Normandy invasion of Europe in 1944, and was one of only eight officers ever promoted to five star rank (General of the Army/Admiral of the Fleet). Eisenhower served as Army Chief of Staff until 1948. He was president of Columbia University from 1948 until 1952 when he was elected President on the Republican ticket.

Gerald Ford (1913–   ), term of office: 1974–77

On April 20, 1942, at the age of 29, Ford enlisted in the U.S. Navy reserve as an ensign. At first Ford was in charge of physical training for new recruits but his request for combat was granted in June of 1943.

Ford was assigned as a gunnery officer on the USS *Monterey* (CVL-26), a light aircraft carrier in the Pacific. He remained until December 1944. Ford saw sufficient combat in central Pacific campaigns to earn 10 Battle Stars. He was discharged as a lieutenant commander in 1946 after 47 months of active service. He was noted by his superiors as a fine officer and a team player.

He was elected to Congress from Michigan in 1949 and served until being appointed Vice President by Nixon in 1973 upon the resignation of Spiro Agnew. When Nixon resigned in 1974 Ford became the only man to serve as President without being elected.

James Garfield (1831–81), term of office: 1881

At the beginning of the Civil War, Garfield enlisted in an Ohio regiment, the 42nd Volunteer Infantry, as its lieutenant colonel. He performed so well on the field, most notably at the Battle of Middle Creek on January 10, 1862, that within a year he was promoted to brigadier general of volunteers.

He was at Shiloh, and served as chief of staff to General Rosecrans and the Army of the Cumberland. He was promoted to major general of volunteers prior to resigning his commission to take the congressional seat of the 19th District of Ohio in December 1863. This was done at Lincoln's request. Lincoln stated that this was necessary because it was easier to get major generals than it was to find loyal Republican Congressmen.

Ulysses S. Grant (1822–85), terms of office: 1869–77

Upon graduation from West Point in 1843, "Sam" Grant was commissioned a second lieutenant, and served at a succession of frontier posts from Louisiana to Texas. During the Mexican War of 1848, he served as a regimental quartermaster and saw action alongside fellow officers Robert E. Lee and Jefferson Davis. By 1854 Captain Grant's drinking had become such a problem (a common experience for army officers serving in isolated frontier posts) that his resignation was requested in July of 1854. He experienced repeated failures as a civilian.

With the outbreak of the Civil War in 1861, Grant took over drilling a company of Galena, Illinois, volunteers. After serving briefly as a colonel with an Illinois regiment in Missouri, he was appointed a brigadier general by Lincoln in August of 1861.

He served with the Army of Tennessee, seeing action at Ft. Donnelson, Shiloh, Vicksburg, and ultimately assuming command of all Union forces as a newly promoted lieutenant general in 1864. He led federal troops to victory in the Civil War, and served as commanding general of the postwar army until his election as President in 1868.

Benjamin Harrison (1833–1901), term of office: 1889–93

In 1862 Harrison was commissioned a colonel of a regiment of Indiana volunteers serving with Sherman, mostly on garrison duty behind the lines. A strict disciplinarian who was little-loved by his troops, he finished the war as a brevet brigadier general.

William H. Harrison (1773–1841), term of office: 1841

Harrison enlisted in the army in 1791 as a second lieutenant. He served at Fort Washington and was present at the Battle of Fallen Timbers against the Shawnee Indians in 1794. He resigned from the army with a rank of captain in 1798.

He returned to the army in 1811 in command of 90 troops, again against the Shawnee. He made military history at the Battle of Tippicanoe.

As a major general in the War of 1812, he went on to rout the British at the Battle of Thames in Canada (1813). He resigned from the army in 1814.

Rutherford B. Hayes (1822–93), term of office: 1877–81

Hayes was appointed a major of infantry upon the outbreak of the Civil War in June of 1861, and was shortly thereafter promoted to lieutenant colonel in the 23rd Ohio under Colonel Rosecrans.

He saw action and was wounded in battle four times. He led a charge at the Battle of Winchester, and campaigned with Crook and Sheridan in the Shenandoah Valley. By 1864 he was a brigadier general, and at the end of the war in 1865 he had the rank of brevet major general. Although elected to Congress by the people of Ohio late in the war, Hayes remained in the army until Lee's surrender.

Andrew Jackson (1767–1845), terms of office: 1829–37

Jackson served with a mounted militia unit during the Revolutionary War. He began at age 13, and at 14 was captured at the Battle of Camden. He received a saber wound from a British officer for refusing to clean his boots, and was subsequently paroled to his mother's custody.

During the War of 1812 he commanded troops as a major general of volunteers on the frontier. His army was composed of local militia, French pirates, freed slaves, and Choctaw Indians. On April 19, 1814, he was commissioned a brigadier general in the U.S. Army. Promoted to major general on May 1, 1814, Jackson signed a treaty with the Creek Indians on August 9, and went on to capture Pensacola and Ft. Michael in Florida.

At the Battle of New Orleans on January 8, 1815, he successfully defended the city from the British even though he was outnumbered two to one. Unfortunately, a treaty had already been signed and the war was over, although word did not reach New Orleans in time. This did not however affect his popularity. He received the thanks of Congress and a Gold Medal by resolution.

In 1817–18 Jackson led troops against the Seminole Indians in Florida on a punitive expedition and (contrary to instructions) captured several Spanish forts.

Andrew Johnson (1808–75), term of office: 1865–69

Johnson served as military governor of Tennessee from May 4, 1862, until March 3, 1865, with the rank of brigadier general. He was appointed by President Lincoln and served until assuming the vice presidency March 4, 1865.

Lyndon Baines Johnson (1908–73), terms of office: 1963–69

In the spring of 1940 Congressman Johnson of Texas promised that if he voted to send American men to fight in a foreign war, he would resign and join them. On December 7th, he requested and received unanimous approval for a leave of absence from Congress to go active. He was the first member of Congress to do so. His reserve navy commission as a lieutenant commander was activated on December 9, and he began a tour of naval shipyards to report back to the President.

In mid-1942 Johnson, convinced he needed combat experience for political reasons, was assigned to meet with General
MacArthur in Australia on a fact-finding mission. Against orders designed to keep him safe, Johnson insisted on accompanying a bomber mission over enemy territory. The mission was
delayed by Johnson's late arrival, and delayed again when the
Congressman had to relieve himself. This saved his life! He was
bumped from his seat on the bomber *Wabash Cannonball* and
reassigned to the bomber *Heckling Hare*.

On the subsequent mission, the *Wabash Cannonball* was shot
down and the whole crew was lost. The *Heckling Hare* was dis-
abled by enemy fire and barely returned. It was for this action
and Johnson's "coolness under fire" that he was awarded a Silver Star. After a Presidential directive ordering all serving members of Congress to return home or resign their seats, Johnson
returned in July of 1942.

Of the seven members of Congress affected by this order,
four chose to resign and remain on active duty. Johnson kept his
promise to go with "the boys"; he never promised to remain with
them. He was elected to the Senate in 1949 and was Vice President in the Kennedy administration.

John Fitzgerald Kennedy (1917–63), term of office: 1961–63

In the summer of 1940 Kennedy was studying business administration at Stanford University in California. He left school
and was visiting South America when the U.S. instituted a military draft late in 1940. Foreseeing that war was coming, Kennedy
first tried enlisting in the army, then the navy. He was rejected
because of a back injury sustained playing football. He began an
accelerated fitness program, and in September 1941 was accepted
into the navy.

Initially Kennedy was given a direct commission as an ensign and was assigned to the Office of Naval Intelligence (ONI).
He served at a desk in Washington DC but wanted a combat
assignment. He volunteered for PT (Patrol Torpedo) boat duty in

October 1942, and was sent to the Motor Torpedo Boat Training School at Melville, Rhode Island, where he trained to command a PT boat.

Kennedy saw the PT boats as a modern-day cavalry. In 1943 Kennedy, now a lieutenant (j.g.) in charge of *PT-109*, was sent to the South Pacific. His boat was rammed and sunk by the Japanese destroyer *Amagari* while on patrol in the Solomon Islands on August 2, 1943.

His heroism in saving an injured crewman, and leading his 10-man crew to safety after 15 hours in the water, resulted in being awarded the Navy Medal and a Purple Heart. Kennedy was the first President to serve in the navy.

When asked by a schoolboy in 1959, "How did you become a war hero?" he replied, "It was easy, they sunk my boat."

Abraham Lincoln (1809–65), term of office: 1861–65

Lincoln served three months as the elected captain of a company of militia in northwestern Illinois during the Black Hawk War of 1832. In Lincoln's own words, he "drew no blood other than mosquitoes."

Lincoln was President and commander in chief of federal forces during the Civil War, and actively participated in determining strategy and tactics while searching for a general in chief.

James Madison (1751–1836), terms of office: 1809–17

Although Madison never served in the military, he was the only President to actively command troops. During the War of 1812 he commanded Barney's Battery, a unit assembled to keep British troops out of the Capital. He was also the only President to come directly under enemy fire while serving as President.

William McKinley (1843–1901), term of office: 1897–1901

McKinley was the last Civil War veteran to become President. He enlisted as a private in an Ohio regiment, served as a commissary sergeant at the Battle of Antietam, and ended the war with the rank of major.

James Monroe (1758–1831), terms of office: 1817–25

Monroe was commissioned a second lieutenant in the Third Virginia Regiment on September 28, 1775. He was wounded at Harlem Heights, White Plains and again at Trenton in December 1776. After being promoted to captain by Washington for "bravery under fire," Monroe fought on at Brandywine, Germantown, and Monmouth.

In 1780 he was promoted to lieutenant colonel by the Governor of Virginia, Thomas Jefferson. He was 22 years old. He held that rank until he resigned to be elected to the Virginia legislature.

Richard M. Nixon (1913–95), terms of office: 1969–74

In 1942 Nixon entered the U.S. Navy at the age of 29 and was commissioned a lieutenant (j.g.). He served as executive officer at a naval air station in Iowa until his transfer to the South Pacific in late 1942.

Assigned to the Air Transport Command, Nixon supervised the loading and unloading of cargo on New Caledonia, and saw combat when his area was bombed by the Japanese 28 times the first month alone. He was well-liked by his men and was a proficient poker player, amassing a $10,000 nestegg by the end of his tour.

He returned stateside in July 1944, and was a lieutenant commander by the time of his discharge in January of 1946.

Franklin Pierce (1804–69), term of office: 1853–57

Pierce enlisted as a private in the Mexican War of 1846, but was subsequently appointed a brigadier general by his friend, President Polk. He led his brigade at Contreros and Churubusco under General Winfield Scott during the advance on Mexico City.

Ronald W. Reagan (1911–), terms of office: 1981–89

Already a popular star in the movies, Reagan was kept from combat in WWII because of poor eyesight. He spent the war assigned to the Army Air Corp's 1st Motion Picture Unit narrating training films in Culver City, California. He also found time to act in the movies, such as Irving Berlin's *This Is the Army* in 1943. He was the officer who signed Major Clark Gable's honorable discharge in June 1944. Reagan was discharged as a captain in December of 1945.

Franklin D. Roosevelt (1882–1945), terms of office: 1933–45

As a boy, Roosevelt hoped for an appointment to Annapolis and a naval career. In April 1898, while a student at Groton, Roosevelt planned to sneak off to Boston with two friends and enlist in the navy during the Spanish-American War, but they all contracted scarlet fever and their plan was never realized.

The only four-term President, Roosevelt served as Commander in Chief during WWII, but the closest he came to military service was a term as Assistant Secretary of the Navy from 1913–20. (FDR wanted to resign and seek a naval commission, but Secretary of the Navy Josephus Daniels felt he was more valuable as his assistant and refused to accept his resignation.)

Theodore Roosevelt (1858–1919), terms of office: 1901–09

Upon the outbreak of the Spanish-American War, Roosevelt resigned as Assistant Secretary of the Navy to help form the 1st Volunteer Cavalry Regiment (the Rough Riders) in 1898. As the regiment's lieutenant colonel, he led his men (cowboys, college men and the sons of the famous) on foot to charge Kettle Hill in Cuba (the horses were late in arriving).

Roosevelt returned a hero and was elected Governor of New York. He was recommended for the Medal of Honor for his action in Cuba but it was never awarded.

Zachary Taylor (1784–1850), term of office: 1849–50

After a short stint as an enlisted man in the Kentucky militia, Taylor entered the army in 1808 as a first lieutenant. He was a major by the War of 1812, and a colonel by the Black Hawk War in 1832. He campaigned in the Second Seminole War of 1836–37 as a brigadier general.

During the War with Mexico (1846), Taylor served as a general at Palo Alto. Known by his troops as "Old Rough and Ready," he became a national hero at the Battle of Buena Vista in 1847 and that fame would propel him into the presidency.

Harry S. Truman (1884–1972), terms of office: 1945–53

On June 14, 1905, a nineteen-year-old Truman enlisted in the Missouri National Guard as a private. He was assigned to Battery B, Field Artillery. He reenlisted in 1908 and was discharged as a corporal at the end of his second three-year hitch on June 13, 1911.

Harry S. Truman

On June 17, 1917, at the age of 33, Truman was appointed a first lieutenant in Battery F, Field Artillery, Missouri National Guard. On August 5 his unit was federalized for service in the First World War, and redesignated as Battery F, 129th Field Artillery.

Lt. Truman was sent overseas aboard the SS *George Washington* on March 30, 1918, for service in France. He was promoted to captain in April, and attended artillery school at 2nd Corps School at Chatillon sur Seine from April 27 to June 5.

He rejoined the 129th while it was attached to the 35th Division in the Gerardmer Sector, and served as part of the reserve of the First Army during the St. Mihiel Offensive from September 12–16, and the Meuse-Argonne Offensive from September 26 until the armistice in November.

Truman returned to the U.S. on April 20, 1919, and was given an honorable discharge at Camp Funston, Kansas, on May 6, 1919. He was appointed a major in the Field Artillery Reserve Corps on January 10, 1920, and was reappointed in 1925. He was promoted to lieutenant colonel in May 1925, and colonel on June 17, 1932. He served in the active reserves until 1949, attending annual training. He was transferred to the Honorary Reserve on November 5, 1951, and officially retired on January 20, 1953, as a colonel at the age of 69.

George Washington (1732–99), terms of office: 1789–97

In 1753 Washington was commissioned a major in the Virginia militia, and went on to serve as a member of the British Expedition against the French at Fort Duquesne (Pittsburgh) under British General Edward Braddock in 1755. He also helped organize the retreat therefrom!

He was appointed colonel of a regiment of Virginia militia, and commander in chief of Virginia forces protecting the frontier against the French and Indians in August 1755. He resigned in December 1758, after being elected to the House of Burgesses from Frederick County.

Washington was appointed commander in chief of the Continental army on June 15, 1775, and assumed command on July 3rd. He led the country to victory before returning to private life in December 1783. In July of 1798 he was briefly appointed lieutenant general and Commander in Chief of the United States Army during the Adams administration.

Politics and Government

Spiro T. Agnew. Vice President of the United States.

Born in Baltimore, Maryland, on November 19, 1919, Agnew enlisted in the U.S. Army as a private on September 24, 1941. He served as an enlisted man until May 22, 1942, when upon completing officer's training he was discharged as a corporal and commissioned as a first lieutenant on May 23, 1942. Agnew served as a company commander with the 10th Armored Division (the "Tiger" Division) during WWII. The division, whose battle cry was "To terrify and destroy as they claw and maul their way through all of their enemies," first saw combat in November 1944 as part of General Patton's Third Army. The division was rushed to Luxembourg at the start of the Battle of the Bulge. The unit slowed the German advance sufficiently for the 101st Airborne to reach and secure Bastogne. The unit continued to fight across Germany, capturing numerous cities, ending the war near Innsbruck, Austria.

Agnew saw combat in France and Germany, and was discharged on February 14, 1946, with a Bronze Star. He was recalled to active duty during the Korean War on October 11, 1950, and served until his discharge as a first lieutenant on May 14, 1951.

Agnew served as Vice President under Richard Nixon, and resigned after pleading no contest to federal income tax violations on November 10, 1973.

Joel Barlow. American poet and politician.

Born in Redding, Connecticut, on March 24, 1754, Barlow served as a military chaplain during the American Revolutionary War. He later served as U.S. Ambassador to France. He is best remembered for writing *The Columbiad* in 1807.

Thomas Hale Boggs. Congressman, majority leader.

Born in Louisiana on February 15, 1914, Boggs was serving in Congress when he was defeated for re-election in 1942. He enlisted in the navy reserve and was commissioned an officer. He served stateside with the Potomoc River Naval Command and the U.S. Maritime Service.

After his discharge in 1946, Boggs was re-elected to Congress in 1947, where he remained until his death in a plane crash in Alaska in 1972.

John Cabell Breckinridge. U.S. Senator, Vice President.

Born in Lexington, Kentucky, on January 21, 1821, Breckinridge served as a major with the Third Kentucky Volunteers during the Mexican War (1847–48).

After serving as Vice President under Buchanan (1857–61), and unsuccessfully running for President, Breckinridge was expelled from the U.S. Senate at the start of the Civil War.

Breckinridge was appointed a brigadier general (1861) and then major general (1862) of Confederate forces. He served at Vicksburg, Shiloh, Murfreesboro, and Jackson before resigning to take the position of Confederate Secretary of War, which he held to the end of the war.

Maurice Britt. Longtime Lt. Governor of Arkansas, professional football player.

Born in 1919, Britt, a professional ballplayer for the Detroit Lions before the war, was drafted into the army at the start of WWII.

He was sent to Italy as a second lieutenant of infantry, and on November 20, 1943, was outside Mignano, Italy, in the midst of a German offensive. During the battle, Britt went forward alone and engaged the enemy with rifle fire and hand grenades. He continued to press the attack, although he was wounded several times. In the course of his actions, he threw 32 grenades, fired numerous discarded weapons after he ran out of ammunition for his own weapon, and liberated captured Americans. He is credited for single-handedly breaking the offensive for which he was awarded the Medal of Honor.

A subsequent wound resulting in the loss of his arm ended both his military and football career. As a result, Britt went to law school on the GI Bill after the war and entered politics. He served several terms as lieutenant governor of Arkansas. He was the first soldier in WWII to be awarded the three highest decorations (the Silver Star in September 1943, the Medal of Honor in November 1943, and the Distinguished Service Cross in January 1944).

William Jennings Bryan. Political orator, three-time candidate for President.

Born in Salem, Illinois, on March 18, 1860, Bryan raised the 3rd Regiment of Nebraska Volunteer Infantry for service during the Spanish-American War in May 1898. He was commissioned as its colonel and commanding officer by the Governor. The unit was never sent overseas, and Bryan resigned when the treaty with Spain was signed. He served five months.

Prior to WWI, Bryan served as Secretary of State (1913–15) under President Wilson but resigned after the sinking of the *Lusitania* because Wilson's response was in conflict with his pacifist beliefs.

Bryan ran unsuccessfully as the Democratic party's candidate for President in 1896 against McKinley, again in 1900 against McKinley-Roosevelt, and in 1908 against Taft. Bryan is most remembered for his courtroom battle against Clarence Darrow on the issue of evolution during the "Scopes Monkey Trial" in 1925. He died in Dayton, Tennessee, on July 26, 1925.

Aaron Burr. U.S. Senator, Vice President of the United States.

Born to a distinguished family in Newark, New Jersey, on February 6, 1756, Burr graduated in 1772 from the College of New Jersey (later Princeton) where both his father and grandfather had served as president.

He enlisted in the Continental army at the start of the American Revolution. He served under Colonel Benedict Arnold at Quebec, and was rewarded with a promotion to captain after he successfully carried a message to General Montgomery through enemy lines.

After serving as an aide to General Putnam, and briefly for General Washington, he took part in the fighting around Long Island and New York (1778–79). He resigned from the army on March 10, 1779, with the rank of colonel. He resigned due to ill health, but he also may have been frustrated because his poor relations with Washington may have kept him from being promoted to general.

Burr tied Jefferson in the election for the presidency in 1801 through the first 35 ballots, but was defeated on the 36th ballot largely through the efforts of Alexander Hamilton. He served as Vice President from 1801–05, but his famous duel with Hamilton on July 11, 1804, resulted in the death of Hamilton, and Burr's political career. He was tried and acquitted for treason in 1807 for his support of General James Wilkinson's plan to seize territory from Spain to form a new republic. He died on September 14, 1836.

Frank Church. U.S. Senator, presidential candidate.

Frank Forrester Church was born in Boise, Idaho, on July 25, 1924. He was a grandson of pioneers who settled Idaho after the Civil War. After graduating high school with honors in 1941, he won a scholarship to Stanford, but withdrew during his first semester to join the U.S. Army.

Private Church was accepted for officer's training in 1944, and was commissioned a second lieutenant of infantry. He served with military intelligence in Asia until the end of the war.

Discharged from the army, he returned to Stanford, earned his LLB degree, and was elected to the U.S. Senate from Idaho in 1956, at the age of 32. He would go on to become a leader of the anti-war element in Congress during the Vietnam War. He was a Democratic candidate for President in 1976 and was instrumental in passing the Panama Canal Treaty in 1978. He died on April 7, 1984, in Bethesda, Maryland.

William Colby. Director of the Central Intelligence Agency.

Born William Egan Colby on January 4, 1920, in St. Paul, Minnesota, Colby was the only child of a career army officer. He grew up at a series of army posts, and graduated Phi Beta Kappa from Princeton University in 1940.

Colby enrolled in Columbia law school, but left in 1942 to enlist in the U.S. Army. Despite poor eyesight, he was commissioned a staff lieutenant with the 462nd Parachute Artillery Battalion.

Answering a call for French speaking officers, Colby volunteered for the Office of Strategic Services, the wartime intelligence agency. He parachuted into occupied France in August 1944 and coordinated a resistance unit. In 1945 he commanded an American paratroop unit in Norway, disrupting German rail operations. After the war, Colby was discharged with the rank of major, and earned a Silver Star and the French Croix de Guerre.

After his discharge, he completed law school and went to work in the law firm of his former OSS commander, Bill Donovan. With the start of the Korean War, Colby followed Donovan into the CIA. He later served as its director from September of 1973 until early 1976 when he was replaced by George Bush.

John Connally. Lawyer, Governor of Texas.

Born in Floesville, Texas, on February 27, 1917, Connally was already an officer in the navy reserve at the start of WWII. He officially resigned from Congressman Lyndon Johnson's staff in March 1941 and went on active duty. As a new ensign, he was assigned as a legal assistant in Under Secretary of the Navy James Forrestal's office.

He wanted to see action, and in mid-1943 was transferred to Eisenhower's staff in Algiers, North Africa, helping to prepare for the invasion of Sicily.

By June 1944 Connally was in the South Pacific, assigned as a fire direction officer aboard the USS *Essex*, "the fightingest ship in the Navy." He saw action at Iwo Jima, Okinawa, and the Philippines and endured over 380 kamikaze attacks. In June of 1945 he served as CIC (Combat Information Center) officer on the USS *Bennington*, earning a Legion of Merit award.

By the war's end, he was a lieutenant commander with two Bronze Stars. He was discharged in February 1946 at the age of 29 and remained in the reserves until 1954. Connally served as Secretary of the Navy under President Kennedy, Governor of Texas from 1963 to 1969, and Secretary of the Treasury under President Nixon. He was riding in the same convertible and was wounded when President Kennedy was assassinated in 1963.

David "Davy" Crockett. Congressman, frontiersman.

Born in Greene County, Tennessee, in 1786, Crockett enlisted as a scout under General Andrew Jackson during the Creek War (1813–14). Unhappy with military life, he hired a substitute to take his place (a common and legal practice at the time) prior to the end of the campaign.

Elected as colonel of a militia regiment in 1821, Crockett served two times in the U.S. Congress (1827–31 and 1833–35). Defeated for re-election, he told the people of Tennessee that they could go to hell—he was going to Texas.

Crockett arrived at the small garrison of a mission outside of San Antonio, and declined a commission in the Texas army, preferring instead to serve as a "high private." His service at the Battle of the Alamo (in which he died) helped delay the Mexican army under General Santa Ana long enough for the new nation to organize an army under Sam Houston. Texas won its independence from Mexico after defeating the Mexican army at the Battle of San Jacinto in 1836.

Jefferson Davis. Secretary of war, Confederate president.

Born in Fairview, Kentucky, on June 3, 1808, Davis was commissioned a second lieutenant upon graduation from West Point in 1828. He served in the Black Hawk War (1830–31) and was promoted to first lieutenant in the 1st U.S. Dragoons on March

4, 1833, for "gallant service." He resigned from the army on June 30, 1835, for a life on the plantation.

After serving in Congress, he resigned in June of 1846 to command the 1st Regiment of Mississippi Riflemen in the War with Mexico. He served under General Taylor at Monterrey and afterward at Buena Vista, distinguishing himself at both battles.

He was promoted to brigadier general in May 1847 but declined the appointment to accept a vacancy in the U.S. Senate. He served as Secretary of War under President Pierce.

At the start of the Civil War, he was commissioned a major general of state militia in the Confederate army on January 25, 1861. He resigned to accept the Confederate presidency where he served for the duration of the war. He was imprisoned after the war at Fortress Monroe (1865–67). He was indicted for treason but never tried. He died peacefully in New Orleans, Louisiana, on December 6, 1889.

David Norman Dinkins. Mayor of New York City.

Born in Trenton, New Jersey, on July 10, 1927, Dinkins tried to enlist in the Marine Corps after his graduation from Trenton High School in 1945, but was rejected because the quota for Negroes was filled. Drafted into the army, he transferred to the marines. After 13 months at Camp Lejeune, North Carolina, where he served as the colonel's chauffeur, he was discharged in August 1946. He attended Howard University on the GI Bill.

In 1990 Dinkins replaced Ed Koch as mayor of New York City, becoming that city's first black mayor.

Everett Dirksen. U.S. Congressman and Senator.

Born in Pekin, Illinois, on January 4, 1896, to German immigrant parents, Dirksen was a student at the University of Minnesota when hostilities were declared against Germany in April 1917.

In January of 1918, at the age of 22, Dirksen enlisted in the army for service during WWI. After a three-week training course at Fort Custer, Michigan, he was promoted to sergeant and sent overseas to France.

After attending French artillery school, he was promoted to second lieutenant and assigned to the 328th Field Artillery. The shortage of balloon observers caused his transfer to the St. Mihiel Sector, assigned as an observer with the 69th Balloon Company attached to the 4th Army Corps.

He served at the front under enemy fire. His duties consisted of going aloft in an open basket to estimate coordinates for artillery support. After the armistice he served briefly with the army of occupation in Germany. He was discharged in October 1919, returned to work at his brother's grocery store, and became involved in local politics.

He was elected to his first congressional seat in 1930, and went on to support the New Deal, even as a Republican. As a Senator from Illinois, he was a major architect in the passage of civil rights laws. He died in Washington DC on September 7, 1969.

Robert J. Dole. U.S. Senator, presidential candidate.

Born in Russell, Kansas, on July 22, 1923, Dole enlisted as a private in the army reserve corps on December 15, 1942, and was called to active duty on June 1, 1943. He was promoted to corporal on July 13 and attended OCS (Officer Candidate School) from July 17 until November 18, 1944, at Fort Benning, Georgia. Upon graduation he was honorably discharged to accept a commission as a second lieutenant in the infantry.

Sent to the Mediterranean theater of operations, Dole was assigned as a platoon leader in Company I, 3rd Battalion, 85th Mountain Infantry Regiment, part of the 10th Mountain Infantry Division ("Mountaineers"). The 10th was the sole infantry division trained specifically for mountain operations.The division was sent to Italy in December 1944, and saw action at Mt. Belvedere near Bologna in February 1945. In March they were fighting fiercely in the mountains, and by April had crossed the

Po River and cut off Brenner Pass, thereby cutting off the remaining German forces in Italy and forcing their surrender on
May 2, 1945. In an action near Castel d'Aiano, Italy, on April 14,
1945, Dole was wounded twice, a severe wound in the right shoulder causing the loss of use of his right arm. The delay in getting
medical aid while pinned down resulted in temporary paralysis
from the neck down. He was not expected to recover. He was
awarded the Bronze Star for his actions.

He spent 39 months recovering in military hospitals, and
was awarded a Bronze Star with Oak Leaf Cluster and two Purple
Hearts before being discharged as a captain on July 30, 1948. He
earned a law degree from Washburn University in 1951 and was
admitted to the Kansas bar a year later.

Dole served as the Republican Senator from Kansas from
1969 until 1996, when he resigned from the Senate in his unsuccessful bid against incumbent Bill Clinton for presidency of the
United States.

Allen Welsh Dulles. Director of Council of Foreign Relations,
CIA director, attorney.

Born in Watertown, New York, on April 7, 1893, the brother
of John Foster Dulles, Dulles graduated Princeton University with
a B.A. degree in 1914, and began a ten-year tour with the Diplomatic Corps (1916–26). He earned his LLB degree from George
Washington University and served as a member of the American delegation to the Paris Peace Conference in 1918–19.

During WWII, Dulles was chosen by General William
Donovan to serve as chief of the OSS in Switzerland, a neutral
country where a lot of intelligence activity took place during the
war. Because of his knowledge of European finance and experience gained in the diplomatic service, Dulles was very effective
in this post. He served from October 1942 until V-E Day.

He then served as chief of the OSS in occupied Germany
until November 1945. He received awards from the U.S., Italy,
Belgium, and France. As chief in Switzerland, he helped negoti-

ate the surrender of German troops in Italy, code named "Operation Sunrise."

He went on to help form the CIA from various wartime intelligence agencies, and served as its deputy director (1951–53) and later as director (1953–61). He died in Washington DC on January 29, 1969.

Barry M. Goldwater, Sr. U.S. Senator, presidential candidate.

Born in Phoenix, Arizona, on January 1, 1909, Goldwater graduated from Staunton Military Academy in Lexington, Virginia, in 1928, winning the honor of "Most Outstanding Cadet."

Goldwater entered the U.S. Army reserve in 1930 as a second lieutenant. A licensed pilot, he applied for the Air Corps, but was rejected for his eyesight (astigmatism) as well as bad knees. It was only through persistence, and the intervention of both Arizona Senators, that he was assigned to the infantry. He went on active duty in August 1941, prior to Pearl Harbor.

During WWII he served as a pilot with the Army Air Corps stationed in India, ferrying aircraft and supplies to all theaters of operation. He was discharged from active service in November 1945 as a lieutenant colonel.

After the war, Goldwater organized the Arizona National Guard, and served as its chief of staff. Promoted to brigadier general in the U.S. Air Force reserve in 1959, and major general in 1962, Goldwater retired in 1967 after 37 years of service. He also served as the Republican Senator from Arizona for 34 years (1953–87). He unsuccessfully ran for President against Lyndon Johnson in 1964 and was defeated in a landslide.

Wilson Goode. Mayor of Philadelphia.

Born in a wooden shack outside Seaboard, North Carolina, on August 19, 1938, the son of a sharecropper, Goode's family moved north after WWII. An honor student, Goode enrolled in ROTC while a student at Morgan State University in Baltimore.

After graduating in 1961, he was commissioned a lieutenant in the army, and served a two-year tour of active duty (1962–63). He commanded a company of military police, and was discharged as a captain, earning the Army Commendation Medal. He returned to civilian life, earning a master's degree in public administration from the University of Pennsylvania in 1968. He was elected the first black mayor of Philadelphia in 1984 and served until 1991.

Albert "Al" Gore. Vice President of the United States.

Born Albert Gore Jr. in Washington DC on March 31, 1948, Gore was opposed to the war in Vietnam as a student at Harvard. Nonetheless, he entered the U.S. Army as a private in 1969 at the height of the Vietnam War. After basic training, he was assigned as a reporter with the 20th Engineer Battalion stationed just outside Saigon. He completed his tour of duty and was discharged in 1971.

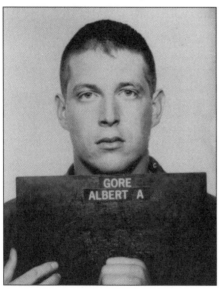

Albert Gore

Gore was elected to the U.S. Senate from Tennessee in 1985 and served until 1992 when he resigned to accept the Democratic Party's nomination for Vice President under Bill Clinton. They were both re-elected in 1996.

Alexander Hamilton. Statesman, founding father.

Born on the Island of Nevis in the Leeward Islands on January 11, 1757, the illegitimate son of unwed parents, Hamilton was commissioned a captain of artillery in the Continental army at age 19.

He became aide de camp to General Washington in 1777, and enjoyed the older man's confidence and patronage. He ended his war service with the rank of colonel.

Later, in a crisis with France that arose in 1798, he was appointed a major general of the army, and upon Washington's unexpected death, commander in chief, until his resignation with the restoration of peace. He died in a duel with Aaron Burr on July 11, 1804.

Phil Hart. U.S. Senator.

Born in Bryn Mawr, Pennsylvania, on December 12, 1912, Hart was practicing law in Detroit when he entered the U.S. Army in 1943. He was commissioned a captain of infantry, and served with the 4th Infantry Division (nicknamed the "IVY" Division from the Roman numeral for four: IV). The 89th Infantry Regiment was in the first wave that landed on Utah Beach during the Normandy invasion on June 6, 1944. Hart was wounded during the landing. After Normandy, the division followed Free French forces in the liberation of Paris, and in September became the first American combat unit to enter the Third Reich when it penetrated the Siegfried line. After heavy losses in the Huertgen Forest, a short rest was interrupted by the Battle of the Bulge.

Hart was back with the division in time for the Battle of the Bulge in December 1944 in which the division again suffered heavy losses. The unit crossed the Prum River in February 1945 and captured the city of Prum. They crossed the Rhine in March capturing Wurzburg, crossed the Main River and were advancing across Bavaria when the war ended. Hart was decorated for bravery several times, including the Bronze Star, Purple Heart, and Croix de Guerre for valor. He was discharged in 1946 with the rank of lieutenant colonel. Called "the conscience of the Senate," Hart served as Senator from Michigan from 1958 until his death in 1976.

Richard Helms. Director of the CIA.

Born Richard McGarrah Helms on March 30, 1913, in St.

Davids, Pennsylvania, Helms moved as a child with his family to Europe where he became fluent in German and French. Returning to the U.S., he graduated Phi Beta Kappa from Williams College in 1935.

From graduation until 1942, Helms worked as a journalist for United Press in Europe. His assignments included the 1936 Olympics in Berlin, and interviews with Sonja Henie and Adolph Hitler. He returned to the U.S. in 1937 writing for the *Indianapolis Times*.

Helms enlisted in the navy in early 1942, and was commissioned a lieutenant. In 1943, possibly because of his experience in Europe and his language skills, Helms was transferred to the OSS (Office of Strategic Services), the wartime intelligence service under Major General Bill Donovan. After desk assignments in New York and Washington, Helms was assigned overseas, first to England, then Europe. With the German surrender, he was posted to Berlin where he worked under Allen Dulles. He was discharged from the navy in 1946 with the rank of lieutenant commander.

Helms remained in intelligence work after the war, first as a staff member of the strategic services unit of the War Department, then as a member of the central intelligence group under the National Intelligence Authority. In 1947 all wartime intelligence agencies were combined to form the CIA. Helms was a key architect and staff member of the new agency. He survived the U-2 and Bay of Pigs incidents to become the agency's director. He also served as ambassador to Iran (1973–76).

Sam Houston. Congressman, president of Texas.

Born in Lexington, Virginia, on March 2, 1793, Houston enlisted as a private in the 39th Regiment, U.S. Infantry during the War of 1812. Promoted to ensign in 1813, he served under General Jackson in the 7th Regiment, Regular Army. He was seriously wounded at Horseshoe Bend and was discharged shortly thereafter.

He was accepted again into the Regular Army in 1815 and was posted to New Orleans. He served on General Jackson's staff in Nashville in 1816 and was promoted to first lieutenant in 1817. He resigned his commission in 1818 amidst charges of engaging or assisting in the slave trade.

In 1836, after serving as a district attorney, Congressman, and Governor of Tennessee, from which he resigned to become a member of the Cherokee nation, Houston traveled to Texas, which was then part of Mexico.

He served as commander in chief of the Texas army when the Republic of Texas declared its independence, and led the army to victory against President/General Santa Ana at the Battle of San Jacinto on April 21, 1836.

He served as the first president of the Republic of Texas, and later as a U.S. Senator to the newly admitted state of Texas. Elected Governor in 1859, Houston opposed secession and was deposed when he refused to take an oath of allegiance to the Confederacy. He died in 1863 during the Civil War.

Daniel Ken Inouye. U.S. Senator from Hawaii.

Born on September 7, 1924, in Honolulu, Hawaii, to Japanese parents, Inouye temporarily postponed his studies at the medical school of the University of Hawaii to enlist in the U.S. Army in 1943. During the Japanese raid on Pearl Harbor in 1941, he used his medical training to give aid to the wounded.

He enlisted to join the 442nd Regimental Combat Team, a Japanese American unit authorized by Congress in June of 1942 to allow Japanese Americans the opportunity to "prove" themselves in combat.

After basic training at Camp Shelby, Mississippi, the 442nd was sent to Italy and became the most decorated outfit in American military history. With the motto "go for broke," individuals in the unit earned 4,000 Bronze Stars, 560 Silver Stars, 52 Distinguished Service Crosses, and one Medal of Honor (Sadao Munemori).

Inouye earned a battlefield commission to second lieutenant in August of 1944 after action in the Voges region of southern France where his unit helped relieve a trapped Texas unit. Returning to Italy as a squad leader, he led an assault on a fortified German position two days before the war ended in May 1945. Although wounded in the right arm, stomach and leg, Inouye was able to destroy three separate enemy gun emplacements with hand grenades, saving his unit. His actions resulted in the award of the Distinguished Service Cross, Bronze Star, Purple Heart and the loss of his right arm.

He spent two years recovering in military hospitals, and was discharged as a captain in 1947. Inouye returned to the University of Hawaii on the GI Bill. He was forced, by the loss of his right arm, to change his major from pre-med to government. He thus became the first Japanese American to serve in Congress (1959–63) and was elected U.S. Senator from the new state of Hawaii in 1962. He served as a member of the Watergate Committee (1972–74) and as chairman of the committee investigating Iran-Contra in 1987.

Daniel Inouye

Edward M. Kennedy. U.S. Senator, presidential candidate.

Born in Brookline, Massachusetts, on February 22, 1932, "Ted" left Harvard and enlisted in the army on June 25, 1951. His father, Ambassador Joseph Kennedy, was concerned that Ted might be sent to combat since the Korean War was in progress, so he used his influence with the draft board to get Ted's four-year enlistment reduced to two years with an assignment in Europe.

After basic training at Ft. Dix, New Jersey, Kennedy was

trained in counter-intelligence at Ft. Holabird, Maryland, and was sent to Ft. Gordon, Georgia, for training as a military policeman. He was sent overseas to France where he was assigned to the 520th Military Police Company.

Kennedy was discharged from active duty as a private first class at Ft. Devens, Massachusetts, on March 27, 1953. Upon his discharge, he returned to Harvard.

Kennedy was elected to the Senate from Massachusetts in 1962, where he has continued to serve despite his involvement in the accidental death of Mary Jo Kopechne in a car accident at Chappaquiddick in 1969. He was also an unsuccessful candidate for the Democratic nomination for President in 1980.

Robert Francis Kennedy. U.S. Senator, presidential candidate.

Born in Brookline, Massachusetts, on November 20, 1925, Kennedy was attending Harvard at the beginning of WWII. "Bobby" was an 18-year-old candidate in the naval aviation program in 1943, but by the end of the program there was a surplus of pilots and his class was canceled. He chose not to continue in officer training and instead took sea duty as an ordinary seaman aboard the USS *Joseph P. Kennedy, Jr.* (DD-850), a recently commissioned destroyer named for his brother who was killed in action in Europe. Kennedy served as a Seaman 2nd Class on her shakedown cruise to Cuba in 1946.

He was discharged in 1946 and returned to Harvard. He later served as Attorney General in his brother John's administration and served in the U.S. Senate. He was killed by assassin S. Sirhan while campaigning for President in California on June 6, 1968.

Bob Kerrey. U.S. Senator, presidential candidate.

Born Joseph Robert Kerrey in Lincoln, Nebraska, on August 27, 1943, Kerrey graduated from the University of Nebraska with a B.S. in pharmacology in January 1966. Soon after, Kerrey enlisted in the U.S. Navy. Sent to naval OCS in October, he was commissioned an ensign and accepted for UDT (Underwater Demolition Training).

Friends remember Kerrey being motivated, and supportive of U.S. policy in Vietnam. Rather than avoid service, or obtain a commission as a pharmacist, Kerrey volunteered first for UDT, then the Navy SEALs (SEa Air Land), a special forces unit. Of the 178 candidates in his UDT class, 68 graduated, and of those, 14 were accepted for SEAL duty, including Kerrey.

After completing army airborne and ranger schools, he was sent for pre-deployment training to Coronado, California, home of SEAL team #1. Assigned to a SEAL platoon, Kerrey, now 25 and a lieutenant (j.g.), was sent with his team to southeast Asia.

His mission in Vietnam was to operate in the field and capture important Viet Cong information and personnel. After two and a half months, on March 14, 1969, Kerrey and his team were sent to Hon Tre Island, where intelligence reported a large number of political and military Viet Cong leaders were present. After scaling a 350-foot sheer cliff, Kerrey was wounded by a grenade, but continued to direct the mission.

Although in severe pain, Kerrey remained conscious and directed the counter-attack. The mission was a success, and many VIP prisoners were captured and vital intelligence obtained. His wounds resulted in the partial loss of his right leg and foot, and his award of the Medal of Honor.

Kerrey spent one year recuperating from his wounds at the Philadelphia Naval Hospital until December 1969 when he was honorably discharged. His experience in Vietnam and the wards of the hospital began his questioning of the justification for U.S. involvement in southeast Asia.

Kerrey entered politics and served as both a Senator and Governor of the state of Nebraska, and as a candidate for President.

Henry A. Kissinger. Secretary of State, Nobel Peace Prize recipient.

Born Heinz Alfred Kissinger in Fürth, Germany, on May 27, 1923, Kissinger was drafted into the U.S. Army as a naturalized citizen on February 26, 1943. After basic training at Camp

Clairborne, Louisiana, he was sent to the European theater of operations as a private in G Company, 335th Infantry Regiment of the 84th Infantry Division (the "Railsplitters"). The division entered combat during the Rohr Valley offensive and captured the city of Geilenkirchen after hard fighting, in November 1944. The division was rushed to Belgium for the Battle of the Bulge in December, fighting off repeated German attacks to restore the line in January 1945. The unit crossed the Roer River in February, and after a brief rest, crossed the Rhine and Weser Rivers, captured Hannover, and joined up with the advancing Russian army on May 2, 1945.

Kissinger saw action at the Battle of the Bulge, and recognizing his skill with languages, the army assigned him as an interpreter/interrogator with the 970th Counter Intelligence Corps. He was awarded a Bronze Star.

He was discharged from active duty as a staff sergeant on May 23, 1946, and remained in the army reserve in military intelligence from May 4, 1948, until April 29, 1959, when he was discharged as a captain.

Kissinger became an advisor on national security issues and was appointed Secretary of State under President Nixon. He won the Nobel Peace Prize along with Le Duc Tho in 1973 for his efforts in bringing about an end to the Vietnam conflict.

Frank Knox. Secretary of the Navy during WWII.

Born William Franklin Knox in Boston on January 1, 1874, Knox attended Alma Christian College in Michigan, earning his B.A. in 1898.

With the outbreak of the Spanish-American War, Knox enlisted in the army as one of Teddy Roosevelt's "Rough Riders" (1st Volunteer Cavalry). At the war's end, Knox went to work as a reporter.

During WWI, Knox, now 43, enlisted as a private in the army. Sent overseas to France with the 78th Division, he was a major in field artillery by the war's end. After the war, he was floor manager in General Leonard Wood's campaign for the Republican presidential nomination at the convention in Chicago.

During WWII Knox served as Secretary of the Navy, and died while serving in 1944. He was succeeded by James V. Forrestal.

Ed Koch. Mayor of New York City, Congressman.

Born Edwin Irwin Koch on December 12, 1924, Koch was attending college and working as a shoe salesman before enlisting in the U.S. Army in 1943.

After basic training, Koch was assigned to the European theater as a combat infantryman where he earned two Battle Stars. After V-E Day, he was assigned duties as a denazification specialist in occupied Bavaria.

Discharged as a sergeant in 1946, he entered New York University Law School on the GI Bill. He served as a Congressman from New York for four terms before being elected mayor of New York City in 1978. He served until he was defeated in 1989.

Fiorello La Guardia. Longtime mayor of New York City.

Born in New York City on December 11, 1882, La Guardia absented himself from the House of Representatives on August 15, 1917, upon America's entry into WWI. He was commissioned a first lieutenant in the army air service and commanded U.S. air forces on the Italy-Austria front.

After the war La Guardia was discharged with the rank of major and returned to Congress. He was awarded the Italian War Cross by the Italian government for bravery in action.

La Guardia served as mayor of New York City from 1934 until 1945. During WWII he served as chief of the Office of Civilian Defense (1941–42). He died in New York City on September 20, 1947.

John V. Lindsay. Mayor of New York City.

Born in New York City on November 24, 1921, Lindsay graduated Yale in April 1943, and by May was commissioned an ensign in the naval reserve. After training he was assigned as gunnery officer on a destroyer, the USS *Swanson* (DD-443).

He saw action at both the Sicily invasion of Italy, and the invasion of the Philippines in the Pacific as part of a carrier task group. He earned five Battle Stars, and was discharged as a full lieutenant in March 1946. He served as the Republican mayor of New York City from 1966 to 1974. He campaigned unsuccessfully for the Democratic nomination for President in 1972.

Henry Cabot Lodge. U.S. Senator, statesman.

Born in Nahant, Massachusetts, on July 5, 1902, Lodge was the grandson of Henry Cabot Lodge (U.S. Senator from Massachusetts from 1893–1924). He was a cavalry officer in the army reserve from 1924, and an advocate of a strong and prepared military. In the summer of 1941 Lodge took leave from the U.S. Senate to be part of the largest military maneuvers in American history along with General George Patton and Colonel Dwight Eisenhower, as the nation prepared for possible involvement in the war in Europe. Lodge commanded a reconnaissance company of the 2nd Armored Division ("Hell on Wheels").

In August 1941 the newly promoted Major Lodge was called to "extended active duty," and in early 1942 was sent to the front in Libya. He was in command of a 16-man tank squadron (4 officers, 12 enlisted men) assigned to combat duty attached to the British 8th Army. Lodge's unit arrived at the headquarters of the 30th Corps just in time to participate in the retreat from Tobruk to El Alamein, one of the worst defeats of the war. (The film *Sahara* with Humphrey Bogart was loosely based on Lodge's unit.)

In battle Lodge's tank crews destroyed nine enemy tanks, thereby becoming the first American tankers to fight and win a battle in WWII. Afterwards the unit was withdrawn from combat and returned to Fort Knox, Kentucky, where they shared the knowledge they gained in combat with new armor trainees.

In July 1942 Secretary of War Stimson denied Lodge's request to remain on active duty, stating that "skilled legislators who understand the army's needs are more important to the army than soldiers."

Lodge returned to the Senate and went on a 41,000-mile fact-finding mission with four other Senators. Upon the tour's completion, Lodge resigned from the Senate and returned to active duty in February 1944, becoming the first Senator since the Civil War to resign from the U.S. Senate to go to war.

Major Lodge was assigned to a staff position in London in May 1944. He helped plan the Normandy invasion, and served as a liaison officer with the Free French army during the invasion. He also served as deputy chief of staff with the 4th Corps in Italy, and was present with General Devers to accept the German surrender of Army Group G outside Berlin on May 5, 1945.

Although a staff officer, Lodge frequently came under enemy fire. He was awarded the Bronze Star, the Legion of Honor, and the French Croix de Guerre with Palm for his war service. He was discharged as a lieutenant colonel on December 2, 1945.

Lodge was re-elected to the Senate in 1947 and served until 1953 when he was appointed the American ambassador to the United Nations. He served until 1960 when he ran as the Republican candidate for Vice President under Nixon. Lodge served as the American ambassador to South Vietnam and West Germany before serving as a representative to the Vietnam Peace Talks in Paris. He died in Beverly, Massachusetts, on February 27, 1985.

Russell Billiu Long. U.S. Senator from Louisiana.

The son of Huey P. Long, the "Kingfish" of Louisiana politics, Long was born in Shreveport, Louisiana, on November 3, 1918. After graduating law school at Louisiana State in 1942, he enlisted as an apprentice seaman in the U.S. Navy during WWII.

Long was sent to midshipman's school at Columbia University where he trained to be an officer. After being commissioned an ensign, he was assigned to the amphibious branch. He was in command of landing crafts at North Africa, Sicily, Anzio and

Southern France. He earned four Battle Stars.

After his discharge from the navy as a full lieutenant in November 1945, Long returned to law and politics. He served as the Senator from Louisiana from 1951 until 1986.

Paul Norton McCloskey, Jr. Congressman.

Born in San Bernardino, California, on September 29, 1927, McCloskey graduated San Marino High School in 1945, two months before the war ended. He joined the navy's V-5 pilot training program, but after nine months at California Institute of Technology, McCloskey requested active duty. He was assigned to the Great Lakes Naval Training Center as a seaman first class. He served for ten months and was discharged in 1947. He attended Stanford on the GI Bill.

After graduating with a degree in 1950, McCloskey enrolled in the U.S. Marine Corps platoon leader program, and was commissioned a second lieutenant in February 1951. He was sent to Korea as a platoon leader with the 5th Marine Regiment. Wounded while leading a bayonet charge up Hill #556, McCloskey was awarded the Navy Cross for "daring initiative and inspired leadership." He was also awarded the Silver Star and a Purple Heart.

Upon his return in 1952, he returned to Stanford Law School and earned his law degree in 1953. Throughout his career he remained in the Marine Corps active reserves, and retired as a lieutenant colonel in 1967. That was also the year McCloskey was first elected to Congress when he won the seat from incumbent Shirley Temple Black. He served as a Representative from California until 1983.

During Pat Robertson's presidential campaign, he asserted that Robertson had used his Senator father's influence to avoid combat. Robertson successfully sued him for libel.

George S. McGovern. U.S. Senator, presidential candidate.

The son of a professional ballplayer turned Methodist minister, McGovern was born on July 19, 1922, in Avon, North Dakota. He left college to join the U.S. Army Air Corps in June 1942. After completing flight training in San Antonio, Texas, and Langley Field, Virginia, McGovern was assigned as a B-24 pilot.

He was sent overseas to North Africa, and from there flew 35 combat missions over Germany, Italy and Austria. On one mission over Vienna, his plane was badly damaged by flak, and his navigator killed. McGovern was able to safely pilot the heavy bomber back for a crash landing. For this action he was awarded the Distinguished Flying Cross, the nation's second highest award for valor. He also won an Air Medal with three clusters. McGovern was discharged in July 1945 as a first lieutenant.

McGovern served as a Senator from South Dakota for three terms from 1963 until 1981. He lost the election for President to Nixon in 1972 in the biggest landslide in American history.

Robert Strange McNamara. Secretary of Defense, president of the World Bank.

Born in San Francisco on June 9, 1916, McNamara was teaching accounting at Harvard Business School at the start of WWII. He remained at Harvard instructing Army Air Corps officers in methods of systems control.

In 1943 McNamara was sent overseas to England to set up a statistical control system for the 8th Air Force. On March 12, 1943, he was commissioned a temporary captain in the U.S. Army. Later in 1943 he was sent to Salina, Kansas, to provide planning and logistical support for long-range B-29 operations. After the victory in Europe, he was sent to the Pacific to assess the effects of long-range bombing on Japan. McNamara contracted polio in July 1945. Just a short week later, his wife Margy became ill with the same illness.

He was discharged as a lieutenant colonel at the end of the war. He later served as Secretary of Defense (1961–68) and president of the World Bank (1968–81).

Walter Frederick Mondale. U.S. Senator, Vice President.

Born in Minnesota in 1928, Mondale enlisted in the U.S. Army in 1951, and served for two years at Ft. Knox, Kentucky. He was part of the crew of an armored reconnaissance vehicle, and rose to the rank of corporal by the time of his discharge in 1953. He attended the University of Minnesota Law School on the GI Bill.

Mondale served as state attorney general of Minnesota before being appointed to the U.S. Senate by the Governor of Minnesota in 1964 to replace Hubert Humphrey who left the Senate to become Vice President under Lyndon Johnson. He served in the Senate until he took the position of Vice President under Jimmy Carter in 1977. He lost the election for President to Reagan in 1984.

Elliot Richardson. Attorney General, HEW Secretary.

Born in Boston on July 20, 1920, and descended from a prominent Massachusetts family of physicians, Richardson attended Harvard (where his father was a professor at the medical school). He drew cartoons for the Harvard *Lampoon* and graduated cum laude in 1941.

Richardson was attending Harvard Law School when the U.S. entered the war after Pearl Harbor. He joined the army and was commissioned a first lieutenant with the 4th Infantry Division (the "IVY" Division). After Normandy, the unit participated in the liberation of Paris, fought for its life in the Huertgen Forest, stood firm at the Battle of the Bulge and captured the city of Wurzburg. Richardson was present at the Normandy invasion where his actions earned him a Bronze Star and Purple Heart. He remained with the 4th Division until the end of the war.

Discharged, Richardson returned to Harvard Law School where he was elected president of his class, and was editor of the *Law Review*. He graduated cum laude and served as a law clerk for Appeals Court Judge Learned Hand and Supreme Court Justice Felix Frankfurter. He went on to serve as U.S. attorney for Massachusetts, Lieutenant Governor of Massachusetts, and HEW Secretary.

Richardson also served as attorney general under President
Nixon during Watergate. He resigned on October 20, 1973, rather
than fire Watergate special prosecutor Archibald Cox. His deputy,
William Ruckelhaus, also refused, leaving the task to Solicitor
General Robert Bork. That night became known as the "Satur-
day Night Massacre."

Frank Rizzo. Mayor of Philadelphia, police commissioner.

Born on October 23, 1920, in Philadelphia, Pennsylvania,
Rizzo enlisted in the U.S. Navy after the death of his mother in
1938. Incipient diabetes caused him to be medically discharged
after 13 months. He joined the Philadelphia police department
in 1943.

He worked his way up in city government to serve as police
commissioner (1967–72) and mayor (1972–80). He died while
running for a third term.

David Dean Rusk. JFK's Secretary of State.

Born in Cherokee County, Georgia, on February 9, 1909, Rusk
graduated magna cum laude from Davidson College in 1931, and
was selected a Rhodes scholar. He entered the army reserves as
a captain in December 1940. He served as commanding officer
of the 30th Infantry at the Presidio in San Francisco.

During WWII, Rusk served as assistant operations officer of
the 3rd Infantry Division (the "Marne" Division) at Ft. Lewis,
Washington, and later with army intelligence in Washington DC.
He was discharged as a colonel in February 1946 and went to
work for the State Department.

Paul Simon. U.S. Senator, Congressman, publisher.

Born Paul Martin Simon on November 29, 1928, in Eugene,
Oregon, Simon was the son of a Lutheran minister father and a
Lutheran missionary mother.

In 1948 at the age 19, Simon became the nation's youngest
editor/publisher of a newspaper when he left college and took
out a bank loan to buy the *Troy Tribune* in Troy, Illinois.

POLITICS, GOVERNMENT, LAW 39

Simon entered the U.S. Army in 1951 and spent his two-year tour of duty with a counter-intelligence unit monitoring Soviet activity along the east German border. He was discharged as a corporal in 1953 and returned to Troy to begin a career in politics. He won his first election to the Illinois legislature as an Independent in 1954.

Harold Stassen. University president, Governor, presidential candidate.

Born on April 13, 1907, in West St. Paul, Minnesota, Stassen was in the ROTC program at the University of Minnesota from 1924 to 1927, rising to the rank of cadet lieutenant colonel. He won a competition in the National Rifle Championship, and was elected class president.

In March 1942 Stassen was commissioned a lieutenant commander in the navy reserve while still Governor of Minnesota. In April 1943 he resigned during his second term as governor to go on active duty with the navy.

He served as an aide and flag secretary to Admiral William F. Halsey in the Pacific. He saw combat and was frequently under fire. Stassen was promoted to captain in September 1945 and served as a delegate to the United Nations chartering conference in San Francisco. He was also sent to Japan to coordinate the return of 13,000 POWs on hospital ships.

He received the Legion of Merit for his combat duty, and sought the Republican nomination for President upon his discharge from the navy in November 1945. He became president of the University of Pennsylvania in 1948.

Strom Thurmond. U.S. Senator, judge, Governor.

Born James Strom Thurmond in Edgefield, South Carolina, on December 5, 1902, Thurmond was working as the youngest circuit court judge in South Carolina when he took a leave of absence to enlist in the army on December 11, 1941, four days after Pearl Harbor. It was the day that Germany declared war on the United States.

Thurmond had entered the U.S. Army Reserve Corps in 1924, and was assigned as an officer with the 1st Army in April 1942. He served with the 82nd Airborne (the "All Americans") during the Normandy invasion, and was wounded in action. He continued to see combat in Europe until V-E Day.

Transferred to the Pacific after V-E Day, Thurmond served in the Philippines until his discharge with the rank of lieutenant colonel in January 1946. His awards include the Legion of Merit, Bronze Star, Purple Heart, the Order of the Crown (Belgium), the French Croix de Guerre, and five Battle Stars. He returned to the bench after the war, and was elected Governor of South Carolina in 1948. He has served in the U.S. Senate since 1955.

Stansfield Turner. CIA director.

The tenth director of the CIA was born in Chicago, Illinois, on December 1, 1923. He attended Amherst College in 1941 where he was elected class president, played football, and joined the naval reserve. His friend and classmate was future FBI director William Webster.

In 1943 Turner transferred to Annapolis, where he was an outstanding student, played football, and was a battalion commander. Jimmy Carter was a classmate. Although Turner was in the class of 1947, his class graduated in 1946 under an accelerated program. He graduated 25th in a class of 820 (Carter's ranking was 59).

Stansfield Turner

Turner spent his first year in the navy at sea aboard a cruiser, and then was sent to Oxford University as a Rhodes scholar, earning his masters degree in 1950. He returned to duty aboard destroyers in both the Atlantic and Pacific Fleets. He earned a Bronze Star during the Korean War.

By 1962 Turner had commanded two warships, and had served a tour of duty in the office of the Chief of Naval Operations (CNO) and the office of Assistant Secretary of Defense. In 1967, after attending Harvard business school, Commander Turner was assigned as captain of the guided missile frigate USS *Horne* (CG-30) off the coast of Vietnam.

Promoted to captain, Turner served for two years as a military aide to the Secretary of the Navy. By 1970, following an assignment as aide to Admiral Zumwaldt, Rear Admiral Turner commanded a carrier group of the 6th Fleet in the Mediterranean.

In 1972 Turner was promoted to vice admiral and was appointed president of the Naval War College where he authored numerous policy papers on global strategy and naval power. Late in 1975 he was promoted to full admiral and placed in command of all Allied forces in southern Europe.

In February 1977 Turner was called to Washington DC by President Carter who named him as principal foreign intelligence advisor and director of the CIA. Turner was allowed to remain on active duty, and it was hoped that his prestige would return credibility to the discredited agency.

Mo Udall. Congressman, presidential candidate.

Born in St. Johns, Arizona, on June 15, 1922, Morris King Udall was a law student at the University of Arizona at the start of WWII. He served in the U.S. Army Air Corps in the Pacific from 1942 through 1945.

Udall was discharged as a captain at the end of the war and returned to the University of Arizona where he earned his law degree. He went on to play professional basketball for the Denver Nuggets before beginning a career in politics. He was an unsuccessful Democratic candidate for President in 1976.

Cyrus Vance. Secretary of State.

Born in Clarksburg, Virginia, on March 27, 1917, Vance enlisted in the U.S. Navy at the beginning of WWII after earning his law degree from Yale. He was accepted into the navy's V-7 training program.

Vance was commissioned an ensign and gunnery officer, and served aboard destroyers in the Pacific. He saw action at Bougainville, Tarawa, Saipan, Guam and the Philippines. He was discharged as a full lieutenant in March 1946.

He served as Secretary of the Army (1962), deputy Secretary of Defense (1964) and Secretary of State (1977–80.)

George Corley Wallace. Governor, presidential candidate.

Born in Clio, Alabama, on August 25, 1919, Wallace joined the U.S. Army Air Corps in October 1942 after graduating law school at the University of Alabama. He hoped to be commissioned a pilot, but an illness, possibly spinal meningitis, caused him to be released from pilot training.

Wallace was assigned to the 20th Air Force and spent the war flying missions in the Pacific as a flight engineer aboard B-29s. He was discharged in 1945 with the rank of flight officer (a WWII warrant officer grade).

Wallace served as a four-term Governor of Alabama, twice ran for President, and was paralyzed in an attempted assassination in 1972. He has been confined to a wheelchair since that time. Although he is remembered as the man who blocked the doors to prevent two black students from registering at the University of Alabama on June 11, 1963, he renounced segregation and apologized to the Black community in the 1990s.

Caspar Weinberger. Secretary of defense, politician.

Born on August 18, 1912, in San Francisco, Weinberger entered the U.S. Army as a private soon after graduating from Harvard Law School in 1941. He served with the 41st Infantry Division in the Pacific and on General MacArthur's intelligence staff. (The 41st was nicknamed the "Sunset" Division for its goal to "set" the rising sun of Japan. Weinberger was discharged as a captain in 1945.

Weinberger served as Secretary of Health, Education and Welfare (1973–75) and Secretary of Defense (1981–87).

Coleman Alexander Young. Mayor of Detroit.

Born in Tuscaloosa, Alabama, on May 24, 1918, Young was about to be drafted at the start of WWII, and so volunteered for the U.S. Army Air Corps. He was assigned to the 477th Bombardment Group, a segregated black squadron at Tuskagee.

Young was commissioned a second lieutenant and assigned as a navigator/bombardier. Committed to equal rights, he and about 100 other black officers were arrested for demanding service in the segregated officer's club at Freeman Field, Indiana, on March 15, 1945. Threatened with a court-martial, Young smuggled word out to the black newspapers and the army inspector general. The black officers were released from confinement on April 19, 1945, and the club was thereafter integrated. The 477th Bombardment Group (later Composite Group) was still in training with B-25s and P-47 Thunderbolts when the war ended, and so saw no service overseas.

After the war, Young returned to his job with the U.S. Post Office in Detroit. He was later investigated by the House Un-American Activities Commission (HUAC) for his work with organized labor. He served as Detroit's first black mayor from 1974 until 1993.

Lawmen, Lawyers and the Courts

F. Lee Bailey. Attorney, jurist.

Born in Waltham, Massachusetts, on June 10, 1933, Bailey left Harvard and enlisted in the navy on March 13, 1952. He was accepted into the naval aviation program. On April 21, 1954, he transferred to the Marine Corps reserves as a second lieutenant,

and served first as a jet pilot and
later as a legal officer at Cherry
Point, North Carolina. He was
discharged as a first lieutenant on
December 3, 1956.

Bailey has defended the likes
of Sam Sheppard, Albert De
Salvo (the Boston Strangler) and
O.J. Simpson.

Griffin Bell. Attorney General of the U.S.

F. Lee Bailey

Born in Americus, Georgia, in 1918, Bell grew up within 12
miles of Jimmy Carter. Late in 1941 Bell enlisted in the U.S. Army
Transportation Corps as a private.

He never served overseas, remaining stateside at bases in
Florida, California, and Washington. He returned to law school
after being discharged from the army in 1946 with the rank of
major.

Hugo L. Black. U.S. Supreme Court Justice.

Born in Harlan, Alabama, on February 27, 1886, Black spent
ten years as a U.S. Senator from Alabama (1927–37) and 34 years
on the Supreme Court (1937–71).

During WWI, Black served as an army artillery officer but
he was never sent overseas and was discharged in 1919.

Black wrote the majority opinion in *Korematsu v. United States*
which validated the internment of Japanese Americans during
WWII, stating "war cannot be fought with the courts in control."

William "Wild Bill" Donovan. Lawyer, ambassador, spy.

Born William Joseph Donovan in Buffalo, New York, on January 1, 1883, Donovan wanted to be a priest, but changed to law
while in college. After earning a law degree from Columbia University (where he was a classmate of Franklin Roosevelt),

Donovan organized a cavalry troop for the New York National Guard in May 1912. He was elected captain of Troop I, New York Cavalry.

In June 1916, Donovan went to Europe as part of a war relief mission, but upon learning that his troop had been activated and sent to Texas, he rejoined his command and saw action along the Mexican border. It was during this time that he first met Father Francis Duffy (see entry on Duffy) who was in Texas with the 69th New York, stationed nearby. It was in Mexico that Captain Donovan first acquired the nickname "Wild Bill."

A year later, with America's entry into WWI, Donovan turned down a position as chief of staff of the 27th Division (and a promotion to colonel) to accept command of the 1st Battalion of the 69th New York ("The Fighting 69th") with a promotion to major.

The 69th had a proud history extending back to the Civil War where it participated in seven major engagements and over 50 major battles. In August 1917, the regiment was chosen to represent New York in the newly formed 42nd (Rainbow) Division. The unit was redesignated the 165th Infantry of the New York National Guard. Colonel Douglas MacArthur was the 42nd Division chief of staff.

The regiment was one of the first to be sent overseas to France, and departed from New York in secrecy on October 27, 1917. They sailed to Liverpool, then France, and went "on the line" in Lunville. The unit saw heavy action, and endured a harsh winter, short supplies, gas attacks and almost constant artillery barrages.

During the Aisne-Marne offensive, Donovan scouted the line along Muercy farm. After his aide, Lieutenant Ames, was killed by sniper fire, his intelligence sergeant, Joyce Kilmer (the poet), volunteered to replace Ames as adjutant. Kilmer was killed in the same manner as Ames the following day, July 29, 1918. In eight days of battle, the 42nd Division was able to defeat the elite 4th Prussian Guards, but at a cost of over 5,400 casualties. On September 7, newly promoted Lieutenant Colonel Donovan and others in the division were awarded the Distinguished Service Cross by General Pershing.

Later, during the Argonne Offensive, Donovan's battalion moved against the German positions. Despite a severe leg wound, he refused evacuation and continued to direct his command against strongly fortified positions. They took the position, and withstood the counter-attack. For his actions Donovan was awarded the Medal of Honor five years later in January 1923.

The war ended while Donovan was recovering from his wounds, but the Rainbow Division was chosen for occupation duty in Germany as part of the Third Army. He was assigned to the provost marshall's office (French-speaking lawyers were hard to find) but persuaded headquarters to assign him as the colonel and commanding officer of the 165th regiment in December 1918. The unit was relieved on April 2, 1919, and returned to a hero's welcome with a parade down New York's Fifth Avenue. Donovan returned to his Wall Street law practice.

During the twenties, Donovan served as an assistant district attorney in Buffalo and in President Coolidge's Justice Department. At President Roosevelt's request, Donovan traveled the world during the thirties, gathering information and defining plans for a future military intelligence operation. He foresaw the need for a single agency to coordinate intelligence, as well as conduct special operations. This was opposed by the established intelligence bureaucracies, especially the FBI.

Despite this, Donovan was appointed Coordinator of Information by Roosevelt on July 11, 1941. Following America's entry into WWII, Executive Order 9182 established the Office of Strategic Services (OSS) in June 1942. Donovan was named director. Although he was a colonel in the army reserve, he was technically a civilian until he was commissioned a brigadier general on April 2, 1943. He was promoted to major general on November 10, 1944.

Donovan traveled extensively during the war, and gained firsthand knowledge of OSS operations in all theaters of the war. He was present at the invasion landings at Anzio, Sicily and Normandy. He served as the first and only director of the OSS until it was disbanded by President Truman on September 20, 1945.

Donovan was released from active service as a major general on January 12, 1946. His awards included the Medal of Honor, a Distinguished Service Cross, two Distinguished Service Medals, two Purple Hearts, a Croix de Guerre with a Silver Star, a French Legion of Honor (Commander), and Knight Commander of the Order of the British Empire. He served as Ambassador to Thailand in 1953, and was awarded the National Security Medal in 1957. Donovan died in Walter Reed Hospital on February 8, 1959.

Many were high in their praise of Bill Donovan. Teddy Roosevelt called him "the finest example of the American fighting gentleman." MacArthur said he was "as determined, resourceful and gallant a soldier as I have ever known in my life." Donovan saw things differently. "I do not consider myself a soldier. I am a civilian who did his duty," he said.

John Foster Dulles. Lawyer, diplomat, author.

Born in Washington DC on February 25, 1888, Dulles was the grandson and nephew of Secretaries of State. He was initially rejected for military service during WWI for his poor eyesight but later was commissioned a captain in the army and advised the general staff as the Director of the Economic Section. He also represented the general staff on the War Trade Board. He was discharged as a major at the end of WWI. He represented the U.S. at the Versailles Peace Conference in 1919.

During WWII Dulles served as a member of the New York State Banking Board, and in 1944 as a delegate to the Republican National Convention. In 1948 he served as the acting chairman of the American delegation to the United Nations. He was appointed by President Truman despite the fact that Dulles had actively supported Dewey in the last election. He also served as

48 THEY ALSO SERVED

an interim U.S. Senator before being selected as Eisenhower's Secretary of State.

Felix Frankfurter. Associate Supreme Court Justice.

Born the son of a rabbi in Vienna, Austria, in 1882, Frankfurter graduated Harvard Law School in 1906 and worked in private practice and in the U.S. Attorney's Office before taking a position teaching law at Harvard in 1914. Except for his wartime service during WWI, he taught continuously at Harvard for the next 25 years.

In 1917 Frankfurter was commissioned a major in the army Judge Advocate Corps (army lawyers). He served on a presidential commission negotiating labor contracts with war industries. He also served as President Wilson's investigator on the Mooney-Billings case in San Francisco which involved persons accused in a labor bombing. He was discharged at the end of the war.

Frankfurter was a founder of the ACLU (American Civil Liberties Union), and served on the Supreme Court from 1939 (when he was appointed by FDR) until 1962.

Arthur Joseph Goldberg. Associate Supreme Court Justice, ambassador to the United Nations.

Born on August 8, 1908, in Chicago, Goldberg graduated summa cum laude from Northwestern University Law School. He was instructing at John Marshall Law School and was concurrently qualified to practice before the U.S. Supreme Court at the start of WWII.

Initially, Goldberg served as a civilian special assistant to General William Donovan, the director of the OSS. He helped to organize the newly formed intelligence agency from early in 1942 until 1943 when he joined the army.

Goldberg was commissioned a captain and a promotion to major soon followed. He was sent overseas to Europe and the Middle East on numerous "sensitive" missions. He was discharged as a major in 1944 and returned to his Chicago law practice. After the war, Goldberg was critical of the failure of the U.S. government to provide support to the "democratic forces of the resistance in Europe" and he felt that this limited the effectiveness of the OSS during the war.

Goldberg was appointed to the Supreme Court by President Kennedy and served 1962–65, and as UN ambassador 1965–68.

L. Patrick Gray III. FBI director.

Born Louis Patrick Gray in St. Louis, Missouri, on July 18, 1916, Gray grew up wanting a career in the navy. He joined the naval reserve while a student at Rice University in Houston, and was accepted to the U.S. Naval Academy at Annapolis in 1936. While a midshipman, Gray played lacrosse, football and boxed. He graduated 172nd in a class of 456, and was commissioned an ensign in 1940.

L. Patrick Gray III

During WWII Gray served in the Pacific as an officer aboard the USS *Steelhead* (SS-280), a submarine. He served until the end of the war, and in 1946 was selected to attend George Washington University Law School as a naval post graduate student. He wrote for the school law review and earned his law degree in 1949, graduating with honors.

By the Korean War, Gray was a captain in command of three submarine patrols. After the war ended, he was on the faculty of the Navy School of Naval Justice, and served as an assistant to the Chairman of the Joint Chiefs, and later to the Secretary of

Defense. In these post, Gray served primarily as a liaison between the Pentagon and Congress.

Gray forfeited his position and retirement to leave the navy and accept a position as an aide to Vice President Nixon's Chief of Staff. In May of 1972, President Nixon appointed Gray acting director of the FBI upon J. Edgar Hoover's death. He resigned during Watergate in 1973.

John Marshall Harlan (1833–1911). Supreme Court Justice.

Born in Boyle County, Kentucky, on June 1, 1833, Harlan served as a colonel in the Union army from 1861 until 1863, serving in command of an infantry regiment. He resigned in 1863 to accept the position of attorney general of Kentucky, where he served until 1867. He was appointed as an Associate Justice of the Supreme Court by President Hayes in 1877. He died while on the bench on October 14, 1911.

John Marshall Harlan. (1899–1971) Supreme Court Justice.

Born the grandson of Justice Harlan in Chicago on May 20, 1899, Harlan was already a prestigious attorney at the start of WWII. He enlisted in the Army Air Corps and was commissioned a lieutenant colonel.

Harlan served in Europe during the war as the chief of the Operational Analysis Section of the 8th Air Force. Promoted to full colonel in 1944, he was assigned to the Group Control Council for Germany.

At the war's end, Harlan was discharged with the award of the Legion of Merit, and the French and Belgian Croix de Guerre. He was appointed to the Supreme Court by President Eisenhower in 1955, and served until he resigned for health reasons in September of 1971. He died shortly after on December 29, 1971.

Oliver Wendell Holmes. Jurist, Supreme Court Justice.

Born in Boston, Massachusetts, in 1841, Holmes helped recruit soldiers at the start of the Civil War, then took a commission as lieutenant with the 20th Massachusetts Volunteer Infantry Regiment. He served for three years, and was wounded three times.

He was appointed a lieutenant colonel by the Governor of Massachusetts, but there were no vacancies, and Holmes refused an appointment to major in command of black troops. He was mustered out of the Union Army as a captain on July 17, 1864.

Holmes returned to Harvard Law School and graduated in 1866. He practiced law until appointed a professor of law at Harvard in 1882. He served as Chief Justice of the Massachusetts Supreme Court before being appointed an Associate Justice of the U.S. Supreme Court by Theodore Roosevelt in 1902. He served on the court until his resignation in 1932. He died in 1935, and left half of his estate to the U.S. government. He summed up the experience of his generation that matured during the Civil War, describing it as "being touched by fire."

Leon Jaworski. Warren Commission member, Watergate prosecutor.

Born in Waco, Texas, on September 19, 1905, Jaworski was a successful 36-year-old attorney with three children when he enlisted in the army in June 1942. He went to court daily to completely clear his calendar before enlisting. He was commissioned a captain in the Judge Advocate General's Corps (the army's legal branch).

He attended a three-month school in Washington DC learning the U.S. Army Articles of War (predecessor to the Uniform Code of Military Justice). Afterwards, he was sent to Fort Sam Houston in Texas where he coordinated the arrest, confinement and trial of military personnel charged with crimes by civil authorities. He served as a liaison with the FBI and civilian police. When it was discovered that Jaworski had trial lawyer experience, he was put in charge of prosecuting cases for the 8th Service Command, in charge of "sensitive" cases.

In December 1943 Jaworski was assigned to investigate the murder of a German POW by Nazi prisoners at Camp Chafee,

Arkansas. Meanwhile, he continued to request assignment overseas.

In December 1944 Jaworski, now a lieutenant colonel, was ordered to Europe to help plan and prepare for the war crimes trials that were sure to follow the Allied victory. There was resistance to non-career officers in Europe, so he arranged to personally serve as a courier of 132 pounds of top secret records which he hand-carried to Paris.

Jaworski was assigned as chief of the War Crimes Trial Section charged with investigating and examining evidence related to war crimes. He was recalled to England to view films of concentration camps, and thus was able to celebrate V-E Day in both Paris and London.

His unit was moved to Wiesbaden, Germany, after the war, and his staff compiled evidence for the trials. He passed on the opportunity to prosecute at Nuremberg, preferring to return home for a discharge. He was discharged as a colonel in December 1945. He wrote of his experiences as a prosecutor of Nazi criminals in *15 Years After* (1961). He served as special prosecutor during the Watergate trials.

William Moses Kunstler. Civil rights attorney.

Born in New York City on July 7, 1919, Kunstler entered the army during WWII after graduating Yale. He served as a signal intelligence officer with the 8th Army in the Pacific. He won a Bronze Star for his actions in combat, and was discharged as a major in 1946. He entered Columbia Law School in 1946.

His law practice in later years would include clients Adam Clayton Powell, Father Berrigan, Martin Luther King, and the Chicago Seven.

G. Gordon Liddy. Lawyer, FBI agent, Watergate conspirator.

Born George Gordon Liddy in New York City on November 30, 1930, Liddy was in prep school when WWII ended. He enlisted in the Army ROTC program at Fordham University in 1948.

He chose the military speciality of anti-aircraft artillery since it was the only branch of combat arms offered at Fordham.

Liddy was commissioned a second lieutenant upon his graduation in the summer of 1952 and was ordered to report to Ft. Bliss, Texas, for artillery school in preparation for deployment overseas. Liddy volunteered for combat in Korea, but an injury during a sit-up contest in the BOQ (Bachelor Officer Quarters) resulted in a burst appendix.

Liddy was given convalescent leave and his unit went overseas without him. He was assigned to Battery C, 380th AAA Battalion, assigned to protect the skies over Coney Island. He recalls using a magnifying periscope to observe women in nearby high-rise apartments. He was later assigned as executive officer of the 737th AAA Battalion (one of the earliest integrated units) which was transferred to Brooklyn after a mutiny. With the end of fighting in Korea, and the signing of the Armistice on July 27, 1953, Liddy decided to leave the army after two years of active service. (No peace treaty was ever signed; efforts continue to this date to formally end the war.) Liddy remained in the active reserve and transferred to the Judge Advocate Corps after earning his law degree from Fordham University.

He served as a special agent for the FBI, prosecuted Timothy Leary as an assistant DA, ran for Congress, and earned notoriety as one of the "plumbers" during the Watergate scandal. Since his release after four years in prison for his participation in Watergate, Liddy has authored books, acted in bit parts on television, and hosted a radio talk show.

John Marshall. Chief Justice of the U.S. Supreme Court.

Born in Germantown (Fauquier County), Virginia, on September 24, 1755, Marshall joined a regiment of Virginia militia in 1775, and enlisted in the Continental Army in 1776. He saw service at the Battles of Brandywine, Germantown, Monmouth and Valley Forge. He left the army in 1779 and returned home.

He was appointed to the Supreme Court as Chief Justice by

President Adams in 1801, after serving in Congress and as Secretary of State. During his 34 years on the court he was instrumental in enlarging federal powers under the Constitution.

John Mitchell. Nixon's Attorney General.

Born John Newton Mitchell in Detroit on September 15, 1913, Mitchell joined the U.S. Navy and was commissioned an officer at the start of WWII. He spent three years in the Pacific as commanding officer of several squadrons of PT boats, including the one in which Lt. (j.g.) John Kennedy served in the Solomon Islands.

Mitchell served as Attorney General during the Nixon administration (1969–72), and took the position of Chairman of the Committee to Re-elect the President in 1972. He was convicted of conspiracy, obstruction of justice, and perjury in January 1975 for his involvement in Watergate. Released from prison in January 1979, he lived quietly until his death on November 9, 1988.

Frank Murphy. Supreme Court Justice.

Born in Harbor Beach, Michigan, on April 13, 1890, Murphy served as a captain in the U.S. Army during WWI, primarily in Germany. He also served briefly as a lieutenant colonel during WWII.

Murphy was appointed to the high court by FDR in 1940. His most famous ruling was his dissent in *Korematsu v. United States* where he opposed the majority decision to intern Japanese Americans during WWII.

Patrick V. Murphy. New York City Police Commissioner.

Born the son of a policeman in Brooklyn on May 15, 1920, Murphy entered the navy in 1942 as an aviation cadet. He was commissioned an ensign and awarded his pilot's wings before being assigned as a bomber pilot.

He served in the continental U.S., and overseas in North Africa, but he never saw combat. He was discharged late in 1945 as a full lieutenant. He joined the NYPD in December 1945 and rose through the ranks to become commissioner.

Allan Pinkerton. Detective, secret service agent.

Born in Glasgow, Scotland, in 1819, Pinkerton emigrated to America in 1842 and opened the Pinkerton Detective Agency in Chicago in 1850. It was the first private detective agency in the country. The trademark symbol of an open eye, with the motto "we never sleep," resulted in detectives thereafter being referred to as "private eyes."

Already nationally famous, Pinkerton escorted President-elect Lincoln to his inauguration as his bodyguard in 1861. He served as the first director of the U.S. Secret Service, and concurrently served as director of counter-intelligence for the Union army under General McClellan. He resigned in 1863, upon McClellan's dismissal.

He returned to his agency and was prominent in working against the unions and organized labor like the "Molly Maguires." In his later years he wrote three books about his exploits. He died in 1884.

Lewis F. Powell. Supreme Court Justice.

Born in Suffolk, Virginia, on September 19, 1907, Powell was commissioned a second lieutenant in the U.S. Army Air Corps in May 1942. He served as a combat and staff intelligence officer for 33 months overseas in Europe and the Mediterranean. As an intelligence officer, Powell was involved with the ULTRA intelligence intercepts. He was discharged as a colonel with a Bronze Star, a Legion of Merit and the French Croix de Guerre. He transferred to the army reserve in May 1946.

He was appointed to the Supreme Court in 1971 by President Nixon and served until 1987, often casting the swing vote on many controversial cases.

John Paul Stevens. Supreme Court Justice, law professor.

Born in Chicago on April 20, 1920, Stevens graduated Phi

Beta Kappa from the University of Chicago just prior to Pearl Harbor, late in 1941.

Joining the navy in early 1942, Stevens was commissioned an officer, and stationed in Washington DC. He served throughout the war assigned to the staff of Admiral Chester Nimitz as an intelligence officer. He was assigned the task of breaking the Japanese codes.

Although he never saw combat, Stevens was awarded the Bronze Star for his wartime service before being discharged in 1945. He entered Northwestern University School of Law in Chicago where he graduated first in his class, and served as co-editor of the law review.

He was appointed to the Supreme Court by President Ford in December of 1975.

Potter Stewart. Supreme Court Justice.

Born in Jackson, Michigan, on January 23, 1915, Stewart graduated Yale in 1941, and was called to active duty as an ensign in the naval reserve at the end of 1942. He spent three years in the navy, serving as an officer aboard oil tankers in the Atlantic and Mediterranean. He earned three Battle Stars, and was discharged in 1945 as a full lieutenant.

Stewart was appointed an Associate Justice of the United States Supreme Court by President Eisenhower on May 5, 1959.

Joseph Albert Wapner. Retired judge, television jurist.

Born in Los Angeles on November 15, 1919, Wapner attended Hollywood High School, and dreamed of becoming an actor. He had a brief romance with a student in his drama class, Judy Turner, who later changed her hair color to blond and her first name to Lana.

By the time he graduated USC in 1941, his ambition had changed to law. Rejected by the navy after attempting to enlist after Pearl Harbor, Wapner joined the army in 1942.

After graduating OCS (Officer's Candidate School), Wapner was commissioned a first lieutenant in January 1943. He was sent to the South Pacific the following year as a platoon commander in the 132nd Infantry of the Americal Division.

Wapner saw fighting on the islands of Bougainville, Leyte and Cebu in the Philippines. On one occasion in April 1945, he was saved from a sniper's bullet while crossing a rice paddy. The bullet lodged in a can of tuna he was carrying in his pack.

Two days later, he was wounded by mortar shrapnel and phosphorus while rescuing a wounded and trapped corpsman (medic). Although wounded and under the influence of morphine, he continued to command throughout the night. In great pain, he remained in command until the battle concluded the following day. Taken to a field hospital, Wapner was awarded the Bronze Star and a Purple Heart for his actions. He was discharged in 1945.

His television show, *The People's Court*, which he began after retiring from the bench, is viewed by a daily audience exceeding 20 million.

Earl Warren. Chief Justice of the U.S. Supreme Court, Governor of California.

Born in Los Angeles on March 19, 1891, Warren graduated the University of California law school, and applied for a commission in the army upon America's entry into WWI. He was twice rejected for a commission, the first time because there were too many applicants, and the other because he was ill. As a result, Warren was drafted and sent to Camp Lewis, Washington, in charge of a group of draftees.

He was eventually commissioned a lieutenant in the reserves, and transferred to Camp Lee, Virginia, in January 1918. He was assigned to training replacement troops for service in Europe. He was sent as a bayonet instructor to Camp MacArthur, Texas, in November 1918, when the war ended. Warren never went overseas, and was discharged from the army in December 1918 as a first lieutenant. He retained his commission until 1935 when he left the army reserves as a captain.

He practiced law in Oakland, California, until he was elected attorney general of California in 1938. In 1943 he was elected governor and re-elected in 1946. He was the unsuccessful Republican candidate for Vice President under Dewey in 1948. He was appointed to the Supreme Court in 1953 by President Eisenhower.

William Hedgcock Webster. Judge, third FBI director.

Born in St. Louis, Missouri, on March 6, 1924, Webster's undergraduate studies at Amherst College were interrupted by his enrollment in the midshipman's program at Columbia University during WWII.

Webster served as a naval reserve officer from 1943 until 1946, and was released from active duty at the end of the war with the rank of lieutenant (j.g.). He returned to Amherst and graduated with a B.A. in 1947.

After earning a law degree from Washington University in 1949, Webster was recalled to active duty during the Korean War in 1950. Assigned as a lawyer with the Judge Advocate General's office, Webster defended sailors accused of crimes, and was largely responsible for incorporating the right to remain silent into the UCMJ (Uniform Code of Military Justice). He was discharged as a full lieutenant in 1952.

Appointed to the federal district bench in 1971, and the 8th Circuit Court of Appeals in 1973 by President Nixon, Webster was appointed director of the FBI by President Carter on February 23, 1978.

Byron White. Associate Supreme Court Justice.

Born in Ft. Collins, Colorado, on June 8, 1917, White was studying as a Rhodes scholar at Oxford at the outbreak of WWII. He returned to the United States, joined the U.S. Navy, and was commissioned a lieutenant (j.g.) in May 1942. He was assigned to intelligence duties in the South Pacific and wrote the report on the sinking of *PT-109*. He was discharged from the navy in 1946 with two Bronze Stars, and was discharged from the naval reserve in 1954 with the rank of lieutenant commander.

After being discharged at the end of the war, White attended Yale and played two seasons with the Detroit Lions professional football team. He was appointed to the Supreme Court by President Kennedy on March 30, 1962, and served until he resigned in 1993.

Section 2

Women in the Military

Fae Margaret Adams. First woman doctor to receive a regular commission in the U.S. Army.

Born in San Jose, California, in 1918, Adams received her medical degree from the University of Pennsylvania, and was commissioned a first lieutenant in the Regular Army on March 11, 1953.

Previously, Adams had served as a WAC reserve medical officer. After her discharge she went into private practice.

Louisa May Alcott. Author, army nurse.

Born in Germantown, Massachusetts, on November 29, 1832, Alcott went to Washington DC in January of 1863 to work as a volunteer nurse at the Union Hotel Hospital, a run-down converted hotel. Like many Northern women unable to enlist in the army, Alcott manifested her patriotism by serving as a nurse in army hospitals. She arrived on duty three days before the arrival of the wounded from the Battle of Fredericksburg in Virginia

She found the sight of the often armless or legless wounded disturbing, but the real dangers came from treating diseases like dysentery, typhoid fever, and measles in overcrowded and unsanitary conditions. Disease spread rapidly among patients and staff.

Alcott caught typhoid fever after six weeks and returned home to Concord where she recovered, but the effects of the illness stayed with her for the rest of her life. The head nurse died from the same outbreak. In all, over 3,000 women served as nurses during the Civil War. It was an entry into the all-male world of army hospitals. Previously, all nurses were men, often recovering wounded soldiers.

She went on to write her masterpiece, *Little Women*, in 1868. She also wrote *Little Men* and *Roses in Bloom*. She died in Boston in 1888.

Anna Warner "Mother" Bailey. Revolutionary patriot.

Born in Groton, Connecticut, in 1758, Warner was present on September 6, 1781, when General Benedict Arnold landed a British force near Groton to lay siege to nearby Fort Griswold.

Learning that her uncle, Edward Mills, was a casualty, she traveled to the battlefield and found her uncle mortally wounded. She braved enemy fire to leave the field and return with Mills' wife and infant daughter for a last family meeting. Her actions made her a legend of the Revolution.

Warner married Captain Bailey, the Groton postmaster. In 1813, during the second war with England (the War of 1812), Bailey (nee Warner) was with the soldiers resisting the British blockade of New London. She donated her petticoats for cartridge wadding during the battle. She died in 1851, an acknowledged veteran.

Josephine Baker. Entertainer, humanitarian.

Born in St. Louis on June 3, 1906, Baker was living in France as an expatriate at the outbreak of WWII. She became a valuable member of the French resistance. Since she was too conspicuous a figure to actively participate in underground activities, her chateau served as a liaison center in occupied France. She also accompanied a French intelligence officer in collecting information in neutral Lisbon. Baker acted as a conduit for communications between the Allies and the French government in exile.

Baker was in Casablanca when it was liberated by the Allies in November 1942. She spent the remainder of the war entertaining troops throughout North Africa and the Middle East. She was with the 1st French Army in August 1944 when Paris was liberated. She was awarded the rank of lieutenant and a Croix de Lorraine for her service to France during the war.

Barbara Olive Barnwell. First woman awarded the Navy-Marine Corps Medal for heroism.

Barnwell, a staff sergeant in the marine reserve, was the first woman to be awarded the Navy-Marine Corps Medal for her actions in saving a soldier from drowning in 1952.

Ann Baumgartner. First female jet pilot.

A Women's Auxiliary Ferrying Service (WAFS) pilot during WWII, Baumgartner took off from Wright Field in Ohio in October 1944 in a YP-59, the first experimental jet. She flew at 35,000 feet at speeds in excess of 350 mph.

Florence Blanchfield. Nursing pioneer, first woman commissioned in the Regular Army.

Born in Shepherdstown, West Virginia, on April 1, 1884, Blanchfield studied at the Southside Hospital Training School for Nurses in Pittsburgh, receiving her degree in 1906. She did post graduate work at John Hopkins Hospital, and worked as a nurse in Panama and for U.S. Steel.

Blanchfield enlisted in the Army Nurses Corps (ANC) during WWI. She served briefly at Ellis Island before being shipped overseas to France. She was assigned to three different hospitals from 1917 to 1919 with the "relative" rank of lieutenant. (Women nurses served at lower "relative" ranks with reduced benefits; they were also required to remain unmarried.)

Separated from the army at the end of the war, Blanchfield returned to the Nurses Corps in 1920. She served as an advisor to the Secretary of War before joining the staff of the Surgeon General in 1935. After two decades of service, Blanchfield was promoted to "relative" captain in 1939.

Assigned to the office of Superintendent of the Nurses Corps in March 1942, Blanchfield was promoted to lieutenant colonel. When the superintendent of the Nurses Corps, Colonel Julia Flikke, retired later that year, Blanchfield was promoted to colonel and named superintendent early in 1943. (Flikke was the first woman promoted to colonel.) As superintendent, Blanchfield was responsible for a corps of women 57,000 strong, assigned from Alaska to Australia. (Male colonels commanded units sometimes as small as 500 men.) She went on numerous overseas tours during the war. Despite her rank of colonel, she received the pay of a lieutenant colonel. She was awarded the Distinguished Service Medal at the end of the war.

With the Army-Navy Nurse Act of 1947, relative rank was eliminated and the Army Nurses Corps was integrated into the Regular Army. (The WAC was integrated a year later.) General Eisenhower commissioned Blanchfield the first woman in the Regular Army on July 18, 1947. She was reduced in grade to lieutenant colonel but had her rank restored to colonel by special legislation.

Blanchfield introduced innovations to the Nurses Corps including combat and survival training for nurses, combat surgery teams, air evacuation, and equal opportunity for women in the military. She retired in 1947 after 30 years of service. She died in Washington DC on May 12, 1971, and is buried at Arlington National Cemetery.

Lucy Brewer. First woman marine.

Little is known of Lucy Brewer other than that she concealed her sex and enlisted in the marines as "George Baker" during the War of 1812. She served three years as part of the marine detachment aboard the frigate USS *Constitution*, and was present during the battle between the *Constitution* and the British frigate HMS *Guerriere* on August 19, 1812.

Once during an engagement, Brewer lost her balance in the riggings of her ship (marines fired on the crews of enemy ships from the riggings) and fell into the sea. It took all her effort to keep her shipmates from removing her wet clothing, but she remained undiscovered and completed her tour of duty. The *Constitution* won the engagement.

Margaret Brewer. First female Marine Corps general.

Born in 1930, Brewer graduated from the University of Michigan, Ann Arbor, and enlisted in the Marine Corps. She was later commissioned a second lieutenant, and rose steadily through the ranks.

Brewer was the seventh (and last) director of the Women Marines. (Women began to be fully integrated into the Marine Corps starting in 1948). She served as Director of Information at Marine Headquarters in Washington DC and was promoted to brigadier general in 1978. The marines were the last service to promote a woman to the flag rank of general/admiral.

Margarethe Cammermeyer. National Guard Chief Nurse, gay rights activist.

Born in occupied Norway in 1942, Cammermeyer went on her first military mission at the age of one when her mother and a friend, members of the resistance, smuggled guns in her baby carriage past unsuspecting German troops.

Born the daughter of a prominent neurologist, her family emigrated to the U.S. after the war. In 1961 she enlisted in the Army Student Nursing Program to help pay her college tuition. Cammermeyer graduated, was discharged from the army as a private first class, and commissioned a WAC second lieutenant in 1963.

After duty stateside, Cammermeyer, now a newly promoted captain, was transferred to Germany where she met and married an armor officer. In early 1967 her husband received orders for Vietnam, and Cammermeyer volunteered so that they could serve together. Her orders came through and his were canceled, so she went to Vietnam alone. She spent a 14-month tour of duty as the head nurse of a ward of an evacuation hospital at Long Binh. She earned a Bronze Star and an education in combat medicine.

After becoming pregnant with the first of her four sons, she was required by regulation to resign from the army. She regained her commission when the regulation was changed in 1975, but she opted to remain with the Veteran's Administration and enlist in the Army Reserve rather than return to active duty. She served in Washington state, and after her divorce, in San Francisco.

In 1987 Cammermeyer, by now a full colonel, returned to Washington state to accept the position of Chief Nurse of the Washington National Guard. Her goal was to become Chief Nurse of the entire National Guard. In order to be considered for the position, with the accompanying rank of general, Cammermeyer was required to attend the War College and this required an upgrading of her security clearance. In May 1989, in the course of a routine interview by the Defense Investigative Service, she disclosed her recently discovered sexual orientation by stating, "I am a lesbian."

Slowly but surely, actions were taken to withdraw her federal certification and discharge her for violating army regulations prohibiting homosexuals from serving in the military. In 1993 Cammermeyer, who could have chosen to resign with full benefits, or earlier could have chosen to say nothing, chose to challenge the army's policy towards homosexuals as discriminatory.

As a result, she was discharged without benefits after 26 years of otherwise distinguished service. She thus became the highest ranking officer to date to challenge the military's anti-gay policy. Her case continues in the civilian courts.

Julia Child. Gourmet cook, author.

Born Julia McWilliams in Pasadena, California, on August 15, 1912, she joined the Office of Strategic Services at the start of WWII with ambitions of being a spy. She was instead assigned as a file clerk in Washington DC, Ceylon and China.

It was while she was in Ceylon that she met another OSS

employee, future husband Paul Cushing Child, a painter turned mapmaker. They were both sent to China where they had long chats over Chinese cuisine which her future husband taught her to cook. They were married after leaving the OSS at the end of the war. Child hosted the TV cooking show, *The French Chef*, from 1962–83.

Mary Clarke. First woman major general in the U.S. Army.

Clarke enlisted in the WAAC (Women's Army Auxiliary Corps) at the beginning of WWII. She served as the last commanding officer of the Women's Corps before it was dissolved and integrated into the Regular Army.

Promoted to major general in June of 1978, she was appointed commanding officer of the Military Police and the Chemical Corps Training Schools at Fort McClellan, Alabama, then as Director of Human Resources Development in the office of the Deputy Chief of Staff. She earned her doctorate in military science from Norwich University and retired in 1981, making her the longest serving woman in the military—36 years of service.

Jacqueline Cochran. Record breaking aviator, WASP director, cosmetics executive.

An early woman pioneer in aviation, Cochran was born in Pensacola, Florida, on May 11, 1910, and grew up in poverty as a foster-child, working by the age of eight. She took her first flying lesson in 1932 and earned her commercial pilot's license in 1933. In June of 1941, prior to America's entry into WWII and under the direction of General Hap Arnold, she was granted a commission in the Army Air Corps reserve and became the first woman to pilot a heavy bomber across the Atlantic, proving that women could handle heavy aircraft. She was successful despite sabotage and taunting by some male co-workers.

In England she volunteered for combat, but the only co-pilot who agreed to fly with her was captured by the Germans. While in England she trained 25 American women as transport pilots for the Air Transport Auxiliary of the Royal Air Force. This freed up male pilots for combat. She was named an honorary flight captain.

She then returned to the U.S. to direct women's flight training for the armed forces, merging the Women's Air Force Service (WAFS) with the Women's Air Force Services Pilots (WASPS) in July of 1943, retaining the latter's name.

She was awarded the Distinguished Service Medal in 1945. Towards the end of the war, Cochrane served as a war correspondent for *Liberty* magazine in the Pacific and Europe. She was present at the Japanese surrender aboard the USS *Missouri* (BB-63) and was the first American woman to enter occupied Japan after the war. She met with Madame Chiang Kai-Shek and Chairman Mao Zedong in China, visited the Buchenwald Concentration Camp, and observed the war crime trials at Nuremberg.

She went on to win air races, set world aviation records, and became the first woman to break the sound barrier in 1953 in an F-86 Sabrejet. She unsuccessfully ran for Congress, and saved Senator Lyndon Johnson's life by flying him to a hospital when he became ill on campaign.

She retired from the Air Force Reserve in 1970 as a colonel, headed a cosmetics firm, and died in Indio, California, in 1980.

Cordelia E. Cook. First woman to receive the Bronze Star.

Born in Fort Thomas, Kentucky, Cook was a first lieutenant in the Army Nurses Corps during WWII. She served overseas in Italy in 1943. When the field hospital where she was assigned was attacked, Cook continued to perform her duties despite repeated bombardments from November 1943 to January 1944. For her coolness under fire, Cook was awarded the Bronze Star, the first woman to receive one.

For wounds received during an artillery attack in January 1944, Cook was awarded the Purple Heart, making her the first woman to receive two awards.

Margaret Corbin. First woman to serve as a soldier during the American Revolution.

Born in 1751, Corbin took over for her husband serving an artillery piece when he was killed at the Battle of Fort Washington, New York, in 1776. She continued to fight in the battle until she herself was wounded in the arm by grapeshot, resulting in a permanent disability.

In 1779 Pennsylvania voted her a relief payment, and the Continental Congress gave her half a soldier's disability pay for life. She enrolled in the Invalid Regiment for wounded veteran's and remained in it until it was disbanded in 1783. Dubbed "Captain Molly," she died in 1801.

Sue Sophia Dauser. First woman commissioned in the Regular Navy.

Born in 1888 in Anaheim, California, Dauser attended Stanford University and nursing school, and worked as a surgical supervisor before WWI.

In September 1917 Dauser enlisted in the Navy Reserve, and entered active service in October. In 1918 her appointment as a reserve nurse was terminated so she could be commissioned a chief nurse in the Regular Navy. She served overseas at a military hospital in Scotland from July 1918 until the armistice.

After the war she served in France, Brooklyn, San Diego, and aboard the hospital ship USS *Relief* (AH-1) in the Pacific. She nursed President Harding when he traveled to Alaska in 1923. From 1926–29 she served in increasingly responsible positions in Guam, the Philippines, Puget Sound and Long Beach. Unlike army nurses, navy nurses were neither officers nor enlisted, and didn't receive "relative rank" until an act of Congress in 1942.

In 1939 Dauser was selected as Superintendent of Navy Nurses, and in July of 1942 received the rank of lieutenant commander. In February 1944 she became the first woman to receive a regular commission as a Navy nurse with the temporary rank of captain.

Dorothea Lynde Dix. Founder of the Army Nurses Corps, prison reformer.

Dix was born in Hampden, Maine, on April 4, 1802, and was teaching Sunday school to women inmates at the East Cambridge House of Corrections in 1841 when she first became interested in penal and mental health reform.

In 1861, early in the Civil War, Secretary of War Edwin Stanton appointed Dix to found and direct the Army Nurses Corps which numbered 10,000 members by war's end.

Dix was criticized for her supervision of the corps. She required her nurses to be over thirty years old and "plain." She rejected those whose religious affiliation she didn't agree with, and was heavy-handed in her supervision. However, she was still the superintendent when she died in 1866.

Alene Duerk. First female admiral, director of the Navy Nurse Corps.

Born in Ohio in 1920, Duerk graduated from the Hospital School of Nursing in Toledo in 1941. After Pearl Harbor she enlisted in the Navy Nurses Corps and was later commissioned an ensign. She served stateside and in the Pacific aboard the hospital ship *Benevolence* (AH-13).

Discharged after the war, she remained in the Naval Reserve while earning a B.S. in nursing in 1948. Recalled to active duty during the Korean War in 1951, Duerk transferred to the Regular Navy in 1953.

She served as a nursing instructor, and as an officer recruiter in Chicago in 1958, earning a promotion from lieutenant to lieutenant commander. Promoted to commander in 1962, she served as a nurse in the Philippines and Japan before being assigned to the Bureau of Naval Personnel in Washington DC in 1967. She was promoted to captain and in May of 1970 was appointed Director of the Navy Nurses Corps. Duerk became the first woman in the navy's history to attain flag rank when in 1972 she was promoted to rear admiral. She retired in 1975.

Sarah Emma Edmonds. Soldier, spy, nurse.

Born in New Brunswick, Canada, in December, 1841, Sarah grew up the fifth daughter of a man who was bitterly disappointed at his lack of male heirs. She learned to shoot and ride at an early age. When the Civil War broke out, Edmonds, now 20, cut her hair and enlisted as private "Frank Thompson" in Company F, 2nd Michigan Volunteer Infantry Regiment. She served as a male field nurse in Virginia, then was accepted and trained as a combat soldier. She stood guard, drilled, and did picket duty.

She fought at First Bull Run and Chickahominy, and spied for the Union Army "disguised" as a woman, but in 1863 she deserted when it seemed her secret would be exposed. She authored a book, *Nurse and Spy in the Union Army*, but kept her soldiering a secret, even from her husband, until she was awarded a veteran's pension from Congress in 1882. She died in 1898 and is buried in a Grand Army of the Republic cemetery plot.

Joycelyn Elders. U.S. Surgeon General, physician.

Born Minnie Lee Jones in Schaal, Arkansas, on August 13, 1933, Elders came from humble beginnings. She entered Philander Smith College in Little Rock at the age of 15 on a scholarship from the United Methodist Church. She earned her bachelor's degree in three years while working as a maid to support herself.

After earning her degree in 1952, Elders worked as a nurse's aide in a veterans hospital until she enlisted in the Army in May 1953, using the name Minnie J. Jones. She was sent to Brooke Army Medical Center at Fort Sam Houston where she was the only black person in her class. She was commissioned a second

Joycelyn Elders

lieutenant in the Army Medical Specialist Corps in October 1953, and began her internship as a physical therapist.

She was stationed at Letterman Army Hospital in San Francisco treating returning combat wounded from the Korean War which ended in July of 1953. In April 1954 Elders was licensed as a physical therapist and transferred to Fitzsimmons Hospital in Denver. She was one of two therapists who treated President Eisenhower after his heart attack. She resigned her commission in May 1956.

After her discharge, Elders attended the University of Arkansas Medical School on the GI Bill. She went on to serve as Director of the Arkansas Department of Health under Governor Bill Clinton. When Clinton was elected President in 1992, Elders accepted his appointment of her as Surgeon General.

Ann Leah Fox. First woman to be awarded a Purple Heart.

Born in Canada circa 1918, Fox became the first woman to be awarded the Purple Heart for wounds she received in a combat zone while serving as head nurse for Hickam Field, Hawaii, during the Japanese attack on Pearl Harbor on December 7, 1941.

Irene Galloway. Fourth director of WAC.

Born in Carroll County, Iowa, on September 1, 1908, Galloway enlisted in a surge of patriotism at the start of WWII, but never planned on staying in the army after the war.

She was assigned to the second class of women officer candidates at Ft. Des Moines, Iowa, and graduated in September 1942. She was commissioned a second lieutenant and was assigned to the office of the Assistant Chief of Staff for Personnel in Washington DC.

In November 1943 Galloway was promoted to major and was assigned to inspection tours overseas (1943–44). She visited WAC units and served as the WAC staff advisor to the European Command before returning to the U.S.

In February 1950 Galloway was promoted to lieutenant colonel, and in October 1952 was appointed commanding officer of the Women's Training Center at Ft. Lee, Virginia.

With Colonel Mary Hallaren's resignation in December 1952, Galloway was appointed the fourth Director of the Women's Army Corps. She was promoted to colonel and sworn in on January 3, 1953.

Deborah Sampson Gannett. Soldier, lecturer.

Born Deborah Sampson in Plympton, Massachusetts, on December 17, 1760, Gannett enlisted in May 1782, as a private in the 4th Massachusetts Regiment disguised as a man using the name of "Robert Shurtleff" (some sources say Shirtliff) during the American Revolution.

She was wounded by a saber at the battle of Tarrytown and by a musket ball at East Chester, but she dressed her own wounds so her disguise remained intact. When she was hospitalized for a fever in 1783 she wasn't as fortunate and her sex was discovered. She was promptly discharged from the army in October 1783, and was given a sum of money from General Henry Knox. She was subsequently excommunicated from the Baptist Church for the "sin" of dressing in men's clothing.

She lectured on her military experiences, dressed in her old uniform, until 1802. In April 1785 she married Benjamin Gannett. She wrote a book of her experiences, *The Female Review* (1797). Gannett was awarded a veteran's pension from the state of Massachusetts in 1792, and through the intervention of Paul Revere, a federal pension in 1805. She died on April 29, 1827.

Gale Ann Gordon. First female navy pilot.

Born in Ohio in 1943, Ensign Gordon, the only woman in a training flight of 999 men, became the navy's first woman pilot when she soloed in a propeller driven T-34 trainer on March 29, 1966.

Assigned to the Medical Service Corps at Pensacola Naval

Air Station, Gordon also earned a master's degree in aviation psychology from Michigan State University.

Edith Greenwood. First woman to receive the Soldier's Medal.

When a fire broke out at the military hospital in Yuma, Arizona, on April 17, 1943, Lt. Greenwood and an attendant, Pvt. James Ford, risked their lives to successfully evacuate every patient safely without any injuries. For their heroism they were each awarded the Soldier's Medal, making Greenwood the first female to receive the award.

Mary Agnes Hallaren. First woman commissioned in the Regular Army.

Born on May 4, 1907, in Lowell, Massachusetts, Hallaren attended the state teacher's college in Lowell and earned her teaching certificate. Hallaren was a teacher and world traveler when she enlisted in the WAACs in July of 1942, and was among the first class of WAAC officer candidates at Fort Des Moines, Iowa.

Commissioned a second lieutenant upon graduation, her first assignments were as a battalion commander serving stateside at Camp Devens, Massachusetts, Camp Shanks, New York, and Camp Polk, Louisiana.

In July of 1943 she was promoted to captain and assigned as commanding officer of the 1st WAAC Separate Battalion which was sent overseas to England and assigned to the 8th Air Force. With this overseas assignment to the "wartime" army, "auxiliary" was dropped from the title and the corps was renamed the Women's Army Corps (WAC).

Later that year Hallaren was assigned as Air WAC Staff Director, responsible for all WAC personnel serving with the 8th and 9th Air Forces. While stationed in London, she endured blitz bombings and V-1/V-2 rocket attacks.

She crossed the English Channel with the WAC contingent during the Normandy invasion, and in March of 1945 was promoted to lieutenant colonel and named Director for all WACs in the ETO (European Theater of Operations). In this position she was responsible for 9000 women stationed in England, France, Austria, Germany and Belgium. She was awarded the Bronze Star, Legion of Merit with Oak Cluster and Croix de Guerre for her wartime service.

After the war she was named chief of personnel of the civilian employee section of the War Department, and in June of 1946 was recalled to Washington as Deputy Director of the WAC. In May of 1947 Hallaren was named the third director of the WAC with the rank of colonel in the Army reserve.

With the Armed Forces Integration Act of 1948, the WAC became a corps in the Regular Army, and Hallaren became the first woman to be commissioned in the Regular Army. The act opened all career fields to women except combat arms (i.e., infantry, artillery, and armor).

Oveta Culp Hobby. First Secretary of Health, Education and Welfare, first director of WAAC.

Born on January 19, 1905, in Killeen, Texas, Hobby worked for the War Department prior to the war, helping to plan a women's auxiliary. With the creation of the Women's Army Auxiliary Corps (WAAC) in May 1942, Hobby served as its first director with the rank of major (later colonel). She oversaw the transition of the WAAC into the WAC (Women's Army Corps) as part of the Regular Army in July 1943. She was the director of WAC until 1945.

Hobby was the first woman to be awarded the U.S. Army Distinguished

Oveta Culp Hobby

Service Medal (1945). Seventeen thousand women served overseas during WWII under her command. She was the first woman
officer, other than nurses, to be commissioned as an officer in
the Regular Army.

After the war, Hobby served as executive vice president of
the Houston *Post* before being appointed the first Secretary of
Health, Education and Welfare by President Eisenhower in 1953.
She served until July 1955 when she returned to the Houston
Post as president and editor, and later publisher upon the death
of her husband. Hobby remained influential in Republican politics until her death on August 16, 1995.

Ethel Ann Hoefly. First USAF nurse to become a general.

Born in 1920, Hoefly earned her master's degree from Columbia University and joined the Army Nurses Corps at the start
of WWII. She served throughout the war.

She transferred to the Air Force Nurses Corps (USAFNC)
upon its establishment in 1949. She was named its director in
1958 with the rank of colonel. In 1972 she was promoted to brigadier general becoming the first nurse to hold flag rank. She retired two years later in 1974.

Jeanne M. Holm. First woman Air Force general.

Born in Portland, Oregon, in 1921, Holm enlisted in the
WAAC (Women's Army Auxiliary Corps) at the start of WWII.
She served initially as a truck driver until she was commissioned
a second lieutenant in 1943.

She left the army at the end of the war but was recalled to
active duty in 1948. She supervised manpower needs from 1957
until 1965 when she was appointed Director of Women in the
Air Force (1965–72). She was promoted to brigadier general in
1971 and served as Director of Personnel from 1973–75. Holm
retired again in 1975 with the rank of major general after 33
years of service.

She went on to serve as a special assistant to President Ford and as a member of the Defense Advisory Committee on Women in the Armed Forces. Her book, *Women in the Military,* was used as a resource for this book.

Olive Hoskins. First female army warrant officer.

Born in Pasadena, California, around 1890, Hoskins worked for the U.S. Army as a civilian clerk in 1907 and as an army field clerk in 1916. When that grade was abolished in 1926, she was appointed a warrant officer (a grade between enlisted and commissioned ranks).

During WWI Hoskins was director of personnel for the Judge Advocate General's Office in San Francisco. She served in the Philippines and at the headquarters of both the 7th and 9th Corps before retiring in 1937.

Opha M. Johnson. First woman Marine Corps reservist.

In August 1918 the Secretary of the Navy authorized the Commandant of the Marine Corps to accept the enlistment of women as marine reservists. The next day Johnson was enlisted as the first female marine recruit. She served as a clerk in Washington DC in the quartermaster corps and was discharged in 1919.

(Altogether 1277 women served in the Marine Corps reserves during the First World War.)

Jane Kendeigh. First woman to land on a battlefield in WWII.

Born in Oberlin, Ohio, in 1922, Kendeigh graduated from Cleveland's St. Luke Hospital Medical School and enlisted in the navy. She was later commissioned an ensign and assigned to the Naval Air Transport Service (NATS) during WWII.

The NATS mission was to fly into combat areas and evacuate wounded marines by air. On March 6, 1945, on the sixth day of the Iwo Jima invasion, Lieutenant (j.g.) Ann Purvis was slated to be the first flight nurse to land in a combat area. As fate would have it, her plane became lost and the plane carrying Ensign Kendeigh landed first, after circling the island for 90 minutes during an offshore bombardment of the island.

Jane Kendeigh

The mission was a 15-hour round trip by air in an unarmed C-47 transport. They left from Agana Air Field in Guam carrying medical supplies, and returned from Iwo Jima with seriously wounded marines. They risked attack by enemy aircraft in the air, and enemy artillery and small arms fire while on the ground.

Kendeigh was also the first flight nurse to land on Okinawa in April 1945. (Eighty five women served with NATS in the Pacific, transporting and treating the wounded from the Mariana Islands to Hawaii to the mainland.)

Elizabeth Korensky. First member of WAVES killed in WWII.

At 11 a.m. September 17, 1943, an explosion at Norfolk Naval Base killed 30 people, injured 426, destroyed 15 buildings including six barracks, the CPO club, a hanger, and 33 aircraft. Among the casualties was Seaman 2nd Class Elizabeth Korensky, the only female killed, and the first WAVES member to die in the line of duty in WWII.

The cause of the explosion was overloaded trailers. To save time, a third bomb was transported on trailers designed for two, and one slipped off during transport, detonating itself and 23 others. The resulting explosion broke windows in Norfolk, seven miles away, and could be heard 20 miles away in Suffolk.

Janna Lambine. First female U.S. Coast Guard pilot.

After earning a degree in geology, Lambine enlisted in the coast guard and completed flight school at Whiting Field Air

Station in Florida. In 1977 she was commissioned an ensign and pilot and assigned to search and rescue duties.

Elsie S. Lott. First woman to receive the U.S. Air Medal.

Lott was commissioned a second lieutenant in the Army Nurses Corps at the start of WWII. She was awarded the Air Medal for her actions in June 1943 when she nursed wounded patients being evacuated by air from India to Washington.

Geraldine Pratt May. First Director of Women in the Air Force.

Born Geraldine Pratt in Albany, New York, on April 21, 1895, Pratt graduated from the University of California at Berkeley in 1920. She worked as a social worker until she married in 1928. In July 1942 she enlisted in the WAAC, and was in the first class of woman officer candidates at Ft. Des Moines, Iowa. Pratt, now May, was commissioned a second lieutenant and assigned recruiting duties in Oklahoma.

Lt. May was among the first 18 WAC officers assigned to the Air Corps. In March 1943 May was appointed WAC Staff Director of Air Transport, responsible for 6000 women in 29 continental and 12 overseas commands. May remained in that position until the end of the war. She was promoted to captain in April 1943, and to major toward the end of the war.

In October 1946, May, now a lieutenant colonel, was assigned to the War Department general staff in Washington. After a tour of duty as WAC Staff Director for ground forces, where she was responsible for supervising WAC personnel in six armies, and upon implementation of the Armed Forces Integration Act of 1948, May was promoted to full colonel and was appointed the first Director of Women in the Air Force (WAF).

Although women were not permitted to be pilots, bombardiers or navigators, numerous other technical and administrative opportunities were opened to women. For her war service May was awarded the Legion of Merit.

Mildred Helen McAfee Horton. College president, first director of WAVES.

Born in Missouri in 1900, McAfee attended Vassar College, earned her master's degree at the University of Chicago, and by age 36 was President of Wellesley College.

Shortly after the outbreak of WWII, she was selected to serve on a committee to establish a naval reserve program for women. Upon its creation on July 30, 1942, (under Public Law 689) McAfee was named director of the newly created WAVES (Women Appointed for Volunteer Emergency Service) with the rank of lieutenant commander.

Of her task, she stated "My first assignment was just getting enough women there to start doing something, and what they were to do was as vague to me as it was to the rest of the navy at the time."

She was responsible for creating the code of conduct for WAVES that included no smoking on streets, dating only on leave, and the same alcohol regulations as men. The WAVES performed administrative and technical duties, freeing men for combat duty. Promoted to captain in 1945, she served as head of the Women's Naval Reserve, and was responsible for commanding 86,000 commissioned and enlisted women during the war.

After the war she returned to Wellesley until 1949. She served as a U.S. delegate to UNESCO (United Nations Education, Science and Cultural Organization) as well as numerous corporate boards, and was named co-chair of the National Women's Committee on Civil Rights by President Kennedy. She died September 2, 1994.

Mary McCauley. "Molly Pitcher"

Born in Trenton, New Jersey, in 1754, McCauley accompanied her first husband, John C. Hays, an artillerist in the Seventh Pennsylvania Regiment, into camp in New Jersey during the American Revolution. She did cooking and laundry (a common practice of the time).

At the battle at Monmouth on June 28, 1778, McCauley gained fame and her nickname by bringing water to wounded troops during the battle, often at great personal risk. When her husband was either wounded or overcome by heat, she took his place at the cannon.

Upon the death of her husband in 1792, she married John McCauley, another revolution veteran. In 1822 Pennsylvania recognized her war service by voting her a lifetime pension, making her the first woman so honored.

It is possible that there was another "Molly Pitcher," known as Mary Ludwig.

Anita Newcomb McGee. Physician, founder of the Army Nurses Corps.

Born in Washington DC in 1864 during the Civil War, McGee earned her M.D. from George Washington University and was assigned to screen and train nurses for the army and navy during the Spanish-American War in 1898. These nurses would become the nucleus of the future corps.

McGee was named the Army Nurses Corps first director in 1900 with a concurrent appointment as Assistant Surgeon General, the first women to hold that post. She served as director until the end of 1900. The Army Reorganization Act of 1901 established the Army Nurses Corps as a permanent part of the army. The Red Cross pressured an insertion into the Act requiring that the director be a graduate nurse; so McGee, a physician, was ineligible for serving as director once the Act became law.

After her resignation, she formed the Society of Spanish-American War Nurses and served as its president. She also served as a nurse during the Russo-Japanese War.

Margaret Mead. Anthropologist.

Born in Philadelphia in 1901, Mead worked writing pamphlets (promoting good relations between English and American troops) for the Office of War Information (OWI) during WWII.

Mary Louise Milligan. Women's Army Corps Director.

Born in East Pittsburgh in 1911, Milligan earned a masters degree in education/school administration from the University of Pittsburgh in 1941. She was working as a school administrator before Pearl Harbor.

Upon the formation of the Women's Army Auxiliary Corps (WAAC), Milligan volunteered for service as an officer candidate in July 1942 at age 31 with the rank of "auxiliary private." After graduating officer training with 436 other women at Ft. Des Moines in Iowa, she was commissioned a "Third Officer" or second lieutenant and was assigned the duties of a classification officer.

In March 1943 Milligan was appointed the director of the training center and was in charge of training over 65,000 women over the next three years. The mission of the WAC (the name was changed to Women's Army Corps on July 1, 1943) was to free men for combat assignments.

In 1946 Captain Milligan was reassigned to Washington DC on the general staff after graduating the Army Command and General Staff School at Ft. Leavenworth.

Lt. Colonel Milligan served as deputy director of the WAC (1947–52), WAC staff advisor in Europe (1952–56), and as a staff officer at the Continental Army Command HQ.

In 1957 she was promoted to colonel and appointed Director of the WAC with the responsibility of commanding the corps and advising the Secretary of the Army and general staff on women's issues. She was awarded the Legion of Merit for her service during the war.

Madalyn Murray (O'Hair). Lawyer, atheist.

Born in Pittsburgh, Pennsylvania, on April 12, 1919, O'Hair has been called "the most hated woman in America." She joined the WAAC at the start of WWII, and was assigned overseas as a cryptographer on General Eisenhower's staff. She saw action in

Italy and North Africa, and earned five Battle Stars. O'Hair was discharged from the army as a second lieutenant at the end of the war.

Her courtroom victory in Murray vs. Curlett in 1963 removed and outlawed prayer in public school, but it has been asserted that as long as there are exams, there will always be prayers in school.

Phyllis Ladora Propp. First woman officer in the Judge Advocate General's Office.

Propp enlisted in the WAAC on October 3, 1942. She was commissioned an officer, and was detailed to the Judge Advocate General's Office (JAG) on May 3, 1944, as a captain. Propp served on active duty until September 21, 1949.

Barbara Allen Rainey. First female navy pilot.

Born in Long Beach, California, in 1948, Rainey enlisted in the navy, completed her flight training in one year, and was commissioned and awarded her gold aviator wings in 1974.

She served with the Pacific Fleet and was assigned to Training Squadron #3 at Whiting Field in Florida. She died suddenly at the age of 34 in 1982. Lt. Commander Rainey was buried with full military honors at Arlington National Cemetery.

Mary Jo Shelly. WAF Director.

The second woman to command the WAF, Shelly was born in Grand Rapids, Michigan, on February 17, 1902. After earning her B.A. from the University of Oregon in 1926, and a master's degree from Columbia University in 1929, she worked in the field of education at several colleges.

In September of 1942 Shelly took a leave of absence from Bennington College to take charge of the Women's Reserve of the Navy (WAVES). She was among the first twelve women commissioned as lieutenants. During the war, she was the assistant for women's reserve to the Director of Training for the Navy, helping to set up 32 WAVES training schools across the country. She was a liaison officer to Captain Mildred McAfee, then Director of the WAVES.

At the end of the war, she was promoted to lieutenant commander and assigned as an assistant to the Director of Planning, as which she organized the peacetime demobilization of the WAVES, reducing the number from a wartime 80,000 to about 40,000. She went inactive in March of 1946 as a full commander and returned to Bennington.

On May 31, 1951, General Vandenburg, the Air Force Chief of Staff, announced Shelly's appointment as the second WAF Commander, replacing Colonel Geraldine Pratt May. On June 6, Shelly resigned her naval appointment, and on June 12 was commissioned a colonel in the U.S. Air Force, and named Director of the Women's Air Force.

Margaret Chase Smith. Three-term U.S. Senator.

Born in Skowhegan, Maine, on December 14, 1897, Smith served on the Naval Affairs Committee in Congress during WWII. She was the first woman to sail on a destroyer during wartime.

After the war, she was instrumental in the Women's Armed Services Integration Act which was signed by President Truman on June 12, 1948. It provided for women to be absorbed into the regular military, rather than as WACs, WAVES, WAFs, etc. (This was necessary because women were brought into the military during WWII through emergency legislation that expired after the war. The act made women a permanent, rather than temporary, part of our nation's military in recognition of their outstanding performance during the war.) Smith retired from the U.S. Air Force Reserve as a lieutenant colonel. She holds the record as the longest serving woman in the Senate (1948–72).

Julia Catherine Stimson. Director of the Army Nurses Corps.

Born in 1881 in Worster, Massachusetts, Stimson earned a B.A. from Vassar College, and did graduate work at Columbia before graduating from nurses school in 1908 (her father, brother and sister were all doctors).

With America's entry into WWI, Stimson enlisted as a reserve nurse in the Army Nurses Corps and was ordered to Europe in May of 1917, assigned as Chief Nurse of Base Hospital #21. Upon her arrival, the hospital was assigned to the British Expeditionary Force in Rouen, France.

In April 1918 Stimson was transferred to the American Red Cross Headquarters in Paris where she assumed the duties of Chief Nurse for all Red Cross nurses in France and coordinator of Red Cross and army nurses. She was eventually promoted to captain and Director of Nurses in the Allied Expeditionary Force, supervising 10,000 nurses in the Army Nurses Corps.

The need for nurses during the war prompted the creation of an Army Nursing School, and Stimson was named Acting Superintendent of the school upon her return to the United States in July of 1919. She served concurrently as superintendent of the corps, and was promoted to major, the first army nurse to hold that rank.

During her twenty years as director, Stimson helped define women's role in the military, raising the standards and improving conditions for women. She retired as a major in 1937, but returned to active duty in 1942 during WWII. She was awarded the Distinguished Service Medal, and helped form the American Nurses Association (ANA).

Dorothy Constance Stratton. SPAR Commander, professor.

Born in Missouri in 1899, Stratton earned a B.A. from Ottawa University in Kansas in 1920, taught high school in Washington, and was a vice principal in California. By 1933 she had earned her Ph.D. and was an associate professor of psychology and Dean of Women at Purdue University.

In 1942 she joined the WAVES as a lieutenant because she felt "it was important for women to give a good account of themselves during the war." After graduating from the first naval training class at Smith College in September, she was assigned as assistant to the commanding officer at the training center for radio operators in Wisconsin.

In November she was transferred to the office of Commandant of the Coast Guard to work on a proposal for a Women's Coast Guard Reserve, and was promoted to lieutenant commander. On November 24, 1942, Stratton was sworn in as Commander of the SPAR (Semper Paratus—Always Ready).

The SPARs received the same training as WAVES, but served primarily as stenographers, radio operators, pharmacists, and photographers. They received the same pay as men. (Military women have received equal pay to men since WWI, but often were given different rank, called "relative" rank.) Stratton commanded the SPAR throughout the war and retired as a captain.

Ruth Cheney Streeter. Director of Marine Corps Women's Reserve.

Born October 2, 1895, in Brookline, Massachusetts, Streeter graduated Bryn Mawr College in 1918. She became an accomplished pilot and earned her commercial license in 1942, a rare accomplishment for women at that time.

On February 12, 1943, the U. S. Marine Corps created a Women's Reserve, the last armed service to do so. With an authorized strength of 19,000 (18,000 enlisted, 1000 officers), enlistees were designated as Class 6 Reserves. Unlike WACs, WAFs, or WAVES, women marines preferred the simple title "marine." The only

Ruth Cheney Streeter

other occurrence of women marines was during WWI when there were 300 enlisted women (but no officers) and they were restricted to clerical duties.

Promoted from major to lieutenant colonel in November of 1943, she oversaw the integration of women into a variety of career fields, including the first 43-member Women's Marine Corps Band. These assignments freed male personnel for combat duty. She fought successfully for equal rank and pay for women.

Reba Whittle Tobiason. Only American female POW in the European theater during WWII.

Born in 1920 Reba Zitella Whittle graduated from the Medical and Surgical Memorial Hospital School of Nursing in San Antonio, Texas. She applied for an appointment as a reserve army nurse in June 1941.

After taking her induction physical at Ft. Sam Houston, Texas, on June 10, she was initially disqualified. At 5' 7", she weighed 117 pounds which was below the minimum. This was waived, and she was sworn in and commissioned a second lieutenant in the Army Nurses Corps on June 17, 1941.

She served as a nurse at hospitals in New Mexico and California for the next 27 months. In January 1943 she volunteered for the Army Air Corps Air Evacuation School. The C-47s used in the mission flew troops and supplies in, and wounded soldiers out, of battlefield areas. Because of this two-fold mission, these planes were not considered non-combatant. As a result, service in air evacuation was at great risk, since the unarmed planes were legitimate military targets and often came under direct fire.

Whittle was accepted into the program in August 1943 and reported to Bowman Field, Kentucky, for training in September. She completed the intense six-week training course and graduated on January 22, 1944. She was sent overseas and assigned to the 813th MAETS (Medical Aeromedical Evacuation Transportation Squadron) attached to the 9th Air Force in Nottingham (later Brighton), England.

She flew on 40 missions to Scotland, Belgium and France, including 80 combat hours and 500 hours in the air. On September 27, 1944, while on a routine mission, her plane became lost and was shot down over enemy territory.

Lt. Whittle, her surgical tech, and four crewmen were captured by German troops. Whittle was injured in the crash, and after a series of temporary sites, she was interned in Luft Stalag IX. She was given a solitary cell because there were no provisions for female prisoners. While a prisoner, she performed nursing duties for the male POWs in the camp.

On January 25, 1945, she was part of a prisoner exchange, and was repatriated with 109 other POWs to Switzerland. She returned to Washington DC and received a congratulatory telegram from President Roosevelt. She was awarded the Air Medal, a Purple Heart, and was promoted to first lieutenant. Reassigned to an air base in Miami, she was disqualified for flight status as a result of her wounds.

Whittle married her wartime fiancé, Lt. Colonel Stanley Tobiason, and was released from active duty on January 13, 1946. She tried unsuccessfully for the next 20 years to qualify for a disability retirement due to her wartime injuries and the loss of her health while a prisoner of war. She had two sons, one of whom graduated Annapolis and served as a pilot in Vietnam. She died of cancer in 1981.

Sixty-seven army nurses and 16 navy nurses were POWs in the Pacific during WWII. Only one army nurse was a prisoner in Europe. The Pacific nurses endured combat conditions on Corregidor and Bataan. Whittle flew into combat, but lived in the relative comfort and safety of England. The Pacific nurses surrendered. Whittle was captured. The Pacific nurses had the support and comfort of each other. Whittle was isolated as the only female. The Pacific nurses endured captivity for years. Whittle was a prisoner for about four months. Finally, the Pacific nurses returned to parades and recognition, including three books and a movie. Whittle was not officially recognized as a POW until 1983, two years after her death.

Sally Tompkins. First woman commissioned in the Confederate army (as a woman; see Velasquez).

Born in Poplar Grove, Matthews County, Virginia, on November 9, 1833, Tompkins grew up in Richmond in a wealthy family. As was customary in Southern "society," Tompkins was involved in charity work at an early age, showing a talent for caring for the sick. When the Civil War began in 1861, she turned a large house owned by a friend, Judge John Robertson, into a hospital which she equipped and operated at her own expense.

Because a Confederate government order prohibited private hospitals, Tompkins was commissioned a captain of cavalry in 1861 by Confederate President Jefferson Davis for the sole purpose of keeping Robertson Hospital in Richmond open. In the four years the hospital was in operation, more than 1000 patients were cared for with only 73 deaths, a remarkable feat considering the state of medicine during the Civil War. The last patient was discharged on June 13, 1865, and "Captain Sally" returned to private life.

She was allowed to join a Confederate veteran's organization. In later years she continued to do charity work until financial reverses destroyed her fortune. She died in Richmond on July 25, 1916, and was buried with full military honors.

Katherine Amelia Towle. Second director of the Marine Corps Women's Reserve, educator.

Born in Towle, California, on April 30, 1898, Towle graduated from the University of California at Berkeley in 1920 and did advanced study at Columbia University. She earned a master's degree in political science from Berkeley in 1935 and was working as a senior editor at the University of California Press when the United States entered WWII.

In February 1943 she accepted a commission as a captain in the newly established Women's Reserve of the Marine Corps. She served at marine headquarters in Washington DC and training centers in New York and Camp Lejeune, North Carolina.

In February 1944 she was promoted to major and assigned as deputy director of the women marines. She advanced to lieutenant colonel in March 1945, and in December of that year was named director, succeeding Colonel Ruth Cheney Streeter who retired. Towle was promoted to colonel, and oversaw the demobilization of the women marines after the war. She remained director until June 1946 when the women marine reserve was deactivated.

Towle returned to the University of California as a provost and vice president. With the passage of the Armed Forces Integration Act of 1948, the women's reserves were integrated into the regular corps, and Colonel Towle was recalled to active duty as director in October 1948. She remained as director until her retirement from the military in May 1953. She returned to the UC system from which she retired in 1962. She died on March 1, 1986, in Pacific Grove, California.

Loreta Janeta Velasques. Confederate soldier, spy.

Born in Cuba as a diplomat's daughter, Velasques disguised her sex to enlist in the Confederate army while her soldier-husband was away fighting. She glued on a false mustache and raised a company of infantry as Lieutenant Harry T. Buford. She fought at First Bull Run, Ball's Bluff and Ft. Donelson until she was wounded. Her sex was discovered in New Orleans and she was discharged.

Undeterred, Velasques re-enlisted soon after her recovery. She secured herself a commission in the cavalry and fought at Shiloh. She led raids and patrols before again being wounded, discovered, and discharged. Unable to re-enlist, she served as a spy, disguised at various times as both a male and a female. After the war, and after being widowed four times, Velasques moved west, settling in Austin, Nevada.

Mary Edwards Walker. Physician, reformer, sole female recipient of the Medal of Honor.

Born near Oswego, New York, on November 26, 1832, Walker graduated from Syracuse Medical College in 1855, becoming one of the earliest women doctors. Unable to obtain a commission as an army surgeon at the start of the Civil War, she served as an unpaid volunteer nurse at the Patent Office Hospital, and later at Union battlefields. In September of 1863 she was finally appointed an assistant surgeon with the Army of the Cumberland.

She was assigned to the 52nd Ohio Regiment, and wore an altered officer's uniform. She was commissioned a second lieutenant in the medical corps, making her the first woman to serve in the army as a doctor. Captured on the field by the Confederates, Walker spent four months as a prisoner of war in Richmond from April until August 1864. She left government service in June 1865, and was awarded the Medal of Honor, making her the first, and to date only, woman to be awarded "The Medal."

In 1917 a War Department commission decided that Medals of Honor not awarded for "combat with the enemy" should be recalled. An elderly Walker refused to return hers, and wore it daily for the rest of her life. A fall on the steps of the Capitol while appealing the decision by Congress resulted in injuries that led to her death in Oswego on February 21, 1919. In 1976 her medal was restored by a special act of Congress. Walker was a reformer for equality of the sexes and wore men's clothing throughout her life.

Loretta Walsh. First woman to enlist in the U.S. Navy.

Born in 1898, Walsh was working as a civilian clerk in a Philadelphia navy recruiting station when she enlisted in the navy at age 18 on March 22, 1917. She was required to pass the same tests and exams as male recruits. Walsh became the first woman (except for nurses) to serve as a member of the U.S. Armed Forces.

Walsh was allowed to enlist because the Naval Act of 1916 specified "all persons who are capable of performing useful special service for coastal defense" could enlist as part of the Naval Coast Defense Reserve. Nowhere did the Act specify that the person must be male.

Women were permitted to enlist only because of the greater manpower requirements of a navy at war. The women sailors were restricted to administrative tasks in the continental United States.

Walsh eventually rose to the rank of chief yeoman responsible for recruiting for the Coast Defense Reserve. She fell ill on recruiting duty and was discharged with a disability in 1919. She spent her remaining years in government and private hospitals until her death in 1925.

White House Honor Guard.

On May 17, 1978, largely through the efforts of First Lady Roselyn Carter, women were assigned for the first time as part of the White House Honor Guard. Five women, one from each of the armed services, were selected. They were:

Specialist 4th Class Christine Crews, U.S. Army
Seaman Apprentice Catherine Behnke, U.S. Navy
Sergeant Elizabeth Foreman, U.S. Air Force
Private 1st Class Myrna Jepson, U.S. Marine Corps
Seaman Apprentice Edna Dunham, U.S. Coast Guard

Note: The military academies were opened to women when President Ford signed Public Law 94-106 on October 7, 1975. The first classes entered in June of 1976. One hundred fifty-five women entered the Air Force Academy, 119 went to West Point, and 61 entered the Naval Academy at Annapolis.

Section 3

Entertainment

Music and Musicians

Julian "Cannonball" Adderley. Jazz musician.

Born Julian Edwin Adderley on September 15, 1928, in Tampa, Florida, Adderly explained that "cannonball" was actually "cannibal," a nickname from his school days in Florida when he would eat anything.

In 1950 Adderly enlisted in the army and served as the leader of the 36th Army Dance Band. He was discharged in 1952. After the army, Adderly continued his formal studies in music at the U.S. Naval School of Music in Washington DC. In 1953, as a civilian, he conducted the army band at Ft. Knox, Kentucky.

Desi Arnaz. Bandleader, actor.

Born in Santiago, Cuba, on March 2, 1917, Arnaz was a bandleader married to Lucille Ball when Japan attacked Pearl Harbor. He immediately resigned his commission in the Cuban army and tried to enlist in the U.S. Navy. He was unsuccessful because foreign nationals were not permitted to enlist. They could however be drafted, as Arnaz was in May 1943.

Assigned to the Army Air Corps, he was en route to bombardier training when an injury sustained playing ball resulted in his being transferred to the infantry. He was put on limited duty because of his knee.

Because of his talents, Arnaz was assigned to put on shows at army hospitals, entertaining the wounded soldiers. He served at Birmingham Hospital in the San Fernando Valley near Los Angeles until the end of the war.

Arnaz was discharged as a staff sergeant on November 16, 1945, and formed Desilu Productions with his wife in 1950. He is best remembered for playing "Ricky Ricardo" on the TV show, *I Love Lucy* (1950–55).

Harry Belafonte. Singer, actor.

Born in New York City on March 1, 1927, Belafonte dropped out of George Washington High School in 1944 to enlist in the navy. He was sent to storekeeper's school and served 28 months before being discharged in 1946.

In later years, the popular calypso singer became the first black entertainer to win an Emmy, and his album *Calypso* was the first non-soundtrack LP to sell over a million copies.

Tony Bennett. Singer.

Born Anthony Dominick Benedetto in New York City on August 3, 1926, Bennett was the youngest of three children and was already performing at the age of six. He was called up for the army in 1944 during WWII. After basic training, Bennett was assigned to the 63rd Infantry Division (the "Blood and Fire" Division) where he served in France and Germany.

While in Europe, Bennett encountered an old friend, and invited him to eat with him. The friend was black, and an officer from the south suggested that the friend should take his meal in the kitchen. This suggestion was met with language that resulted in Bennett's demotion from corporal to private, and assignment to a unit disinterring mass graves and preparing the bodies for shipment home.

It was while he was in the army that Bennett got his first opportunity to sing—with a military band. Transferred to special services, he finished the war touring Europe with army shows. Upon discharge, he remained in Europe and studied music at Heidelburg University before returning to the U.S. He studied voice under the GI Bill while supporting himself as an elevator operator. His signature song, "I Left My Heart in San Francisco," was recorded in 1963.

Irving Berlin. Oscar-winning songwriter, music publisher.

He was born Israel Baline in the village of Temun, Russia, on May 11, 1888. His family immigrated to America in 1893 where he grew up in New York City's Lower East Side. He began writing songs while working as a singing waiter, and published his first song in 1907. His song "Alexander's Ragtime Band" in 1911 was an immediate hit, selling over a million copies of sheet music. Berlin was drafted into the U.S. Army in 1917 as a private in the infantry. He was sent to Camp Upton, Long Island, where he trained for the war. In his spare time Berlin wrote songs.

He wrote a camp musical, *Yip Yip Yaphank*, which was so popular that it played in New York and raised $150,000 to build a service center at Camp Upton. He was discharged as a sergeant at the war's end in 1918.

Berlin wrote "God Bless America" in 1939 and won an Oscar for "White Christmas" in 1942.

Dave Brubeck. Pianist, composer, musician.

Born David Warren Brubeck in Concord, New Hampshire, on December 6, 1920, Brubeck served as an entertainment officer in the U.S. Army during WWII.

He played piano in his own jazz quartet from 1951 to 1967.

Charlie Byrd. Guitarist, composer.

A guitarist who can play the musical spectrum from classical to blues, Charles Lee Byrd was born on September 16, 1925, in Chuckatuck, Virginia. He grew up learning to play guitar on the steps of his father's general store.

With America's entry into WWII, Byrd was drafted into the U.S. Army. He was assigned to the infantry, but his musical ability was soon noticed and a transfer to special services was arranged. It was while playing with a GI orchestra in Paris that Byrd first developed an interest in jazz guitar. He continued that interest after he was discharged from the army at the end of the war.

Johnny Cash. Country singer, musician, composer.

Born in Kingsland, Arkansas, on February 26, 1932, Cash enlisted in the U.S. Air Force at age 18 in 1950. He took basic training near San Antonio, Texas, and after he was trained as an intercept radio operator, Cash was sent overseas to Germany.

While overseas, he bought his first guitar in a pawn shop for $5 and taught himself to play. He was honorably discharged in 1954 as a staff sergeant.

John Coltrane. Jazz saxophonist.

Born John William Coltrane in Hamlet, North Carolina, on September 26, 1926, Coltrane enlisted in the navy toward the end of WWII, and served in a navy band from 1945–46 playing the clarinet. Later, as a civilian, he took up the tenor saxophone.

Sammy Davis Jr. Dancer, singer, actor.

Born in New York City on December 8, 1925, Davis enlisted in the army at the start of WWII. He was sent to Ft. Warren, Wyoming, for basic infantry training, and was assigned to one of the first integrated units. One of only two blacks in the unit, he endured taunts, harassment and prejudice.

Already an experienced entertainer before the war, Davis was transferred to special services in 1943 and spent the remainder of the war serving as a writer/producer. He was discharged at the end of the war in 1945.

Jimmy Dean. Country singer.

Born in Plainview, Texas, on August 10, 1928, Dean quit school at age 16 to join the merchant marine toward the end of WWII in 1944. He served for two years as a seaman, and was discharged in 1946. Dean, now old enough, enlisted in the U.S. Air Force and was assigned to Bolling Air Force Base outside Washington DC.

It was while Dean was in the service that he began to work professionally in music. He began playing in the local clubs on the weekends and formed a band. He continued to pursue a music career after his discharge in 1948.

Eddy Duchin. Pianist, orchestra leader.

Born Edwin Frank Duchin in Cambridge, Massachusetts, on January 1, 1909, Duchin and his orchestra were popular and played the best hotels and theaters in the country when he disbanded the orchestra to join the U.S. Navy early in June 1942.

Duchin took basic training at the Great Lakes Naval Training Center, and Midshipmans School at Northwestern University. Because of his perfect pitch as a musician, he was trained in submarine detection devices at Northwestern University, and later at sub-chaser school. He spent some months on patrol duty until he was sent to sound school to learn how to take depth readings. He was then assigned as a sound officer aboard the newly commissioned destroyer escort, USS *Bates*.

Duchin took part in the Normandy invasion of Europe on June 6, 1944. He was also involved in the invasions of Okinawa and Iwo Jima in the Pacific. He attended Commanding Officer's School in Pearl Harbor, and was named operations officer for a destroyer squadron upon his graduation. Duchin served until the end of the war and was discharged with the rank of lieutenant commander in Washington DC, on December 15, 1945. He returned to music performing as a solo pianist after the war.

Arthur Fiedler. Boston Pops conductor, composer.

Born in Boston on December 17, 1894, Fiedler was studying music in Vienna when WWI began and quickly returned to America rather than risk being drafted into the Austrian army. After the U.S. entered the war, Fiedler tried to enlist but was rejected for being too short and underweight.

However, this didn't prevent him from being drafted in the spring of 1918. He served in the army for two weeks before being discharged for flat feet. He returned to the Boston Symphony Orchestra until 1930 when he founded and conducted the Boston Pops Orchestra from 1930 until his death in 1979.

Tennessee Ernie Ford. Singer, entertainer.

Born Ernest Jenning Ford in Bristol, Tennessee, on February 13, 1919, Ford enlisted in the U.S. Army Air Corps after Pearl Harbor. He was commissioned a lieutenant and trained as a navigator aboard bombers. He was stationed at the air base in Victorville, California, where he served as a flight instructor. He never served overseas, and was discharged as a first lieutenant in 1945.

In a long and distinguished career in country music, Ford won the Medal of Freedom in 1984, and was voted into the Country Music Hall of Fame in 1990.

Jerry Garcia. Legendary rock guitarist.

Born Jerome John Garcia in San Francisco on August 1, 1942, Garcia enlisted in the army on April 12, 1960 at age 17 after dropping out of high school in 1959. He was sent to Ft. Ord, California, for basic training, and was then stationed at Ft. Winfield Scott at the Presidio in San Francisco assigned to Headquarters, 30th Artillery Group.

Garcia was trained as a communications specialist as part of headquarters company. He was sent to missile school but discipline problems, including ten AWOLs and two courts-martial, resulted in being dishonorably discharged after only eight months of service on December 14, 1960.

After his discharge, Garcia joined another recently discharged soldier, Robert Hunter, and the two went on to form the "Grateful Dead" rock band. Gardia died on August 9, 1995.

Woody Guthrie. Folksinger, composer, writer.

Born Woodrow Wilson Guthrie in Okemah, Oklahoma, on July 14, 1912, Guthrie was an anti-fascist, pro-union Marxist folk singer before the war. His guitar sported the painted-on slogan "This Machine Kills Fascists."

He was initially exempted from the draft during WWII because he was the sole support of his family. As the war progressed, the increased need for manpower caused Guthrie to be reclassified. Shortly after the publication of his book, *Bound for Glory*, in May of 1943, Guthrie received notice to report in June.

To avoid the draft, Guthrie joined the merchant marine. He shipped out aboard the liberty ship SS *William B. Travis* as a messboy, and helped transport war supplies across the Atlantic. The *Travis* arrived in Sicily in September 1943 where it unloaded its cargo and picked up a unit of 30 military policemen for transport across the Mediterranean to Tunis. The ship was torpedoed en route and barely made harbor in Bizerte, where it sank.

Guthrie returned to the States in November but received another induction notice. He signed up again, this time aboard the SS *Oliver Hazard* on December 7, 1943. He was transferred aboard the SS *Woodrow Wilson* three days later. In January they transported 200 Texas oil workers to Oran.

Guthrie returned in March 1944, but by May he was back at sea aboard the SS *Sea Porpoise*. The ship was transporting 3000 soldiers to Europe. It was a nervous crossing due to increased German submarine activity and because they had lifeboats for only 200 in case of torpedoes. During air raids, Guthrie would go deep into the holds of the ship with his guitar and play for the troops trapped below. They were still en route when Normandy was invaded on June 6. They arrived at Normandy in July and his ship was sunk by a magnetic mine.

Guthrie was home in August and campaigned for FDR's reelection. In March 1945 he received yet another induction notice to report April 9 for a physical.

With victory closer, service in the merchant marine now required an interview with naval intelligence, and possibly because of his previous support of communism, he was unable to sign aboard a ship.

Drafted into the U.S. Army at age 32 on May 8, 1945, the day Germany surrendered, Guthrie took basic training at Sheppard Field, Texas. He couldn't march, couldn't shoot, and the obstacle course was insurmountable. But he could type. He was sent to Scott Field, Illinois, for training as a teletype operator, a job he hated. The war ended in August, but Guthrie wasn't discharged, and he went AWOL in September.

Guthrie returned and was given two weeks confinement. He graduated but was assigned as a sign painter awaiting discharge. He married Marjorie Mazia, a Martha Graham dancer, while on a two week furlough in November, and was discharged from the army as a private on December 20, 1945.

Upon his release, Guthrie enrolled at Brooklyn College under the GI Bill. He wrote over 1000 songs, including "This Land is Your Land" in 1956.

Jimi Hendrix. Rock guitarist, songwriter.

Born James Marshall Hendrix in Seattle, Washington, on November 27, 1942, Hendrix enlisted in the army on June 2, 1961, to avoid being drafted. He was sent to Ft. Ord, California, for basic training where he formed a band with other soldiers in his spare time.

He soon became dissatisfied with military life and attempted to get a Section 8 discharge (mentally unsuitable) several times. He was assigned to the 101st Airborne but broke his ankle during training. He was given a medical discharge on July 2, 1962, after serving 26 months. He was discharged as a private.

Al Hirt. Musician, jazz trumpeter.

Born Alois Maxwell Hirt in New Orleans, Louisiana, on November 7, 1922, Hirt left the Cincinnati Conservatory of Music to enlist in the U.S. Army on October 29, 1942. He spent the majority of his service playing in the 82nd Army Air Force Band. He served briefly overseas before being discharged as a sergeant on January 31, 1946.

Kris Kristofferson. Singer, songwriter, actor.

Born in Brownsville, Texas, on June 22, 1936, Kristofferson

joined the U.S. Army upon returning from England where he completed a Rhodes scholarship at Oxford.

After basic training, Kristofferson went to airborne jump school, ranger training, and flight school before being sent to Germany. He was assigned to an aviation unit as a helicopter pilot.

He disliked the army, but loved flying. He was writing at the time, but a lack of success caused him to change his focus to songwriting. He performed at the enlisted and non-commissioned officer's clubs.

Kris Kristofferson

Kristofferson repeatedly requested a transfer to combat in Vietnam, but was instead assigned to teach English literature at the Military Academy at West Point. Unhappy, he resigned his commission and returned to civilian life.

Henry Mancini. Oscar-winning composer, conductor.

Born April 16, 1924, in Cleveland, Ohio, Mancini was drafted into the army in 1943, and served in both the Air Corps and the infantry overseas during WWII.

Mancini won Oscars for the songs "Moon River" (1961) and "Days of Wine and Roses" (1962), and for the score of the movie *Victor/Victoria* (1982).

Glenn Miller. Bandleader, arranger, musician.

Born Alton G. Miller in Clarinda, Iowa, on March 1, 1904, Miller had the leading Big Band of the 1930s with hits like "In the Mood," "Moonlight Serenade," and "Chattanooga Choo Choo."

With the start of WWII, Miller disbanded his band, and joined the army late in 1942. He was commissioned a captain, but was promoted to major upon his transfer to the Army Air Corps. He organized and led the Army Air Corps Band and traveled to London with this band in June of 1944. He disappeared while on a flight from England to France in bad weather on December 15, 1944.

General Doolittle remarked that next to letters from home, the Glenn Miller Band was the greatest morale builder in Europe. Miller was played by Jimmy Stewart in the 1953 film, *The Glenn Miller Story*.

Willie Nelson. Country singer.

Born in Abbott, Texas, on April 30, 1933, Nelson enlisted in the U.S. Air Force after dropping out of high school in 1950. He was given a medical discharge after only a few months.

As a singer, he has won two Grammys for "Blue Eyes Crying in the Rain" (1975) and "Georgia on My Mind" (1978).

Cole Porter. Composer, musician.

Born to a wealthy family in Peru, Indiana, on June 9, 1892, Porter was educated at Yale where he produced student shows, and Harvard, where under pressure he enrolled in the law school. Despite his family's wishes, he switched to the school of music in 1915, and wrote his first Broadway score, "See America First." The show was less than successful, and a depressed Porter enlisted in the French Foreign Legion. When America entered WWI, Porter was sent to French artillery school to learn gunnery tactics to teach to arriving American troops.

He was awarded the Croix de Guerre by the French government, not so much for valor, but rather for his famous champagne parties in Paris. Porter never went to the front lines during his service in the French army and was discharged after the war.

After the war, he studied music in Paris at the Schola

Cantorum. In 1928 he wrote the score for the musical *Paris* which was a hit. During the 1930s and early 1940s, he had hit after hit on Broadway. His greatest work, *Kiss me Kate*, was written in 1948. He was crippled in a riding accident in 1937, and had a leg amputated in 1958. He died in California on October 15, 1964.

Elvis Presley. Actor, musician, rock and roll legend.

Born in Tupelo, Mississippi, on January 8, 1935, Presley was already an international star when he was drafted into the U.S. Army on March 24, 1958. He was inducted at Ft. Chafee, Arkansas, and took eight weeks of basic and eight weeks of advanced tank training at Ft. Hood, Texas. Shortly after his mother's death on August 14, 1958, Presley received orders for Germany and was en route aboard the USS *General Randall* by September 22.

Presley was assigned to the 1st Medium Tank Battalion, 32nd Armor of the 3rd Armor Division and landed at Bremerhaven, West Germany, on October 1. He was assigned as a guide in a reconnaissance platoon. During the height of the Cold War, combat preparedness was taken seriously and Presley's unit was on almost constant field exercises

Presley performed the basic duties of a soldier, and was described by his former commanding officer, Lt. William Taylor Jr., as a "motivated and dedicated soldier." Presley was discharged as a sergeant with a Good Conduct Medal on March 5, 1960. He enjoyed success in music, film, television, and in Las Vegas.

Tito Puente. Two-time Grammy winning musician.

Born in New York City on April 20, 1923, Puente entered the U.S. Navy in 1942 during WWII. He served for three years in the South Pacific and saw combat serving aboard an aircraft carrier. Discharged after the war ended in 1945, Puente attended the Julliard School of Music on the GI Bill. He won Grammys in 1978 and 1983.

Buddy Rich. Legendary jazz drummer, bandleader.

Born Bernard Rich in New York City on June 30, 1917, Rich

was already playing drums with the likes of Artie Shaw and Tommy Dorsey when WWII began. Although Rich qualified for a 3-A draft deferment as the sole support of his family, he enlisted in the marines early in 1942.

Rich served stateside as a rifleman and judo instructor. He repeatedly requested a combat assignment but was repeatedly turned down. This may have been because Rich refused "suggestions" to form a band. He was never sent overseas and was discharged in 1945.

Pete Seeger. Folklorist, folk singer, musician.

Born in New York City on May 3, 1919, Seeger toured the country with Lee Hays and Woody Guthrie singing and researching sea shanties, folk songs, anti-fascist and pro-labor music.

Drafted into the army on July 24, 1942, at McClellan, Alabama, Seeger spent six months training to serve on the air crew of B-24 bombers. He hoped for an overseas assignment, but an investigation by military intelligence into his left-wing politics resulted in being kept stateside.

In 1943 Seeger was able to transfer to a special services unit, and was eventually sent overseas and put in charge of hospital

Pete Seeger, Eleanor Roosevelt in audience

entertainment on the island of Saipan. He added army songs to his repertoire.

Discharged on December 14, 1945, as a corporal from Ft Dix, New Jersey, he later helped found People Songs, a songwriters union and research center.

John Phillip Sousa. Musician, bandmaster, composer.

Born in Washington DC on November 6, 1854, Sousa at age 13 was invited to join a circus band after the manager heard him play the violin. His father, a former member of the U.S. Marine Corps Band, arranged for him to join the marine band instead. Sousa remained in the band until age 18, when he left to continue his musical studies.

Sousa wrote some of his most famous marches when he returned and served as civilian bandmaster of the U.S. Marine Corps Band from 1880 to 1892. He then formed his own band after leaving the marines band and played at the Chicago World's Fair in 1893. He briefly served as musical director with the U.S. Sixth Army Corps during the Spanish American War. He wrote over 140 marches, his best remembered being "Stars and Stripes Forever" (1897). He died on March 6, 1932, and is buried in the Congressional Cemetery in Washington DC.

Mel Torme. Singer, "The Velvet Fog."

Born Melvin Howard Torme in Chicago on September 13, 1925, Torme was singing with a musical group, the Mel-Tones when he graduated Los Angeles High School at 18. Torme lost his exemption and was inducted into the army during WWII. He took his physical and despite his 5' 7", 129 pound frame and flat feet, was accepted.

Sent to Ft. MacArthur, California, he was offered a position with the Air Corps Band. However, tests showed that he excelled in Morse code, most likely due to his musical "ear," and was transferred to the Signal Corps.

Torme was assigned to the 87th Infantry Training Battalion

for basic training. He was issued 8C size boots for his size 9AA feet, resulting in an injury during a nine-mile hike.

Sent to the hospital, Torme was advised that he was again accepted for the Air Corps Band on the same day was notified that he would be given a medical discharge for flat feet. Torme was discharged as a private after two months of military service. He won a Grammy for "The Christmas Song" in 1983.

Rudy Vallee. Singer, bandleader, actor.

Born Hubert Prior Vallee in Island Pond, Vermont, on July 28, 1901, Vallee enlisted in the U.S. Navy at the start of WWI but was discharged when it was discovered he was under age.

At the start of WWII, Vallee enlisted in the U.S. Coast Guard and rose from chief petty officer to lieutenant senior grade. In 1943 he was appointed bandmaster of the 11th Naval District Coast Guard Band where he served until the end of the war, entertaining troops. During this time, he donated his salary to the Coast Guard Welfare Fund.

Bobby Vinton. Gold record winning singer.

Born Stanley Robert Vinton in Canonsburg, Pennsylvania, on April 16, 1935, Vinton earned a music degree from Duquesne University, then enlisted and served in the army for six months of active duty.

His ability with the organ secured him an assignment as a chaplain's assistant. After his release from the army, Vinton began a career in music with hits like "Roses Are Red," "Mr. Lonely," and "Sealed With a Kiss."

Film, Television, and the Stage

Abbott and Costello. Comedy team.

Although neither Bud Abbott nor Lou Costello served in the military, they spent WWII on tour selling war bonds and entertaining troops. They also "served" in all three branches in film: *Buck Privates* (Army), *In the Navy* (Navy), and *Keep 'Em Flying* (Air Corps).

Charles Addams. Cartoonist, created "The Addams Family."

Born in Westfield, New Jersey, on January 7, 1912, Addams worked as an animator and illustrator for the Signal Corps while serving with the army during WWII.

He earned fame as a cartoonist for *New Yorker Magazine* from 1930 into the 1980s with his "Addams Family" cartoons.

Eddie Albert. Actor, producer.

Born Eddie Albert Heimberger in Rock Island, Illinois, on April 22, 1908, Albert had already enjoyed success as an actor on Broadway, and had a contract with Warner Brother's when he sailed his boat to Mexico in 1938. On one trip he observed Japanese "fishermen" taking hydrographic readings off the coast. His report to army intelligence resulted in his return to Mexico after finishing a film for Warner Brothers. He toured Mexico with the Escalante Brothers Circus where he was the "flyer" (the one who is caught) in a trapeze act. He was also successful in gathering useful information on German activities in Mexico.

Albert enlisted in the navy on September 9, 1942, and served as a seaman until his discharge on January 31, 1943. He was given a direct commission as a lieutenant (j.g.) and attended officer training at Cornell University from February to April 1943. After graduating he was sent to Mare Island, California, and assigned to the newly commissioned USS *Sheridan* (APA-51) on July 31, 1943. The *Sheridan* was a merchant cargo ship reconfigured into an attack transport. The *Sheridan* got underway for the South Pacific in September, arrived in New Zealand, and practiced amphibious landings with the 1st Battalion, 8th Marines.

On November 20, 1943, Allied Forces landed on Tarawa and Albert was assigned as salvage boat officer responsible for refueling and servicing the 26 landing craft and various other small boats. Albert landed his marines early on the second day, but low tides and intense enemy fire made the landing difficult. After unloading his troops, he repeatedly returned to the reefs, altogether rescuing over 150 trapped and wounded marines while under fire from Japanese machine guns and snipers. After the battle, Albert was involved in recovering dead marines in a lagoon. He and others were cited for "outstanding performance of duty" for their actions that day.

The *Sheridan* returned to Hawaii, then San Diego, where Albert was ordered to report to the Training Films Branch on January 10, 1944. He spent the next year and a half on public relations tours across the U.S. He was discharged as a full lieutenant on January 9, 1946.

After the war, Albert returned to Hollywood where he was twice nominated for Academy Awards in *Roman Holiday* (1955) and *The Heartbreak Kid* (1972) but he is best remembered for his role as Oliver Douglas on the TV comedy *Green Acres* with Eva Gabor (1965 to 1971).

Alan Alda. Emmy winning actor and writer.

Born in New York City on January 28, 1936, Alda joined the army reserve sometime after graduating Fordham University. He did the minimum six-month tour of duty as a gunnery officer (captain) during the Korean War. After his discharge, he started acting in film and on television, and is best remembered as "Hawkeye Pierce" on *M*A*S*H*.

Steve Allen. Entertainer, composer, musician, comedian.

Born in New York City on December 26, 1921, Allen was living in Arizona prior to WWII. He moved there in hopes that his asthma condition would improve. It did and he was promptly drafted.

On June 1, 1943, Allen was inducted at Ft. MacArthur in Los

Angeles and sent for basic training to Camp Roberts near Paso Robles. He trained in a heavy weapons company, and states that should the need arise, he is confident he could still competently operate a machine gun or mortar.

Allen served in the U.S. Army for only five months before a return of his asthma forced him to accept a medical discharge. He was discharged as a private on October 15, 1943.

The easy-going comedian was the first host of the *Tonight Show* on television.

James Arness. Actor, "Marshall Dillon."

Born in Minneapolis, Minnesota, on May 26, 1923, the brother of the actor Peter Graves, Arness enlisted in the army at age 19 at the start of WWII. He was wounded in the leg during the Anzio invasion of Italy in January 1944.

Arness kept the peace in Dodge City from 1955 to 1975 as "Marshall Matt Dillon" on TV's *Gunsmoke*.

Ed Asner. Actor, former president of the Screen Actors Guild.

Born in Kansas City, Missouri, on November 15, 1929, Asner was drafted into the army in 1951. After basic training, he was assigned to a Signal Corps unit, and was transferred to France. Asner managed the unit basketball team which was the highest rated army team in Europe.

Upon his discharge, he began acting in repertory theaters in Chicago. The six-time Emmy winner starred on *The Mary Tyler Moore Show* and *Lou Grant*, and served as president of the Screen Actors Guild.

Gene Autry. Singer, cowboy star, baseball team owner, TV station owner.

Born Orson G. Autry in Tioga, Texas, on September 29, 1908, Autry enlisted in the Army Air Corps in July 1942. He was assigned to special services as a staff sergeant, and took flying lessons in his spare time.

He earned his wings and a commission as a lieutenant, and served as the copilot of C-47s with the Air Transport Command, flying missions in Europe, the South Pacific, and the China-India-Burma theaters. He was discharged in September of 1945, and immediately returned to the Pacific on a USO tour.

Jack Benny. Vaudevillian, radio star, actor, musician.

Born Benjamin Kubelsky in Chicago on Valentine's Day, 1894, he enlisted in the U.S. Navy on May 29, 1918, shortly after his mother died in November of 1917. Already working in vaudeville doing ragtime pieces on his fiddle, Benny pursued the usual course of training as a basic seaman at Great Lakes Naval Training Center. In his off-time he performed in shows with other "showbiz" sailors. It was in one of these shows that Benny first did comedy.

He was a hit, and the wife of the base commander (Captain William Moffett) convinced him to do shows for naval relief, traveling to several cities. Also stationed at Great Lakes, though they wouldn't meet until later, were Pat O'Brien and Spencer Tracy. Benny was discharged on September 30, 1921. He began an extraordinary career on stage, radio, film and television, and was still a popular entertainer when he died on December 26, 1974.

Busby Berkeley. Dance director, cinematographer.

Born William Berkeley Enos on November 29, 1895, in Los Angeles, California, Berkeley enlisted in the army on the day that America declared war in April 1917. He was commissioned a second lieutenant, and was sent to France as an artillery officer. He served briefly with the 312th Field Artillery attached to the 79th Division.

Berkeley was transferred to General Pershing's staff at Chaumont, France, where he was assigned as entertainment officer. He had his first experience in coordinating movements of large numbers of people by devising intricate close order drill routines for American troops. By late 1917 Berkeley was out of the army and back in New York City.

Joey Bishop. Comedian, entertainer.

Born in New York City on March 3, 1918, Bishop was drafted into the army in April 1942 at the start of WWII. He was assigned to a special services unit where he served as recreation director at Ft. Sam Houston, Texas.

Bishop served for three and one half years, and was discharged in September 1945 with the rank of sergeant.

Dan Blocker. TV actor, "Hoss Cartwright."

Born in Bowie, Texas, on December 12, 1927, Blocker was drafted into the army in 1950, and sent to Korea. He served in the 45th Infantry Division, rising to the rank of sergeant. He was discharged in 1952.

Blocker starred as the amiable "Hoss" from 1959 to 1972 on the long-running television show *Bonanza*.

Humphrey Bogart. Oscar-winning actor.

Born on Christmas Day, 1899, in New York City to a surgeon father and illustrator mother, Bogart enlisted in the U.S. Navy in May 1918 after America's entry into WWI. He served as a seaman aboard the USS *Leviathan* (SP-1326), a captured German liner impounded and commissioned by the U.S. Navy as a troopship. He reported aboard on November 27, two weeks after WWI ended. In February 1919, Bogart was transferred to the USS *Santa Olivia* (SP-3125), another troopship.

He got his famous scar and lisp when a prisoner he was escorting fought him in an escape attempt. Bogart had to shoot him to prevent his escape. (This is the most likely story. However, one source says the scar was from a splinter while doing carpentry aboard the *Leviathan*.) He was discharged from the navy as a seaman second class on June 18, 1919.

Although he is remembered for movies like *Casablanca* (1943), *The Maltese Falcon* (1941), and *Treasure of Sierra Madre*, (1948) it is for *African Queen* in 1951 that he won the Best Actor Oscar. He was also nominated for his role as Captain Queeg in *The Caine Mutiny* (1954). He died on January 14, 1957.

Richard Boone. Actor, director, "Paladin."

Born in Los Angeles on June 16, 1917, Boone attended San Diego Army and Navy Academy (1929–32) then Stanford in 1934. He was expelled from Stanford when the person upon whom he staged a prank auto accident turned out to be Mrs. Herbert Hoover.

With America's entry into WWII, Boone enlisted in the U.S. Navy and spent three and a half years in the Pacific as an aerial gunner on torpedo planes. He served aboard the USS *Intrepid*, the USS *Hancock* and the USS *Enterprise*, all aircraft carriers.

After his discharge, Boone studied drama in New York City under the GI Bill. He went on to star in movies and on television. He is best remembered for the character "Paladin" on *Have Gun Will Travel*.

Ernest Borgnine. Oscar-winning actor.

Born Ermes Effron Borgnino in Hamden, Connecticut, on January 24, 1917, Borgnine enlisted in the U.S. Navy in October 1935. After initial service as a seaman apprentice aboard the USS *Lamberton* (DD-119), he served as a gunners mate aboard destroyers in both the Atlantic and Pacific Fleets before the war. He also boxed in amateur bouts. He was discharged in October 1941.

After Pearl Harbor, he reenlisted in the navy and spent the majority of the war aboard the USS *Sylth* (PY-12), a patrol gun boat, protecting the East Coast. Besides anti-submarine duties, the *Sylth* was involved in training sonar operators and researching new anti-sub techniques. He was discharged as a gunners mate 1st class late in 1945.

After his discharge, Borgnine began acting and won an Oscar for *Marty* in 1955, and starred on the long-running TV series *McHale's Navy*. He also appeared in *From Here to Eternity* (1953), *The Flight of the Phoenix* (1965), and *The Wild Bunch* (1965).

Walter Brennan. Actor.

The first actor to win three Oscars, Brennan was born in Lynn, Massachusetts, on July 25, 1894. He left home at age 11 to work as a wagon driver, and enlisted in the army the day after America declared war on Germany during WWI.

Brennan spent 19 months overseas in France from 1917 to 1919 assigned to the 101st Field Artillery. He served at the front but found time to perform in camp shows.

Brennan began acting professionally in 1925 and made over 100 movies, many of them westerns. He won three Best Supporting Actor Oscars: *Come and Get It* (1936), *Kentucky* (1938), and *The Westerner* (1940). Too old for service during WWII, Brennan spent the war entertaining troops.

Charles Bronson. Film actor.

Born Charles Buchinsky in Ehrenfield, Pennsylvania, on November 3, 1922(?) (sources differ), one of 15 children, Bronson grew up in poverty and ignorance and was working in the mines by age 15. He enjoyed his experience in the army for its regular meals and clean clothes. He was drafted in late 1942 and was in the army by early 1943.

Bronson served three years in the army during WWII. Although some press releases had him serving as a tail gunner in B-29s in the South Pacific, he actually was assigned as a private first class with the 769th Mess Squadron in Kingman, Arizona. In David Downing's biography of Bronson, he states that while Bronson did serve briefly in Arizona, the press releases were correct and Bronson did complete 25 missions as a tail gunner on B-29s in the Pacific, earning a Purple Heart. Bronson's records were destroyed in the fire at the National Personnel Records Center in 1973.

After his discharge from Camp Atterbury, Indiana, in February 1946, Bronson attended the Huessein School of Art in Philadelphia. He made his screen debut in *You're in the Navy Now* (1951) starring Gary Cooper as the captain. Bronson played a "frolicsome" sailor, handy with his fists. It was also the first screen appearance of another actor and veteran, Lee Marvin.

Joe E. Brown. Actor, comedian.

Born Joe Evan Brown in Holgate, Ohio, on July 29, 1892, Brown, already a popular comedian, performed in USO shows throughout WWII. Brown traveled to Alaska, New Guinea, the South Pacific, the China-India-Burma theater, Iraq, Iran, Egypt and Italy, as well as bases stateside.

He is one of only two civilians to be awarded the Silver Star (the other is Ernie Pyle). General MacArthur once said of him, "There isn't a man in uniform or out who has done more for our boys then Joe E. Brown."

Bugs Bunny. Oscar-winning rabbit.

Born at Warner Brothers studio in Burbank, California, Bugs made his first appearance in the cartoon *A Wild Hare* in July 1940. Like most major stars, he did his bit for war bonds, starring in *Any Bonds Today?*, made in a record three weeks and released on December 15, a week after Pearl Harbor.

It was during WWII that Bugs Bunny cartoons passed Disney in popularity for the first time, as GIs could identify with the rabbit with the Brooklyn accent. Bugs took on the Japanese in *Bugs Nips the Nips* (April 1944) and the Nazis in *Herr Meets Hare* (January 1945) where he crossed swords with Hermann Goering and impersonated Josef Stalin.

Bugs adorned bombers and PT boats, served as a mascot for the 385th Air Service Squadron and the 5th Parachute Battalion as well as the hospital ship USS *Comfort*. He was given an official service record in the U.S. Marine Corps.

Sid Caesar. Comedian, musician.

Born in Yonkers, New York, on September 8, 1922, Caesar enlisted in the U.S. Coast Guard on November 5, 1942. After taking basic seamanship training at Manhattan Beach, he spent the remainder of the war guarding piers in Brooklyn.

When not on guard, Caesar spent his free time writing comedy sketches, and playing in the coast guard orchestra. He was selected for the cast of *Tars and Spars*, a coast guard musical, which toured the country. He was the only cast member selected by director Max Liebman to appear in the Columbia Pictures film of the same name.

Discharged at the end of the war on December 12, 1945, Caesar finished the film for Columbia, then returned to the nightclub circuit. He's made Americans laugh on stage, film and television.

Art Carney. Oscar-winning TV and film actor.

Born Arthur William Matthew Carney in Mt. Vernon, New York, on November 4, 1918, Carney already had two brothers in the service when he was drafted into the army during WWII. As a replacement with Pennsylvania's Keystone Division, Carney was sent to France on July 15, 1944, arriving at Normandy in August 1944. Private Carney joined the 28th Division, and was setting up a machine gun position in the area of St. Lo, and was in the process of filling his canteen, when he was blown off his feet by a German mortar round. The date was August 15, 1944, his fourth wedding anniversary. Wounded by shrapnel in the right thigh, Carney was evacuated from combat without ever firing a shot. He was transported to an American Hospital in the English Midlands. His wife Jean, however, was advised that he was missing in action, and didn't receive any news until two of Carney's letters arrived on September 5.

Carney was transported back to the States where he spent nine months at McGuire General Hospital near Richmond. Despite being in pain and forced to remain immobile, Carney entertained, and because of his age, acted as big brother to the other men on the ward. He was discharged from the army in April 1945 with a Purple Heart and a permanent limp. He began acting after his discharge, and won three Emmys as "Ed Norton" on the *Honeymooners*, and an Oscar for *Harry and Tonto* in 1974.

Johnny Carson. Host of the *Tonight Show*.

The king of late-night TV for over three decades, Johnny Carson was born in Corning, Iowa, on October 23, 1925. He was working as a theater usher at the start of WWII. He enlisted in the U.S. Navy on June 8, 1943, as an apprentice seaman enrolled in the V-5 program, which trained navy and marine pilots.

He hoped to train as a pilot, but was sent instead to Columbia University for midshipman training where he performed magic for his classmates on the side.

Commissioned an ensign late in the war, on July 5, 1945, Carson was assigned to the USS

Johnny Carson

Pennsylvania, a battleship on station in the Pacific. He was en route to the combat zone aboard a troopship when the bombing of Hiroshima and Nagasaki brought the war to a close.

The *Pennsylvania* was torpedoed on August 12, 1945, and Carson reported for duty on the 14th, the last day of the war. Although he arrived too late for combat, he got a firsthand education in the consequences of war.

The damaged warship sailed to Guam for repairs, and arrived eighteen days later. As the newest and most junior officer, Carson was assigned to supervise the removal of 20 dead sailors. He stated that he would never forget the stench of the decaying crewmen.

After temporary duty as officer in charge of a trainload of returning GIs from the Naval Barracks at Swan Island, Oregon, in November 1945, Carson returned to Guam and served as a communications officer in charge of decoding encrypted messages. He recalls the high point of his military career was performing a magic trick for Secretary of the Navy James Forrestal. He returned to the U.S. aboard the *Pennsylvania*, and was released from active duty as a lieutenant (j.g.) on August 13, 1946. He was discharged from the reserves on September 1, 1955

Lee J. Cobb. Actor.

Born Leo Jacob Cobb on December 9, 1911, in New York City, Cobb was 32 years old when he enlisted in the Army Air Corps in 1943. Since he was already an established film actor, Cobb was assigned to a radio production unit in California where he spent the duration of the war. He was discharged as a corporal in 1945.

Bill Cosby. Comedian, actor, adman.

Born William Henry Cosby Jr. on July 12, 1937, in North Philadelphia, Cosby enlisted in the navy in 1956. He trained as a hospital corpsman and served aboard ships and at the marine base at Quantico, Virginia, before being sent to Bethesda Naval Hospital. He was assigned to work with Korean War casualties.

Cosby won awards running on the navy track team, but also experienced racial discrimination, being forced to eat in the kitchen of cafes where the team stopped to eat while on the road. He was honorably discharged after four years of service in 1960. He went on to Temple University on the GI Bill. He has a doctorate in education.

Cosby has entertained with his comedy on records, stage, film, television and in Las Vegas. He is one of the highest paid entertainers in the world.

Wally Cox. Actor, comedian.

Born Wallace Maynard Cox in Detroit, Michigan, on December 6, 1924, Cox was a botany student at City College in New York when he was drafted into the U.S. Army in 1942.

Sent to Camp Walters, Texas, for training, Cox was hospital-ized with heat stroke, and spent four months as a barracks guard before being given a medical discharge.

While learning how to silversmith, Cox joined a theater group doing impressions of soldiers. He was a hit and a star was born. He starred as "Mr. Peepers" in the 1950s and was a regular on *Hollywood Squares.*

Tony Curtis. Oscar-nominated film actor.

Born Bernard Schwartz on June 3, 1925, in New York City, Curtis left high school to enlist in the navy in 1943, during WWII. He took basic training in Buffalo, New York, and signal school at Champaign, Illinois, where he was promoted to signalman 3rd class upon completing training. Legend has it that a visit to the Hollywood Canteen caused Curtis to fall in love with the mov-ies.

Curtis was assigned as a signalman 3rd class aboard the USS *Proteus* (AS-19), a submarine tender, and as a relief torpedoman aboard the USS *Dragonette* (SS-293), a submarine. Injured when a winch chain broke while cleaning the side of the *Dragonette*, he spent four days in the ship's infirmary before later serving in Guam. Curtis was aboard the *Proteus* in Tokyo Bay during the Japanese surrender in September 1945.

After his discharge, Curtis attended drama classes at New York City's Dramatic Workshop under the GI Bill. He appeared in over 80 movies including *Houdini* (1953), *The Defiant Ones* (for which he received an Oscar nomination in 1958), *Some Like it Hot* (1959), and *The Boston Strangler* (1968).

Kirk Douglas. Film star.

Born Issur Danielovitch Demsky on December 9, 1916, in Amsterdam, New York, Douglas was determined to attend the Academy of Dramatic Arts in New York City. He met with the director and demanded a scholarship, even though no such pro-gram existed. After an audition, Douglas was granted the first special scholarship in the history of the institution. After graduating in 1941, Douglas made his first appearance on Broadway as a bellboy singing "Yankee Doodle" in *Spring Again*.

Drafted into the U.S. Navy as an enlisted man on December 10, 1942, Douglas spent his first year at midshipman's school at Notre Dame University, and was commissioned an ensign on February 27, 1943. He was assigned as a communications officer in an anti-submarine unit upon his graduation. He served aboard Patrol Craft #1139, a 175-foot sub-chaser in Algiers.

The premature detonation of a depth charge on February 24, 1944, while en route from California to Hawaii, caused internal injuries that resulted in a five-month hospital stay at Balboa Hospital in San Diego, and a medical discharge on July 27, 1944.

Douglas starred in more than 70 films, including *Act of Love* (1953), *Gunfight at the O.K. Corral (1957)*, *The Man from Snowy River* (1982), and was nominated for an Oscar on three occasions. He earned the American Film Institute's Lifetime Achievement Award in 1991. He married actress Diana Dill during the war on November 2, 1943.

Hugh Downs. Newscaster, writer.

Born Hugh Malcolm Downs in Akron, Ohio, on February 14, 1921, Downs was anxious to enlist after Pearl Harbor. He tried to enlist in the U.S. Navy, Coast Guard and Air Corps before being drafted into the U.S. Army in 1942. He was sent to Ft. Lewis, Washington, and was assigned to the 123rd Infantry in a heavy weapons company.

His unit was part of an experiment to accelerate basic training and condense the regular 13-week course into four weeks. Downs was among the many soldiers who collapsed from exhaustion. He was hospitalized for several weeks and given a medical discharge in 1943.

Donald Duck. Oscar-winning Disney star.

The world's most famous duck made morale-raising war films

during WWII, including *The Vanishing Private* and *Sky Trooper* (1942), *Donald in Nutzy Land* (1943), and *Commando Duck* (1944). He didn't win the Silver Star, but he did win an Oscar for the song *Der Fuhrer's Face.*

Clint Eastwood. Actor, Oscar-winning director/producer.

Born Clinton Eastwood Jr. in San Francisco, California, on May 31, 1930, he was the older of two children whose family traveled across Northern California during the Great Depression. He took up competitive swimming and basketball during high school. After graduating, he worked as a lumberjack and forest firefighter in Oregon, and a steelworker in Seattle.

Drafted into the U.S. Army in 1951, during the conflict in Korea, Eastwood was sent to Ft. Ord in California for basic training. When his unit was sent overseas to combat, Eastwood's name was not on the list. Instead, he lucked into a job as a swimming instructor and remained at Ft. Ord.

Eastwood recalls that it was "tough duty," working all day by the pool so he could spend nights and weekends as a bouncer at the NCO club. Although there was a war on, it was a trip home to Seattle that almost got Eastwood killed.

Too poor to afford a commercial flight, Eastwood caught a ride aboard a navy plane at Moffett Field to Seattle to visit his parents and a girlfriend. On the ride back aboard a navy torpedo bomber, the plane developed engine trouble forcing it to make a water landing off San Francisco. Eastwood was forced to swim over a mile through the tide to shore.

It was while on duty at the Ft. Ord pool that Eastwood met fellow soldiers and actors Martin Milner (*Route 66*), David Janssen (*The Fugitive*), and Richard Long (*The Big Valley*).

After his discharge in 1953, Eastwood attended L.A. City College and studied drama under the GI Bill. He landed a $75-a-week contract with Universal Studios, and played bit parts in *Francis the Talking Mule* and *Revenge of the Creature.* International fame followed from his "spaghetti westerns," "Dirty Harry" movies, and his Oscars for *The Unforgiven*.

Buddy Ebsen. Vaudeville and broadway actor, dancer.

Born Christian Rudolph Ebsen Jr. in Belleville, Illinois, on April 2, 1908, Ebsen was already a star on Broadway and in Hollywood musicals at the start of WWII.

An avid yachtsman, Ebsen offered the services of his sailboat and himself to the navy, but they refused him a commission, so Ebsen joined the U.S. Coast Guard. He was commissioned a lieutenant (j.g.) and after indoctrination in anti-submarine warfare techniques, was assigned as the executive officer of the newly commissioned USS *Pocatello* (PF-9), a sub-chaser patrolling the Pacific, involved primarily in weather monitoring.

To relieve the boredom, Ebsen organized and performed in variety shows. In October 1945, after the war ended, Ebsen was transferred to the Coast Guard District Office in Seattle, having never seen combat. Upon his discharge as a lieutenant in January 1946, he returned to Broadway in *Showboat* in the role of song-and-dance man "Frank." His career in television included *The Beverly Hillbillies* (1962–71) and *Barnaby Jones* (1973–79).

Douglas Fairbanks Jr. Actor, adventurer.

Born on December 9, 1909, in New York City, the son of silent film star Douglas Fairbanks, Fairbanks was already a well known actor (*The Dawn Patrol, Gunga Din*) and a lieutenant (j.g.) in the naval reserve by April 1941. With the approach of WWII, he was sent on a goodwill tour of South America by the State Department. Officially he was there to counter Nazi Germany's influence, but he also collected intelligence, reporting directly to Assistant Secretary of State Sumner Welles.

Upon his return, and upon finishing the movie *The Corsican Brothers*, Fairbanks was called to active duty. It was suggested that with his extensive contacts, he should be posted to naval intelligence, but he requested sea duty.

After training aboard a supply ship in Boston, and convoy duty off Newfoundland aboard the USS *Ludlow* (DD-438), Fairbanks was assigned as "Staff Officer: Communications and Signals" aboard the battleship USS *Mississippi* (BB-41), which patrolled the North Atlantic and escorted convoys. He was considered a popular and capable officer, received good evaluations and fitness reports, and was promoted to full lieutenant.

After Pearl Harbor, Fairbanks was transferred to naval intelligence early in 1942, but the resulting publicity resulted in his return to sea duty. After a tour of duty as the executive officer of the USS *Goldcress* (AM-80), a minesweeper stationed off Staten Island, Fairbanks was assigned as an aide to Admiral Giffens. He served as "flag lieutenant" aboard the battleship USS *Washington* (BB-56), the flag ship of Task Force 99. He was responsible for signals and radio messages.

Douglas Fairbanks Jr.

Fairbanks was assigned special duty aboard the carrier USS *Wasp* (CV-7) as part of a convoy taking planes and supplies to the besieged island of Malta. He did similar duty aboard the cruiser USS *Wichita* (CA-45) en route to Murmansk to supply the Russians. In both instances there was constant danger from enemy submarines, ships and planes.

Fairbanks developed an expertise in small boat operations, and served in planning, and often participating in, diversionary raids. He set troops ashore in Yugoslavia, Egypt, Tunisia, Italy and the southern coast of France during the invasion in August of 1944.

Fairbanks was awarded the Croix de Guerre, the British Distinguished Service Cross, the Legion of Merit with a "V" for valor, and the Silver Star. He was also awarded two tins of anchovies by Marshal Tito of Yugoslavia. He was discharged from active duty on February 5, 1946, as a lieutenant commander. He retired from the navy reserve on July 1, 1969, as a captain.

Henry Fonda. Oscar-winning actor.

Born in Grand Island, Nebraska, on May 16, 1905, Fonda was already a popular film star when he enlisted in the U.S. Navy as a seaman, despite being exempt from the draft because he was 37 years old and married with three children.

Like "Mr. Roberts," a character he would play years later, Fonda wanted to be in the "real war." His enlistment was delayed as a result of Darryl Zanuck's influence. Zanuck was reluctant to lose his star, and convinced Washington that his next film, *The Immortal Sergeant*, was necessary to the war effort.

Upon the film's completion, Fonda went to San Diego for basic training. He turned down a direct commission and instead trained as a quartermaster/signalman 3rd class. He was sent in May 1943 to Seattle for duty aboard the USS *Saterlee* (DD-626), a newly commissioned destroyer. Its first mission was to escort a British aircraft carrier from the Pacific to Virginia.

Late in 1943 Fonda was ordered to Washington DC where he was honorably discharged from the navy as an enlisted man, and commissioned a lieutenant (j.g.) assigned to making training films. Instead, he convinced a commander in personnel to assign him to officer's training in Rhode Island. Fonda graduated top of his class, and was given his choice of assignments. He chose air combat intelligence, and again graduated near the top of his class from the training school.

In February 1944 Fonda was assigned to the carrier USS *Essex*

(CV-9), Admiral Nimitz' flagship. Although a celebrity, he was a respected and competent officer. Transferred to the USS *Curtis* (AV-4), a seaplane tender, Fonda survived submarines, air attacks and kamikazes at Guam, Iwo Jima, and Saipan. At Saipan his actions in tracking and trapping a submarine earned Fonda a Bronze Star. By all accounts Fonda was a competent naval officer. He was fortunate that he was off the ship when a kamikaze struck the side of the *Curtis*, destroying the cabin where he slept. (Mr. Roberts would die in a similar manner.) The day after Japan's surrender, Fonda was again ordered to Washington and promptly discharged as a full lieutenant four weeks later in October 1945.

Fonda appeared in over 60 films including *Grapes of Wrath* (1940), *The Ox Bow Incident* (1943), and *My Darling Clementine* (1946), before finally winning an Oscar for *On Golden Pond* in 1982. He died in Los Angeles on August 12, 1982

Glenn Ford. Actor.

Born Gwyllyn Samuel Newton Ford in Quebec, Canada, on May 1, 1916, Ford enlisted in the U.S. Marine Corps as a sergeant and photographic specialist on December 13, 1942, and took basic training at San Diego in March 1943. After basic, Ford was assigned to the Marine Corps Schools Detachment (Photographic Section) at Quantico, Virginia. In February 1944 he was transferred to the Radio Section of Headquarters Battalion at San Diego, assigned to public relations. He was honorably dis-

Glenn Ford

charged as a sergeant on December 7, 1944. Despite printed stories of Ford serving with the OSS, or liberating Dachau, Ford remained stateside doing as he was ordered during WWII.

Ford enlisted in the naval reserve on December 30, 1958, and was commissioned as a lieutenant commander. He served as a public affairs officer for the 11th Naval District where he earned outstanding fitness reports. He was promoted to commander in 1963 and captain in 1968. Ford served on active duty for 30 days when he volunteered with his reserve unit for duty in a forward combat area in Vietnam. He advised marine combat camera teams filming a Marine Corps documentary in the Mekong Delta. For his actions, Ford was awarded the Navy Commendation Medal, and was decorated with the Vietnamese Legion of Merit First Class by Premier Nguyen Cao Ky on February 4, 1967. He retired from the reserve on October 1, 1978.

Bob Fosse. Oscar-winning choreographer.

Born Robert Louis Fosse in Chicago on June 23, 1927, Fosse enlisted in the U.S. Navy after graduating Amundson High School in Chicago in 1945. He was assigned to an entertainment unit in the South Pacific. He performed in Guam, Wake Island, and Okinawa, and was discharged in 1947.

He won Oscars for his choreography in *Cabaret* (1972) and the autobiographical *All That Jazz* (1979).

Allen Funt. Creator of *Candid Camera*.

Born in Brooklyn, New York, on September 16, 1914, Funt graduated high school at 15 and earned a degree from Cornell University. He was working in radio as a sound effects man at the start of WWII.

Funt enlisted in the U.S. Army in 1943, and was initially assigned to teach infantry tactics to Japanese American soldiers. He also performed in special services stage shows. Funt was transferred to the Signal Corps where he recorded soldier's voices for the folks back home. It was in this assignment that he first discovered the potential of covert recording.

To overcome nervousness, Funt would start the tape early after he disconnected the red light indicating that a recording was in progress. He found that his subjects would be more re-laxed and natural. After his discharge, he brought the concept first to radio, then television with *Candid Camera*.

Clark Gable. Oscar-winning screen actor.

Born William Clark Gable in Cadiz, Ohio, on February 1, 1901, Gable won an Oscar for the film *It Happened One Night* in 1934. He also had the lead role of Rhett Butler in *Gone With the*

Wind (1939), a film made from a book of the same name authored by Margaret Mitchell. Mitchell said she wrote the character of Butler with Gable in mind.

Shortly after the death of his wife, actress Carole Lombard, in a plane crash on a war bond tour in January of 1942, Gable announced his intention of enlisting as a buck private after the completion of the film *Somewhere I'll Find You*.

Clark Gable

On August 12, 1942, at age 41, Gable enlisted in the U.S. Army Air Corps as a private, and was sent to (Officers Candidates School) in Miami, Florida. He took the regular course, competing against younger men, and was commissioned a second lieutenant and aerial gunner on October 28, 1942.

Sent overseas to Europe with the 8th Air Force, Gable (now a captain) participated in five combat bombing missions over Germany for which he received the Distinguished Flying Cross and the Air Medal. Goering offered a $5000 bounty and immediate promotion to the pilot who shot down Gable. He returned stateside, was promoted to major, and was discharged in 1945. His discharge papers were signed by Captain Ronald Reagan.

The last words Gable received from Lombard were in a telegram that read, "Hey Pappy, you'd better get in this man's army."

James Garner. Television and film actor, "Maverick."

Born James Scott Bumgarner in Norman, Oklahoma, on April 7, 1928, Garner became the first draftee inducted from the state of Oklahoma during the Korean War in 1951. He spent 14 months in Korea assigned to the 5th Regimental Combat Team of the 24th Division (the "Victory" Division), and was wounded twice. The first instance was a shrapnel wound received while on patrol. The second wound occurred when his unit was surprised and overwhelmed by Chinese troops. During a nighttime withdrawal, Garner was separated from his unit, and with 30 other stragglers observed a navy jet attack on enemy positions. He was wounded by friendly fire when the group he was with was mistaken for a concentration of enemy troops. Going over the side of a ridge to avoid being hit, Garner was wounded in the buttocks by shrapnel, dislocated a shoulder and both knees, and suffered phosphorus burns over his body, especially the back and neck.

Isolated and weaponless with only one other South Korean soldier, they were able to fool the Chinese troops into thinking that Garner was the other soldier's prisoner, as they walked in the distance with Garner's hands raised, making it back to friendly lines.

After recovering from his wounds, Garner was assigned to a postal unit in Japan where he used his talents as a scrounger and scavenger to equip the post office building with a bar, theater, and hot showers.

Awarded the Purple Heart, Garner returned stateside and was discharged in June 1952. He returned to Los Angeles to lay carpet with his father. Garner won an Emmy for his longtime TV series *The Rockford Files* (1974–80).

John Gavin. Actor, U.S. Ambassador to Mexico.

Born John Anthony Golenor on April 8, 1928, in Los Angeles, California, Gavin grew up speaking Spanish due to a Mexican mother and a father with mining interests in Mexico. He attended St. John's Military Academy and Beverly Hills High School before entering Stanford. While at Stanford, he enrolled in Navy ROTC, and upon graduation in June of 1951, Gavin began his four years of active service in the navy. He saw combat service in Korean waters aboard the USS *Princeton* (CV-37), serving as assistant air intelligence officer. After attending Air Intelligence School at Alameda Naval Air Station in California, he returned to Korea aboard the *Princeton* in February 1953.

Because of his knowledge of Spanish and Portuguese, Gavin was transferred to Panama, and assigned as a civil affairs aide to Admiral Miles, commandant of the 15th Naval District. He was released from active duty in June 1955.

After the navy, he applied for a job as a technical advisor on a navy film, but instead was given a screen test, beginning a long and distinguished film career. His interest in Latin affairs earned him positions in the Kennedy and subsequent administrations. He served as U.S. Ambassador to Mexico during the Reagan administration.

Arthur Godfrey. Radio and TV broadcaster.

Born in New York City on August 31, 1903, Godfrey ran away from home at 14, and worked as a coal miner, cab driver and office boy before enlisting in the U.S. Navy in 1920.

After taking technical radio classes and graduating naval radio school at Great Lakes Naval Base, Godfrey took and passed the entrance exams for Annapolis. He chose instead to volunteer for duty aboard a destroyer as a radio operator. He was discharged in 1924.

Godfrey worked in a vaudeville troop, sold cemetery plots and insurance, and in 1927 signed up for a three-year hitch with the U.S. Coast Guard where he obtained further training in radio. He remained in the navy reserve.

At the outbreak of WWII, Godfrey was a lieutenant commander in the reserve, but was prevented from going active duty by injuries sustained in a 1931 car accident. He served in recruiting drives and as a war correspondent.

Dick Gregory. Comedian.

Born Richard Claxton Gregory in St. Louis, Missouri, on October 12, 1932, Gregory left Southern Illinois University to enlist in the U.S. Army. He spent two years as a comedian assigned to special services.

Gene Hackman. Oscar-winning actor.

Born Eugene Alden Hackman in San Bernardino, California, on January 30, 1931, Hackman lied about his age to enlist in the U.S. Marine Corps in 1947 at age 16. After basic training at Parris Island, South Carolina, Hackman was sent to China where he served as a disc jockey for Armed Forces Radio but communist victories on the mainland forced the relocation of his unit to Hawaii, and later Japan. He loved athletics, and played on the football, track and swim teams.

Toward the end of his four-year tour, Hackman was in a motorcycle accident at Camp Pendleton, and broke both legs. It was fortunate that this made him ineligible to reenlist, as his unit was sent to Korea and suffered 90% casualties. Hackman loved the adventure of the Corps, but had difficulty with the discipline and regimentation. Although he was promoted to corporal three times, he was discharged in 1950 with the rank of private first class.

Hackman has won an Oscar twice, for *The French Connection* (1972) and *The Unforgiven* (1992).

Paul Harvey. Radio and TV news commentator.

Born Paul Harvey Aurandt in Tulsa, Oklahoma, on September 4, 1918, Harvey enlisted in the U.S. Army Air Corps in December 1943. He expected to be assigned as an Air Corps cadet, but was surprised when he was assigned to the infantry.

In March 1944, after four months of service, Harvey lacerated his heel on the obstacle course sufficiently to receive an honorable discharge for medical reasons.

Sterling Hayden. Film star, author.

Born Sterling Relyea Walter in Montclair, New Jersey, on March 26, 1916, Hayden received his last name from his stepfather, James Hayden. Sterling dropped out of school at age 16 to go to sea aboard fishing and sailing vessels. By age 20 he was first mate on the schooner *Yankee* when he was struck with the desire to be an actor. He went to New York, arranged for a screen test, and signed a contract with Paramount Pictures in 1940.

In November 1941 he traveled to England and trained in Scotland as a commando in the English army. He broke his ankle during a parachute jump, and was discharged.

He returned to the U.S. and tried to enlist in the navy, hoping for an assignment to PT boats, but his tenth grade education disqualified him for a commission as a lieutenant. He declined a commission as ensign to enlist as a private in the marines.

He wished to avoid celebrity and legally changed his name to John Hamilton. After basic training at Parris Island in the winter of 1942, he applied for officers training at Quantico and was one of only three selected from a class of 270 for the OSS (Office of Strategic Services). He was familiar with the director, Bill Donovan, for whom he had informally collected information in the thirties.

He was sent to Cairo, Egypt, where he reviewed intelligence reports, then to Yugoslavia where under Tito he assumed command of 400 Yugoslavian partisans and established a base of operations in Monopoli. Because of his sailing experience, he was put in charge of 22 small schooners, ketches and brigs running the German blockade across the Adriatic to the Island of Vis off the coast of German-occupied Dalmatia. He landed supplies, captured Italian war material, and acted as liaison.

Hayden returned to the U.S. in November of 1944, and dined

with FDR in January of 1945. He then returned to Europe as part of the intelligence section of the 1st Army. He performed clandestine missions in Italy, Germany, and other parts of Europe. He was discharged as a captain in 1945 with a Silver Star and a medal from Tito. He returned to Hollywood after the war.

He survived an investigation into his Communist associations by the House Un-American Activities Commission in 1951, occasionally made movies, traveled the world aboard his yacht, *Wanderer*, and authored several books. He died of prostate cancer in 1986.

Van Heflin. Oscar-winning actor.

Born Emmett Evan Van Heflin in Walters, Oklahoma, on December 13, 1910, Heflin enlisted in 1942 and after OCS was assigned as a second lieutenant in field artillery. Because of his experience in film, he was transferred to the duties of combat cameraman with the 9th Air Force in Europe.

Heflin won an Oscar in 1942 for *Johnny Eager*. He died in 1971.

Charlton Heston. Oscar-winning actor, Screen Actor Guild president, National Rifle Association vice president.

Born Charlton Carter in Evanston, Illinois, on October 4, 1924, Heston left Northwestern University as a drama student to enlist in the Army Air Corps at age 19 in 1943. He took basic training at Greensboro, North Carolina, and attended aerial gunnery school. He was sent overseas in March 1944 and spent two years assigned as a radioman aboard B-25s serving with the 77th Bombardment Squadron of the 11th Air Force on the island of Attu in the Aleutian Islands. The 77th was primarily involved with attacking the Japanese northern Kurile islands of Shumushu and Paramushiri and harassing Japanese shipping. Air operations in this theater of operations was especially hazardous because the severe climate made it extremely unlikely for crews in battle damaged or mechanically failing aircraft to make it back to Attu. Their options were Russian internment or survival in the artic sea below. The aircraft flew to the limit of their range in some of the worst weather in the world in what has been called the "forgotten war." In June 1944 all forces in the Aleutians were involved with "Operation Wedlock," a massive deception to convince Japan that five American and a Canadian division were preparing to invade the Kurile islands, thereby distracting them from the invasion of Saipan.

Later in the war, Heston was switched to B-29s. His unit was preparing for "Operation Downfall," the invasion of mainland Japan, when the war ended. He ran the control tower at Elmendorf Air Base in Anchorage, Alaska, before being ordered home in March of 1946. He was discharged with the rank of staff sergeant.

He won an Oscar for *Ben Hur* in 1959, played Moses in *The Ten Commandments* and was president of the Screen Actors Guild (1966–71). He twice traveled to Vietnam, visiting troops in remote forward areas, often within range of enemy weapons. He has been a steadfast proponent of the Second Amendment's right to bear arms.

Hal Holbrook. Actor, dramatist, "Mark Twain."

Born Harold Rowe Jr. in Cleveland, Ohio, on February 17, 1925, Holbrook graduated the Culver Military Academy in Culver, Indiana, in 1942. He was attending Denison University when he was drafted.

He served in the U.S. Army from May of 1943 until March of 1946. He was assigned as a private in the corps of engineers stationed in Newfoundland. To fight the boredom, Holbrook became involved in amateur theater groups, an interest he pursued after the war.

He won a Tony award for his one-man show, "Mark Twain."

William Holden. Oscar-winning actor.

Born William Franklin Beedle on April 17, 1918, in O'Fallon, Illinois, Holden had already starred in a dozen films including

Golden Boy (1939) and *Our Town* (1941) when the Japanese attacked Pearl Harbor. He is credited with being the first married Hollywood star to enlist.

He enlisted in the army as a private on April 21, 1942, and was assigned to the Air Corps at Tarrent Field near Ft. Worth, Texas. After training, he was transferred to the Signal Corps school at Ft. Monmouth, New Jersey.

Holden was accepted for officers training, and was sent to Florida. Upon his graduation on January 20, 1943, he was commissioned a second lieutenant, and was sent back to Tarrent Field as a public relations officer. He was assigned to the 1st Motion Picture Training Command, and his roommate in the BOQ (Bachelor Officers Quarters) was football star Hank Greenberg. He spent his time making training films and making appearances at war bond drives.

On New Years Day, 1944, Holden had a premonition of tragedy. Calls to his wife and parents assured him that all was well, but on January 4, he learned that his brother Robert, a naval aviator, was shot down on January 1 while flying a mission over Kavieng, New Ireland, in the South Pacific. Holden both wanted and requested a combat assignment, but his request was repeatedly denied as he was considered too valuable to morale to risk in combat.

Early in 1945, Holden was transferred to the Army Air Corps unit at Hal Roach Studios in Culver City. He recalls taking an instant dislike to the unit's "martinet adjutant," Captain Ronald Reagan, who had him stand at attention for 25 minutes while he recited regulations. He was discharged as a first lieutenant at the end of the war on December 8, 1945.

In 1953 Holden won the Oscar for Best Actor for his portrayal of a cynical captured airman in *Stalag 17*.

Tim Holt. Legendary cowboy star.

Born in Beverly Hills, California, on February 5, 1918, Holt was the son of actor Jack Holt and was already appearing in westerns by the age of ten (*The Vanishing Pioneer*, Paramount, 1928). He attended Culver Military Academy in Culver, Indiana. While there he excelled in sports and drama and graduated cum laude in 1936.

Late in 1942 Holt enlisted in the U.S. Army Air Corps. After training at Victorville, he was commissioned a second lieutenant and was briefly assigned as a flight instructor before being sent to the Pacific.

Holt flew combat missions as a bombardier aboard B-29s. While returning from his twenty-second mission, he viewed the mushroom cloud of Hiroshima in the distance. He was forced to bail out of a damaged aircraft on the last day of the war, August 14, 1945. He earned the Distinguished Service Cross and an Air Medal with three clusters. He was discharged as a major on December 8, 1945, and returned to Hollywood.

Holt made 52 movies, mostly RKO pictures, including *Stagecoach* and *My Darling Clementine* for director John Ford, and *Treasure of Sierra Madre* for director John Huston. He died in Shawnee, Oklahoma, on February 15, 1973.

Bob Hope. Showman, comedian, legend.

Born in London in 1903, Bob Hope has traveled over a million miles entertaining U.S. servicemen in three wars, although he never served in the military.

It can be argued that Hope did the first show of WWII when, while aboard the *Queen Mary* crossing the Atlantic on September 1, 1939, he put on an improvised show to calm the nerves of passengers who had just learned of Hitler's invasion of Poland. He traveled to all theatres of WWII with the USO, often putting himself at risk. He continued this tradition through Korea, Vietnam, and Desert Storm, as well as the peaceful periods in between. If current legislation in Congress passes, Hope will become the nation's first (and only) "Honorary Veteran."

Rock Hudson. Actor, leading man.

Born Roy Scherer Fitzgerald in Winnetka, Illinois, on November 17, 1925, Hudson enlisted in the U.S. Navy during WWII upon graduating high school in 1943. After basic training, he shipped out on the SS *Lew Wallace* for the Philippines.

Assigned to AROU-2 (Aviation Repair Overhaul Unit 2) on Samar Island, Hudson's duties consisted of unloading naval planes from aircraft carriers. In August 1945 a serious accident Hudson may have caused resulted in his transfer to laundry duties where he spent the remainder of his time in uniform. He was discharged from the navy in San Francisco in 1946.

Hudson enjoyed a successful film career and was nominated for an Oscar for his part in *Giant* (1956). He died of AIDS in 1985.

James Earl Jones. Actor, world's greatest voice.

Born in Arkabutla, Mississippi, on January 17, 1931, Jones enrolled in the ROTC program in 1952 while a student at the University of Michigan. After graduation, he entered the U.S. Army as a second lieutenant toward the end of the Korean conflict. He was sent to ranger training at Ft. Benning but wasn't able to complete the program.

Jones was then sent to the Cold Weather Command in Colorado where he excelled in the mission. He seriously considered making the army a career, but was advised to get more life experience before committing himself, so he accepted a discharge as a first lieutenant in 1955.

In his acting career, Jones has earned two Tonys, one Emmy, and the National Medal of the Arts in 1991.

Buster Keaton. Stage and screen comedian.

Born Joseph Francis Keaton in Piqua, Kansas, on October 4, 1895, Keaton spent his early years in vaudeville and was working in the movies when the U.S. entered WWI. He served in the army for seven months in France, but was never sent to the front lines because headquarters felt that the "Great Stoneface" was more valuable entertaining troops. He returned to California and the movies in 1919. He died in Hollywood in 1966.

Robert James Keeshan. "Captain Kangaroo."

Born in Lynbrook, New York, on June 27, 1927, Keeshan enlisted in the Marine Corps on June 14, 1945, shortly after graduating high school. After taking basic training at Parris Island, South Carolina, he was trained as a rifleman/paymaster clerk and transferred to Camp Lejeune, North Carolina, on September 18, 1945. The war ended while Keeshan was at Camp Lejeune and he remained there until May 1946 when he was transferred to San Diego for service with the Fleet Marine Force. He served aboard the USS *Rockridge* and the USS *Thomas Jefferson* before being discharged as a private first class on August 26, 1946.

He took a job at NBC after his discharge. He hosted *Captain Kangaroo*, the longest running children's show, from 1955 to 1984.

Gene Kelly. Oscar-winning dancer, choreographer.

Born Eugene Curan Kelly in Pittsburgh, Pennsylvania, on August 23, 1912, Kelly worked as a part-time dance instructor while attending the University of Pittsburgh. He enlisted in the navy after finishing the film *Anchors Aweigh* with Frank Sinatra in November 1944.

After basic and officer's training and a commission as an ensign, Kelly was disappointed that his first assignment was to make a movie about battle fatigue. This led to rumors in the trade papers that Kelly had seen combat and was suffering from battle fatigue.

He transferred to the photographic division of Naval Aviation in Washington DC. He was assigned to various photography projects, and was poised to participate in the invasion of Japan when two atomic bombs made the exercise unnecessary.

He was discharged on May 13, 1946, as a lieutenant (j.g.). In

1952 he starred in the film *Singing in the Rain*. Other films include *An American in Paris* and *That's Entertainment*.

Alan Ladd. Actor, leading man.

Born on September 3, 1913, in Hot Springs, Arkansas, Ladd graduated from North Hollywood High School in 1933. By 1942 he had appeared in 27 movies, mostly in bit parts, and in his first hit, *This Gun for Hire*, with Veronica Lake.

Although he was initially classified 4-F because of a diving accident, Ladd was anxious to serve and persisted until he was accepted by the Army Air Corps in January of 1943. The brass at Paramount Studios made sure that Ladd was sent off "to war" with plenty of publicity.

Sent to Ft. MacArthur, outside of Los Angeles, for basic training, Ladd's military career was publicized extensively by *Modern Screen*, *Photoplay* and other fan magazines. However, he was hospitalized with a double hernia and given an honorable discharge after only weeks of military service. He returned to Hollywood and made war movies for the duration.

Burt Lancaster. Oscar-winning actor.

Born Burton Steven Lancaster in New York City on November 2, 1913, Lancaster had a contract for $6,000 a year with CBS radio when he was drafted into the U.S. Army in June 1942. He reported for duty on December 26, 1942, and was ordered to report to Ft. Riley, Kansas, on January 2, 1943. Because of his show business background (he had performed in the circus), Lancaster was assigned to the 21st Special Services Unit of the 5th Army, and charged with directing and acting in shows.

The unit was sent overseas, and Lancaster put on the show "Stars and Gripes" in North Africa, Sicily, Italy and Austria. He was promoted to tech 5/corporal on March 1, 1943 and tech 4/ sergeant on April 1, but ended the war as a private first class due to insubordination. While in Italy, he met and later married USO entertainer Norma Anderson.

After the victory in Europe, Lancaster's unit returned to the U.S. and was en route to Japan, in transit at Camp Patrick Henry, Virginia, when the war ended. Lancaster was discharged from Ft. Dix on October 10, 1945.

He won an Oscar in the film *Elmer Gantry* (1960) and was nominated for an Oscar on three other occasions. He died in 1994.

Jack Lemmon. Two-time Oscar-winning actor.

Born John Uhler Lemmon III on February 8, 1925, in Boston, Massachusetts, Lemmon entered the Navy's V-12 training course and received the lowest marks of any officer commissioned by the Harvard ROTC program. He was first assigned to the aircraft carrier USS *Lake Champlain* (CV-39) as an ensign on February 12, 1946, where he served as its communications officer only for the time it took to sail her to be mothballed after the war.

With no overseas service or decorations, Lemmon, like his counterpart "Ensign Pulver," was able to wrangle himself a soft desk job, first in Washington DC, then Boston. He was discharged in the summer of 1946 after seven months in the navy. Lemmon has won an Oscar on two occasions: *Mr. Roberts* (1955) as Best Supporting Actor and for *Save the Tiger* (1971) as Best Actor. He received the American Film Institute Lifetime Achievement Award in 1988.

Fredric March. Oscar-winning actor.

Born Ernest Fredric McIntyre Bickel in Racine, Wisconsin, on August 31, 1897, March enlisted in the U.S. Army upon America's entry into WWI. After officer training school, he was commissioned a second lieutenant in the artillery and was discharged in February of 1919.

He played in films like *Death Takes a Holiday* (1934) and *A Bell for Adano* (1944) and won two Oscars for *Dr. Jekyll and Mr. Hyde* (1932) and *The Best Years of Our Lives* (1946).

Lee Marvin. Oscar-winning actor.

Born in New York City on February 10, 1924, the grandson of Civil War General Seth Marvin, Marvin dropped out of high school and enlisted in the marines on August 12, 1942. After basic training at Parris Island, South Carolina, and quartermasters school, he was sent to San Diego and then the South Pacific where he was assigned to I Company, 3rd Battalion, 24th Marines, 4th Marine Division.

Lee Marvin

He served in the engineers and later as an infantry scout, and saw action at Saipan, the Marianas, and Marshall Islands. He was involved in the capture of several small islands as part of a reconnaissance unit and was almost killed on two separate occasions. He was wounded in the buttocks on Saipan in June 1944, and narrowly missed being paralyzed. Marvin was in the hospital for 13 months before being given a medical discharge from the naval hospital at Chelsea, Massachusetts, on July 24, 1945. Although he rose to the rank of corporal, he was discharged as a private first class. He earned a Purple Heart and a Presidential Unit Citation.

Marvin worked in over 45 films and won an Oscar for Best Actor in *Cat Ballou* (1965). He also made legal history in 1976 as the defendant in the first "palimony" suit with Michelle Triola. He died of a heart attack on August 29, 1987.

Raymond Massey. Film actor.

Born in Toronto, Canada, on August 30, 1896, to an American mother and Canadian father, Massey can trace his ancestors to Salem in 1629. Members of his mother's family fought in the American Revolution and both sides of the Civil War.

With the outbreak of WWI, Massey enrolled in the Canadian officer's training corps while at the University of Toronto. In 1915 he was commissioned a lieutenant in the Canadian field artillery. He was sent to France in 1916 and was wounded at Ypres. After a six-month recovery, he was assigned to the British Military Mission in the United States where he served as a gunnery instructor at Yale and Princeton Universities.

He also served with the Expeditionary Force in Siberia from 1918 to 1919, where he earned recognition for organizing minstrel shows. He was discharged as a lieutenant in 1919 and went to Oxford.

He began a distinguished career in the theater, performing in plays by Eugene O'Neill and George Bernard Shaw. He was an established actor by the time WWII began.

After finishing the film *Action in the North Atlantic*, Massey applied to the U.S. Marines for a commission in intelligence. While waiting at the Hay-Adams Hotel in Washington DC for his commission to be processed, he received a telegram from the Canadian Minister of Defense.

Massey promptly rejoined his old regiment with a commission as major in November 1942. He served for one year as a recreation and entertainment officer, and was discharged for medical reasons in 1943. He returned to making films.

Walter Matthau. Oscar-winning actor, comedian.

Born Walter Matuschanskavasky in New York City on October 10, 1920, Matthau grew up in New York's Lower East Side, the son of Russian-Jewish immigrants. He enlisted in the Army Air Corps in April 1942. After basic training, he was trained at the Army Air Force radio school at Savannah, Georgia, as a radio operator and gunner. (All flight crew members were required to take gunnery training.) After training, he was assigned to the 453rd Bomb Group and went overseas to RAF station 144, Old

Buckenham, near Attleborough, England as part of the 8th Air Force.

Matthau was a ground radio operator and cryptographer, and saw service in France, Belgium, Holland and Germany. He remembers serving with Jimmy Stewart, who was an operations officer giving mission briefings to the group. He returned to Reno, Nevada, as part of the Air Transport Command, and was discharged in October 1945 from Sacramento, California, as a staff sergeant.

He took up acting after the war and appeared in his first film, *The Kentuckian*, in 1955. He has appeared in over 50 films including *The Odd Couple* (1965), and *Grumpy Old Men* (1993) with Jack Lemmon. He won an Oscar in 1972 for *The Fortune Cookie*.

Victor Mature. Film actor.

Born in Louisville, Kentucky, on January 29, 1916, Mature was already a popular star who had played opposite stars like Betty Grable, Rita Hayworth and Lucille Ball, and was making $1,200 a week when WWII broke out.

Mature enlisted in the U.S. Coast Guard in July 1942, and was initially stationed at San Pedro, California. He was transferred to Boston five months later at his own request for duty aboard an armed cutter on Atlantic convoy duty. He was assigned to the icebreaker USS *Storis* (WMEC-38) on November 28, 1942.

For 14 months he escorted ships and patrolled the North Atlantic. In 1944 he returned to acting in the all-coast guard musical, *Tars and Spars*, which toured the country to encourage enlistment. This assignment lasted a year.

When the war ended in Europe, Mature transported troops from Europe to the Pacific via the Panama Canal aboard the transport USS *Admiral Mayo* (AP-125). During the war Mature also participated in numerous war bond tours.

Discharged as a chief boatswain's mate at the end of the war, in November 1945, Mature took a part in John Ford's *My Darling Clementine* (1946). He retired in 1960 after a long career in film.

Ed McMahon. Co-host, commercial spokesperson.

Born Edward Lee McMahon in New York City on March 6, 1923, McMahon enrolled at Boston College as an electrical engi-

neering student. On February 9, 1943, he enlisted in the navy's V-5 program, designed to train navy and marine pilots. After he graduated, he worked in radio while waiting for an assignment.

On April 4, 1944, McMahon earned his wings and a commission as a second lieutenant in the Marine Corps. He served stateside at Lee Field as a flight instructor and test pilot. He received orders for overseas duty, but the war ended and he was processed out. He attained the rank of major. In 1951 he was recalled to active duty, assigned to the First Marine Division in Korea as an artillery spotter and forward air controller. He flew 85 missions over combat zones and was awarded seven Air Medals (six Oak Leaf Clusters). He began his career in show businesses as a circus clown in *Big Top* in 1950. He retired from the marine reserves as a colonel on March 6, 1983, his sixtieth birthday.

Ed McMahon

Steve McQueen. Film actor.

Born Terrance Steven McQueen on March 24, 1930, in Beech Grove, Indiana, McQueen enlisted in the Marine Corps at age 17 on April 28, 1947. After basic training at Camp Lejeune, North Carolina, he was trained as an auto mechanic and tank driver. He served in Labrador, where he rescued five marines when their Amtrac (amphibious tracked vehicle) overturned in freezing water.

He served the majority of his tour at Quantico, Virginia, where he was part of the honor guard protecting President Truman's yacht. McQueen was repeatedly promoted and demoted on account of numerous incidents of drunkenness and going AWOL. He spent six weeks in the brig, and was discharged as a private first class on April 27, 1950. McQueen once stated that the only way he'd make corporal in the Corps would be if all the Pfc's died at the same time.

McQueen's long and distinguished film career included movies like *The Great Escape* and *The Getaway*.

Burgess Meredith. TV and film actor.

Born on November 16, 1907, in Cleveland, Ohio, Meredith was already a successful actor when he enlisted in the army at the beginning of WWII. He was serving as a private in Santa Ana, California, when he was called to New York to perform in a revival of *Candida* at the request of General Marshall.

After being sent to the Air Corps intelligence school, he was commissioned a lieutenant, and sent to London where he was promoted to captain and put to work making films promoting Anglo-American and French-American relations.

An aide to President Roosevelt arranged for Meredith to be discharged in 1944 so that he could play the lead in the film, *The Story of GI Joe*, about the life of beloved war correspondent Ernie Pyle who was killed in action during the war. After the war, Meredith had a long distinguished career in television and film. He was nominated for an Oscar for *Rocky* (1976) and won an Emmy for supporting actor in 1977 for *Tail Gunner Joe*, a T.V. movie. He died in Los Angeles on September 9, 1997.

Robert Mitchum. Oscar-winning actor.

Born Robert Charles Duran Mitchum in Bridgeport, Connecticut, on August 6, 1917, Mitchum was deferred from the draft until March of 1945 so that he could finish filming *The Story of GI Joe* (he won an Academy Award for Best Supporting Actor in 1945). In April he was sent to Camp Roberts, California.

He served as a drill instructor and medical assistant at Ft. MacArthur, and was given a dependency discharge in November after serving only eight months.

Tom Mix. Cowboy star.

According to legend, Tom Mix enlisted in the army during the Spanish-American War, went to Cuba where he served as a scout and courier, was wounded in the neck at the Battle of Guaymas, and was hospitalized until the war's end.

Then in 1899, he was sent to the Philippines, then China during the Boxer Rebellion, where he was again wounded in battle. He was decorated for valor, but deserted prior to completing his second enlistment. He later trained horses for the British Army in South Africa during the Boer War. He deserted and joined the Boer side, but was captured by the British and returned to the United States. So goes the legend.

According to his son Paul Mix in his biography of his father, the legend was created by studio executives in the February 1925 issue of *Photoplay* magazine, much to his father's embarrassment.

The truth is that Thomas Edwin Mix was born on January 6, 1880, in Mix Run, Pennsylvania. After the battleship *Maine* was sunk in Havana on February 15, 1898, Mix traveled to Washington DC to enlist in the army. He took his induction physical on April 25, the day the U.S. declared war on Spain.

He was assigned to Battery M, 4th Regiment, U.S. Army artillery, and put to work guarding the Du Pont Powder Works outside of Montchanin, Delaware. In May he was assigned to a coastal artillery unit at Battery Point, Delaware. He was promoted to corporal on July 1, and was promoted to sergeant on New Year's eve, 1898.

In April 1899 Mix was transferred to Battery O at Ft. Monroe, Virginia, where he was put to work drilling recruits, and upgrading the facilities. He was promoted to quartermaster sergeant on July 12, 1899. In August Battery O was relocated to Ft.

Terry, New York, during an outbreak of yellow fever. On November 18, Mix was promoted to first sergeant.

By July of 1900, Battery O was sent to Ft. Hancock, New Jersey, where records show Mix was honorably discharged on April 25, 1901, and re-enlisted on April 26, 1901. He married a Norfolk, Virginia, schoolteacher named Grace I. Allen while on furlough on July 18, 1902. On his next furlough in October 1902, he didn't return. He was officially declared AWOL on October 25, and listed as a deserter on November 4. He was never apprehended or returned to army custody. He moved west to Oklahoma, before going on to star in 93 films, primarily for Universal Pictures.

Robert Montgomery. Film actor.

Born Henry Montgomery in Beacon, New York, on May 21, 1904, Montgomery made his Broadway debut in 1924 and was a popular film star in the 1930s, earning two Oscar nominations. He worked with the American Field Service in the summer of 1940 and was assigned to an ambulance unit in Europe where he witnessed ambulances being bombed. He was an early proponent of America entering the war.

He returned to the U.S. after the Germans invaded France, and applied for a naval commission. On April 28, 1941, Montgomery was commissioned a lieutenant (j.g.), and was sent to the American embassy in London as a naval attaché several months before Pearl Harbor. He was responsible for tracking American and British ships.

In November 1941 he was recalled to the U.S. to set up a similar program at the White House, where he served only briefly. He continued to volunteer for sea duty, requesting assignment to a PT boat squadron. He was accepted, and after training was sent first to Panama then to the South Pacific.

He saw action at Guadalcanal and the Marshall Islands, earning a promotion to lieutenant commander. In the summer of 1943 he returned to the U.S. for training as a deck officer on a destroyer. He was assigned to the Atlantic Fleet aboard the destroyer USS *Barton* (DD-722), and was part of the Normandy invasion on D-Day. His ship was part of a task force that provided offshore fire support. He was ordered back to Washington DC on August 19, 1944, where he worked on film until his discharge as a commander at the end of the war.

He earned a Bronze Star, and was recalled to the U.S. to be released from service on October 5, 1945 to star in the war film *They Were Expendable* with John Wayne. (The film was the true account of Navy P. T. skipper Lt. John D. Bulkeley, a Medal of Honor winner who evacuated the MacArthurs from the Phillippines. The film was written by WWI naval aviator Frank "Sprig" Wead and directed by Commander John Ford who was on leave from the navy.) After the war Montgomery did some acting and directing, was involved in conservative politics, and served on the boards of Macy's and The Lincoln Center for the Performing arts. His daughter is actress Elizabeth Montgomery. He died in 1981.

Zero Mostel. Comedian, painter, writer.

Born Samuel Joseph Mostel on February 28, 1915, in New York City, Mostel was already a popular entertainer before WWII. In 1943 *Life* magazine described Mostel as the "funniest American now living." In March of that same year, Mostel was drafted into the U.S. Army and went from a salary of $5,000 a week, to a private's pay of $21 a month.

After taking basic training at Camp Croft in South Carolina, Mostel applied for a position as an entertainment director with army special services; however, there was concern because Mostel was suspected of being "leftist" or "subversive."

Even after a favorable investigation by military intelligence, which described Mostel as "a good soldier," "intelligent," and "an apt and willing soldier," statements made to investigators alleging that he was a communist resulted in his being found "not qualified." He was subsequently given an honorable discharge in August 1943 after only six months for "unspecified physical disabilities." Mostel would later go overseas to entertain troops as a civilian with the USO.

He would be blackballed from working during the McCarthy era, but would win long-standing fame for his portrayal of the father in *Fiddler on the Roof* on Broadway.

Audie Murphy. Film actor, most decorated soldier of WWII.

Born in Kingston, Texas, on June 20, 1924, Audie Leon Murphy was born into poverty, one of twelve children of a sharecropper. He quit school in the fifth grade to go to work to help support his family. He also hunted to put meat on the dinner table.

He was at the movies on a date, when Pearl Harbor was announced. The 17-year-old Murphy promptly tried to enlist in the service. He was rejected by both the paratroopers and the marines. He returned after his eighteenth birthday, and enlisted as a private in the U.S. Army on July 19, 1942.

After training in the States, Murphy was sent overseas to North Africa on February 8, 1943, but arrived too late to see action. He was assigned to Company B, 15th Regiment of the 3rd Infantry Division (named the "Marne" Division from its service in WWI). The Third Division saw action in North Africa, Italy and Southern France across the Rhine into Germany and Austria making it the only American division to engage the Germans on all fronts. Murphy's unit landed in Sicily on July 10, 1943. He was promoted to corporal during the Salerno campaign and his single-handed destruction of a tank earned him a Bronze Star. From September of 1943 until June of 1944, he saw almost continuous combat. He was part of the amphibious invasion of Anzio, and was a sergeant by the time Rome was liberated.

In August of 1944 Murphy's unit landed in the south of France at St. Tropez. In a skirmish, Murphy's best friend was killed by German troops pretending to surrender by displaying a white flag. Enraged, Murphy lost control, killed the "surrendering" troops, and destroyed the machine gun position. For his disregard of his own safety, Murphy was awarded the Distinguished Service Cross.

On January 26, 1945, Murphy earned the Medal of Honor for his actions in the Colmar pocket of eastern France. With his outnumbered command concealed in the woods, Murphy mounted a burning tank destroyer and, manning its machine gun, held off a German force of six tanks and 250 infantry. After killing fifty troops, and forcing a withdrawl, Murphy led the counterattack despite a leg wound.

Murphy won the Medal of Honor and also a battlefield commission to second lieutenant. At the war's end, after thirty months of combat, Murphy had over 28 combat decorations including the Medal of Honor, the Distinguished Service Cross, three Silver Stars, the Legion of Merit, the Bronze Star, three Purple Hearts, the French Legion of Honor, and the Croix de Guerre. He was discharged as a first lieutenant.

After the war he was a national figure and signed an agreement with James Cagney to begin acting lessons. In all, Murphy acted in 40 movies, mostly westerns. He played himself in the film *To Hell and Back* (1955), the story of his life. But success was difficult, and Murphy suffered from what would later be referred to as post traumatic stress syndrome. He drank heavily, gambled, had nightmares, and slept with a loaded gun. He died in an airplane accident on May 28, 1971, and was buried at Arlington National Cemetery with full military honors.

Paul Newman. Oscar-winning actor, businessman.

Born on January 26, 1925, in Cleveland, Ohio, Newman was a 17-year-old student attending Ohio University when WWII began. He enlisted in the navy's V-5 preflight program for training pilots. He was dropped from the program when it was discovered he was colorblind. Newman was trained as a radioman/gunner and served the next two years as a radioman 3rd class aboard Grumman TBM Avengers (naval patrol torpedo planes) in the Pacific. He saw little action, flying a few missions over Japan toward the end of the war while stationed on board the

USS *Hollandia* (CVE-97). On one occasion in Hawaii, Newman was in a pool of replacements, and all the crews were ordered to the USS *Bunker Hill* (CV-17). Newman's pilot got an ear infection, and so his crew was left behind. A kamikaze crashed into the briefing room of the *Bunker Hill* during the mission briefing, killing many of the squadron. Otherwise, Newman recalled his war service as pretty much "uneventful." He was discharged from the navy in April 1946.

The six-time Oscar nominated actor who starred in films like *Butch Cassidy and the Sundance Kid, The Sting,* and *Cool Hand Luke,* won his first Oscar for *The Color of Money* in 1987. He also races Formula One race cars.

Chuck Norris. Martial arts expert, actor.

Born Carlos Ray Norris in Los Angeles on March 10, 1940, of mixed Irish and Indian ancestry, Norris wanted to grow up and become a policeman. After graduating high school, he enlisted in the U.S. Air Force on August 13, 1958.

After basic training and air police school at Lackland Air Force Base in Texas, he was assigned first to Arizona, then in April 1960, to Osan, Korea, as an air policeman with the 6314th Air Police Squadron.

Unable to arrest a battling drunk without pulling his weapon, Norris became interested in martial arts. He earned his black belt in Tang So Do karate before his discharge as an airman first class from March AFB in California on August 12, 1962. He was awarded the Good Conduct Medal. Norris never became a policeman, but he did meet Bruce Lee who helped him and gave him work.

Hugh O'Brian. Actor, "Wyatt Earp."

Born Hugh J. Krampe in Rochester, New York, on April 19, 1925, O'Brian was the son of a retired Marine Corps captain. He attended both Roosevelt Military Academy in Illinois, and Kemper Military School in Kentucky, before entering the University of Cincinnati.

Interrupted by WWII during his sophomore year, O'Brian enlisted in the U.S. Marine Corps, and at 18 became one of the youngest drill sergeants in marine history.

Desiring combat duty, he volunteered for transfer to a tank company, but instead was selected for appointment to Annapolis. He barely missed the entrance requirements, and was studying to retake the exam the following year when the war ended. O'Brian subsequently decided against a military career, and was discharged as a sergeant.

He worked odd jobs while studying theater, appeared in some 34 movies, and starred in the television series *The Life and Legend of Wyatt Earp* from 1955 to 1961.

Carroll O'Connor. Television actor.

Born in New York City on August 2, 1924, O'Connor spent three years as a seaman in the merchant marine during WWII. He served aboard tankers and transported fuel supplies to the combat zones in the North Atlantic. Because the cargo was so volatile, this was a significantly hazardous duty, even without the mines and German U-boats.

O'Connor is best remembered for the role of "Archie Bunker" in the ground-breaking television series *All in the Family*.

Jack Paar. Entertainer, *Tonight Show* host.

Born May 1, 1918, in Canton, Ohio, Paar took basic training at Camp Custer in Michigan as well as infantry training before he was assigned to the 28th Special Services Company. The unit was comprised of musicians, actors and athletes. Infantry and small arms training was required for such units since they often entertained in the forward areas and frequently came under enemy fire (talk about your hostile audience!). He spent two years entertaining troops in the South Pacific.

Paar earned a reputation for mocking officers in his comedy routines. On one occasion, his remarks onstage resulted in being placed under guard by order of a navy commodore offended by a joke. Paar kidded that the USO girls would be unable to perform the "Dance of the Virgins" as planned because they had been quartered in the officer's club and had their "contracts" broken.

Bert Parks. Showman, entertainer.

Born December 30, 1914, in Atlanta, Georgia, Parks was working as a staff announcer at CBS radio in New York at the start of WWII. He enlisted as a private in the army in 1942 and was sent overseas to China as an infantryman.

In China, Parks was assigned dangerous reconnaissance missions establishing underground radio stations behind enemy lines. He sometimes would spend weeks at a time in the field. He also served briefly as a staff officer for General Stilwell. By the time of his discharge in 1946, Parks was a captain. He was awarded a Silver Star and returned to CBS after the war. He hosted the Miss America Pageant from 1954 until 1979.

George Peppard. Film and TV actor.

Born in Detroit on October 1, 1928, Peppard entered the U.S. Marine Corps in 1951, and spent 18 months serving in the artillery. He worked with 105 mm and 155 mm cannons and was discharged in 1952 as a corporal.

After his discharge, Peppard began acting in films like *Breakfast at Tiffany's*, and the television series, *The A Team*.

Sidney Poitier. Oscar-winning actor.

Born in Miami, Florida, on February 2, 1924, Poitier enlisted in the U.S. Army in 1943 to escape living on the street. He took basic training at Camp Upton, Long Island.

After basic training, Poitier was assigned to the 1267th Medical Detachment, the all-black military unit attached to the veteran's hospital at Northport, Long Island. He was responsible for caring for psychiatric patients suffering from shell shock.

Disillusioned with the army after nine months of service, in

1944 Poitier feigned a violent mental disorder to obtain a discharge after one year and 11 days of service.

Poitier enjoyed better success in his acting career. He gave noteworthy performances in films like *To Sir with Love* (1969), and *Guess Who's Coming to Dinner* (1969). He was nominated for an Oscar for *The Defiant Ones* (1958) and won an Oscar for Best Actor in 1963 for *Lilies of the Field*. He was the first black since Hattie McDaniel to win an Oscar. In 1992 he became the first black to win the American Film Institute's Lifetime Achievement Award.

Tyrone Power. Film actor.

Born in Cincinnati, Ohio, on May 5, 1914, Power acted in over two dozen films prior to WWII. He was unable to obtain a commission in the navy, and was unwilling to accept a commission as a "Culver City Commando" in the Signal Corps unit commanded by Darryl Zanuck, so he enlisted as a private in the U.S. Marine Corps in August 1942. Upon reporting to Camp Pendleton in California for basic training, he was informed that he had been granted four months leave to complete the film *Crash Dive.*

After basic training in San Diego, and officer's training at Quantico, Virginia, Power was commissioned a second lieutenant. He took flight training in Corpus Christi, and served 16 months at the naval air station in Atlanta, and the marine air station at Cherry Point, North Carolina.

In late 1944 Power was sent overseas to the South Pacific as a marine transport pilot flying the Curtiss R5C Commando with Transport Squadron VMR-353. (The R5C was the Marine Corps version of the army's C-46.) He saw action at Saipan flying supplies in under fire in his plane *Blythe Spirit,* logging over 1100 hours flight time. After brief service with occupation forces in Japan, Power was discharged as a captain in January 1946.

His postwar films include *The Long Gray Line* (1955), and *Witness for the Prosecution* (1958). He died of a heart attack while filming *Solomon and Sheba* in Madrid in 1958.

Robert Preston. Actor, "The Music Man."

Born Robert Preston Meservey on June 8, 1917 (or 1918, depending on source), in Newton Heights, Massachusetts, Preston was raised in Hollywood and quit school to join a Shakespearean company. He enlisted in the Army Air Corps in 1942 and served in Europe as a captain in military intelligence. He set routes, reviewed data, and briefed aircrews. He was discharged in 1945 with the rank of captain.

As an actor he is remembered best as "Professor Harold Hill," a character he performed in 1,375 performances of *The Music Man* on Broadway and in the 1962 film of the same name. He was nominated for an Oscar for his role in *Victor/Victoria* (1982). His last film was *The Last Starfighter* (1984). He died in 1987.

Tony Randall. Actor, half of "The Odd Couple."

Born Leonard Rosenberg on February 26, 1924, in Tulsa, Oklahoma, Randall enlisted in the U.S. Army as a private during WWII in 1942. He was assigned to the Signal Corps and was sent to OCS (Officer's Candidate School) at Ft. Monmouth, New Jersey. Upon graduation, Randall was commissioned a second lieutenant and served as a courier of classified documents. He was discharged as a first lieutenant in 1946.

As an actor he is best remembered as Felix, the clean member of *The Odd Couple* on television.

Jason Robards. Award-winning actor.

Born on July 22, 1922, in Chicago, Robards was the son of an actor who moved his family to Hollywood. Soon after graduating Hollywood High School in 1940, he enlisted in the U.S. Navy reserve at the age of 17. He was called to active duty as an apprentice seaman.

He served overseas in the South Pacific as a radioman aboard cruisers. He was present at 13 major engagements, and was twice on torpedoed ships. He was aboard the *North Hampton* (CV-26) at Guadalcanal when it was sunk by torpedoes, and also on the

Honolulu when it was torpedoed near Formosa toward the end of the war.

Although some accounts have him at Pearl Harbor aboard the USS *Honolulu* the day of the Japanese attack, ships muster rolls show him aboard the USS *North Hampton* as a radioman third class. The *North Hampton* was at sea on the day of the attack, returning to Pearl Harbor from escorting the USS *Enterprise* (CV-6) to Wake Island, and returning on December 8, the day after the attack.

Discharged in 1946 as a radioman first class, Robards took up acting. He won a Tony for "Disenchanted" in 1959, married Lauren Bacall, and won two Oscars for Best Supporting Actor in *All the President's Men* (1976) and *Julia* (1977).

Edward G. Robinson. Oscar-winning tough guy actor.

Born Emanuel Goldenberg on December 12, 1893, in Bucharest, Romania, Robinson came to the United States as a child. In July 1918, armed with a letter of introduction from George M. Cohan, Robinson enlisted in the U.S. Navy with the hope of working for naval intelligence.

After seamanship training at Pelham Bay, Robinson spent his time in traditional military pursuits like KP and "shovel details." He turned down opportunities to join entertainment units because he wanted to make a significant contribution to the war effort. He still hoped for a transfer to naval intelligence.

Robinson's transfer to intelligence came through shortly before the war ended on November 11, 1918. With the war over, he hoped to be swiftly demobilized but was to be disappointed. Miserable with the boredom of the peacetime navy, Robinson accepted invitations to entertain troops at camps and hospitals. It was his experiences in the burn and casualty wards that gave Robinson his real introduction to war. "What I saw made me hate war with every fiber of my being," he recalled. He was discharged from the navy in 1919.

Robinson enjoyed a long career in film, becoming a legend for his gangster roles in *Little Caesar*, *Key Largo*, and *Brother Orchid*. He was awarded a special Oscar in 1972.

Mickey Rooney. Oscar-winning actor.

Born Joe Yule Jr. in Brooklyn on September 23, 1920, Rooney first performed at the age of seven months. After making 15 Andy Hardy films, he was voted the most popular actor of 1939 and 1940. He was dating Ava Gardner and earning $125,000 a year when WWII began.

Neither Rooney nor studio boss Louis Meyer were anxious for Rooney to enter the service, and the studio continued to get extensions while studio lawyers tried to get Rooney an exemption, arguing that the Andy Hardy movies were necessary to the war effort and morale. In September 1942 the local draft board classified Rooney 4-F (unfit for military service) for high blood pressure.

By mid-1943 Rooney was so uncomfortable being out of uniform that he requested that the draft board review his case, and he was reclassified 1-A. Shortly afterwards, in June of 1944, Rooney was inducted into the army at Ft. MacArthur. He was sent to the cavalry training center at Ft. Riley, Kansas, for basic training. In September he was sent for chemical warfare training to Camp Siebert, Alabama.

During this time, the army was seeking entertainers for service overseas, and Rooney was transferred to special services. Assigned to the 6817th Special Services Battalion, Rooney was en route to Europe by November 1944 aboard the *Queen Mary*. He served in France as part of a "jeep show" under the command of Broadway producer and army major Joshua Logan. "Jeep shows" were a team of three entertainers who put on shows on the front lines, often under hazardous conditions. On more than one occasion Rooney came under enemy small arms fire. All entertainers took infantry weapons training and carried small arms.

Rooney was very popular with the troops, and would tell jokes and do imitations. He served in Europe until the war ended. After the war, he served as an announcer for Armed Forces Radio in Frankfurt until he earned enough points for a discharge. He declined a commission to remain in the army, and was discharged as a technician 3rd class (equal to staff sergeant) from Ft. Dix, New Jersey, on March 6, 1946. He served for 20 months and earned a Bronze Star and a Good Conduct Medal. He won a Best Supporting Actor Oscar for *Black Stallion* (1979).

Dan Rowan. Comedian, co-host of *Laugh In*.

Born Daniel H. David in Beggs, Oklahoma, on July 2, 1922, Rowan joined the U.S. Army Air Corps early in 1942 and trained as a fighter pilot. Upon completion of flight training, he was commissioned a second lieutenant assigned to the 8th Fighter Squadron, 49th Fighter Group of the 5th Air Force in New Guinea. He flew Curtiss P-40 fighters.

He survived a plane crash and served until his discharge at the end of the war. He entered "Show Biz" as half of the comedy team of "Rowan and Martin" and won four Emmys for the television show *Laugh In* (1968–72). He died in 1987.

Robert Ryan. Film actor.

Born on November 11, 1909 (some sources say 1913), in Chicago, Ryan was already a leading man in the movies when he enlisted in the Marine Corps in January 1944. RKO Pictures guaranteed his salary throughout the war.

Ryan spent his entire tour of duty as an infantry drill instructor at Camp Pendleton, California. He was discharged in November 1945 as a private first class. Ryan stated that watching the casualties of war returning turned him into a pacifist.

He had a long career in film in starring roles, mostly war movies like *The Longest Day* (1962), *The Battle of the Bulge* (1965), and *The Dirty Dozen* (1967). He died of cancer in 1973.

Soupy Sales. Entertainer, comedian.

Born Milton Hines in Wake Forest, North Carolina, in 1926, Sales enlisted in the U.S. Navy upon graduation from high school.

After basic training, he was sent to the Pacific theater where he was assigned aboard the USS *Randall*, an attack transport in the 7th Fleet. Sales was present at the invasion of Okinawa and served until the end of the war. After the war he attended college on the GI Bill.

George Campbell Scott. Oscar-winning actor, "Patton."

Born in Wise, Virginia, on October 18, 1927, Scott graduated Redford High School and promptly joined the U.S. Marines. While taking basic training at Parris Island, he had his nose broken in a fight with a drunken sergeant major over the acting ability of Ava Gardner. He was training in expectation of having to invade mainland Japan when the war ended.

With 45 months yet to serve, Scott was sent to language school, then assigned to Washington DC. He served from 1945 to 1949 assigned to the Honor Guard at Arlington National Cemetery performing burial details, and taught a creative writing correspondence course. By all accounts Scott was the picture of the hard drinking, hard fighting marine.

After his discharge, Scott attended the University of Missouri on the GI Bill. He was nominated for Oscars on two occasions: *Anatomy of a Murder* (1959), and *The Hustler* (1961) before winning for *Patton* in 1971. He is the first actor to refuse an Oscar, stating that the awards are "professionally demeaning."

Red Skelton. Clown, artist, comedian, author.

Born in Vincennes, Indiana, on July 18, 1913, Richard "Red" Skelton was exempt from the draft during WWII because he was 28 and married with one child. He was earning $12,000 a week doing shows and movies. When his wife divorced him in February 1944, Skelton's status changed and he was drafted into the army as a private.

He was sent to Entertainers Specialist School at Lee University in Virginia where he served as the resident clown. In March 1945 he was assigned as an entertainer on the troopship SS *General Altman* in Naples. Skelton entertained so continuously that he collapsed from exhaustion, and returned to the U.S. aboard a hospital ship.

He was in the hospital for four months until given a medical discharge on September 18, 1945. Skelton would later kid that he was the only major star to emerge from WWII as a "buck private." He returned to show business and continued to entertain audiences for the next 52 years until his death in Los Angeles on September 18, 1997.

Rod Steiger. Oscar-winning actor.

Born Rodney Steven Steiger on April 22, 1925, in Long Island, New York, Steiger began his acting career in school plays. He dropped out of Newark's West Side High School and lied about his age (he was 16) to enlist in the navy in 1941.

He spent four years as a torpedoman, rising to torpedoman 1st class assigned to the newly commissioned destroyer USS *Taussig* (DD-746) in the South Pacific. He was present at many major engagements of the 3rd and 5th Fleets. His ship was awarded Battle Stars for operations at Okinawa and Iwo Jima but the ship was not actually present at those battles. It was involved in escorting aircraft carriers attacking nearby enemy airstrips in support of the operations. Steiger left the *Taussig* on March 17, two weeks before the invasion of Okinawa.

Steiger was given a medical discharge in August 1945 for acute skin disease, two weeks before the Japanese surrendered. He studied acting after the war on the GI Bill. He was twice nominated for Oscars for *On the Waterfront* (1954) and *The Pawnbroker* (1965) before winning with *In the Heat of the Night* (1967).

James "Jimmy" Stewart. Oscar-winning actor.

Born James Maitland Stewart in Indiana, Pennsylvania, on May 20, 1908, Stewart won the Oscar for Best Actor in 1940 for

The Philadelphia Story. As early as 1939, with the outbreak of WWII in Europe, Stewart had been accumulating flying hours as a civilian as fast as possible in order to qualify as a military pilot.

After accepting his Oscar in February 1941, Stewart enlisted in the U.S. Army Air Corps as a private in March. After basic training at Ft. MacArthur in Los Angeles, Stewart was sent to Moffett Air Corps Training Base in Northern California. His experience as a pilot earned him a promotion to corporal.

Jimmy Stewart

After nine months of flying on 4-engine bombers, Stewart was promoted to lieutenant in December 1941. He served as a pilot-instructor for B-17s in Idaho before being sent overseas to England as a captain in November 1943. He flew over 20 missions in his B-24 Liberator. Promoted to major, he was assigned as group operations officer for the 453rd Bombardment Group. He was responsible for 50 bombers.

By April 1945 Stewart was a colonel and chief of staff of the 2nd Combat Wing, 8th Air Force. By the time he was released from active duty in September, he had over 18,000 hours flight time. He was awarded the Distinguished Flying Cross for his leadership of the 703rd Squadron on a raid over Brunswick, Germany, on February 20, 1944. He also was awarded the Croix de Guerre and an Air Medal with an Oak Leaf Cluster. Stewart remained in the reserves and retired a brigadier general in 1968. Men who flew under his command remember him as a good and competent officer. He died in August 1997.

Note: At the start of the war, only 25% of B-17 and B-24 crews completed the 25 required missions. The average was 15 before being shot down, killed or captured. Aircrews had a one-in-four chance of surviving. The number of required missions increased as the war progressed.

Robert Taylor. Film actor.

Born Spangler Arlington Brugh on August 5, 1911, in Filley, Nebraska, Taylor was a civilian pilot before WWII. After basic training at the Naval Air Station in Dallas, and flight training at NAS New Orleans, Taylor was commissioned a lieutenant (j.g.) and naval aviator on January 11, 1944.

Although he repeatedly requested combat assignments, Taylor was considered too old and spent the war making training films in Livermore, California, and as a flight instructor. He was discharged in November 1945 as a full lieutenant. He returned to Hollywood and a career as a leading man for MGM.

Gregg Toland. Oscar-winning cinematographer.

The director of photography on films like *Citizen Kane*, *Grapes of Wrath*, and *Best Years of Our Lives*, Toland was born in Charleston, Illinois, on May 29, 1904. He left school at 15 to go to Hollywood where he found work as an office boy at a film studio.

Toland was an established cameraman when WWII began, and was commissioned a lieutenant in the navy, attached to Commander John Ford's OSS Field Photographic. Toland's documentary on Pearl Harbor, *December 7th* (1943) was critical of America's preparedness before the war. The film was confiscated by the navy and was never released, except as an industrial film as part of the "Industrial Incentive Program." Disgusted, Toland requested and was assigned as the head of the Field Photographic in Rio de Janeiro for the rest of the war. Toland died of a heart attack on September 28, 1948.

Rip Torn. Actor, director.

Born Elmore Torn Jr. in Temple, Texas, on February 6, 1931,

Torn enlisted in the U.S. Army in 1953 at the height of the Korean War. He served for two years as a military policeman and was discharged in 1955. He married Geraldine Page in 1961.

Spencer Tracy. Nine-time nominated, Oscar-winning actor.

Born Spencer Bonaventure Tracy on May 5, 1900, in Milwaukee, Wisconsin, Tracy considered the priesthood, but changed his mind with the outbreak of WWI.

He tried to join the Marine Corps, but was too young. Tracy's boyhood friend Bill O'Brien (later known as Pat), enlisted in the navy and advised Tracy that he could join too, if he could get parental permission. Tracy's parents gave their consent with his promise to return to school after the war.

Tracy was in the navy for seven months, stationed at Great Lakes Naval Station near Chicago. He studied boat handling, seamanship and other nautical skills.

After his discharge, he returned to school and began a long career in film, winning Oscars for *Captain Courageous* (1937) and *Boys Town* (1938).

Eli Wallach. Film actor.

Born on December 7, 1915, in New York City, Wallach had already earned a master's degree in education by the age of 26, when Pearl Harbor was attacked. He enlisted in the U.S. Army and was assigned to the medical corps after basic training. He served as a Medical Services Officer throughout the war being discharged as a captain at the end of the war.

Jack Warner. Oscar-winning studio executive.

Born in London, Ontario, on August 2, 1892, Warner enlisted with his brother Sam into the U.S. Army during WWI. He produced documentaries for the Signal Corps. After the war, he founded Warner Brothers Studios with his brothers Harry, Albert and Sam in 1923.

After the start of WWII, Warner accepted a commission of

lieutenant colonel in April 1942. He was assigned to the Motion Picture Unit of the U.S. Army Air Force where he produced both military and commercial films such as *Yankee Doodle Dandy* with James Cagney in 1942.

Dennis Weaver. TV Actor, "Chester" on Gunsmoke.

Born June 4, 1925, in Joplin, Missouri, Weaver enlisted in the U.S. Navy reserve at 18. He served as a flier, but set records while on a navy track team. He was discharged with the rank of ensign, then attended the University of Oklahoma as a drama major. He just missed qualifying for the 1948 Olympic team.

Jack Randolph Webb. Actor, director, producer.

Born John Farr in Santa Monica, California, on April 2, 1920, Webb joined the U.S. Army Air Corps as an aviation cadet in 1943. After taking preflight training at Camp St. Cloud in Minnesota, Webb served as a pilot of B-26s briefly before receiving a dependency discharge in 1945. While in the service, he served on two occasions as the master of ceremonies for USO shows.

Webb's most famous role was that of "Sgt. Joe Friday" on *Dragnet* the radio show (1949–55), and on *Dragnet* the television show (1952–59 and 1967–70).

James Allen Whitmore. Oscar-nominated actor.

Born in White Plains, New York, on October 1, 1921, Whitmore was enrolled in the prelaw program at Yale when WWII began. He left Yale (where he played football under Coach Gerald R. Ford) to enlist in the marines. He earned his B.A. while he was in the service.

He saw combat at Saipan, the Mariana Islands, and Tinian, eventually earning a battlefield commission to lieutenant. He decided that he wanted a career in theater rather than law, so after he was discharged he joined a USO tour and returned to the Pacific to entertain troops serving with the occupation forces.

He returned to the U.S. and performed in small theater groups. He later gained fame with his one-man shows, "Will

Rogers" and "Give 'Em Hell, Harry." The latter earned him an Oscar nomination.

Montel Brian Williams. Talk show host, motivational speaker.

Born in Baltimore, Maryland, on July 3, 1956, Williams enlisted in the U.S. Marines upon graduating high school in 1974.

He took basic training at Parris Island, South Carolina, where he was promoted to platoon guide. After basic training, he was sent to the Desert Warfare Training Center at Twenty-nine Palms, near Palm Springs, California.

While at Twenty-nine Palms, his superiors became impressed with his leadership skills, and he was recommended for, and accepted to, the Naval Academy Preparatory School at Newport, Rhode Island. He completed the one-year course, and was accepted to the U.S. Naval Academy at Annapolis.

Montel Williams

When he arrived at Annapolis on July 6, 1976, he was honorably discharged as a corporal from the marines, and enlisted into the navy as a midshipman. It was at Annapolis that Williams first began to shave his head. Upon his graduation in 1980, he became the first black enlisted marine to complete and graduate both the Academy Prep School and Annapolis.

Commissioned an ensign, he spent the next one and a half years in Guam as a cryptologic officer for naval intelligence, where he served both at sea and ashore. In 1982 he was transferred to the Defense Language Institute in Monterey, California, where he studied the Russian language for one year. In 1983 he was transferred to Ft. Meade in Maryland, where he worked with the National Security Agency. What Williams did there is vague, due to the sensitive nature of intelligence work, but he performed various intelligence missions. He was offshore aboard ship during the invasion of Grenada.

After three years aboard submarines, Williams, now a full lieutenant, was made supervising cryptologic officer with the Naval Security Fleet Support Division at Ft. Meade. It was while counseling his crew that he discovered a gift for public speaking. Occasional talks to high school students led to a career change, and eventually the *Montel Williams Show* on television. He left the navy with the rank of lieutenant, and received the Navy Achievement Medal, the Meritorious Service Medal, and the Navy Commendation Medal.

Flip Wilson. Comedian.

Born Clerow Wilson in Jersey City, New Jersey, on December 8, 1933, Wilson dropped out of school and lied about his age to enlist in the U.S. Air Force in 1950 at age 16. He was trained as a clerk, but his reputation for being a clown led to an opportunity to entertain troops. He was sent on a tour of Pacific bases until his discharge in 1954. It was in the air force that Wilson got the nickname "Flip" for being "flipped out."

Jonathan Winters. Comedian.

Born Jonathan Harshman Winters III in Dayton, Ohio, on November 11, 1925, Winters enlisted in the marines on November 17, 1943. After basic training at Parris Island, he was trained as a light anti-aircraft crewman with a secondary skill as a machine gun crewman. After sea school at Portsmouth, Virginia, Winters was assigned to the 3rd Marine Fleet Landing Forces and was sent overseas on November 26, 1944.

He served as part of the marine detachment aboard the USS *Wisconsin*, and later the carrier USS *Bon Homme Richard*. While overseas, he was in almost continuous operations against the enemy. To relieve the tension, he entertained his buddies with

Jonathan Winters

improvisations. Winters was among the first marines to occupy Japan when his group took control of Yokosuka Naval Base in Tokyo Bay on August 30, 1945. He was returned to San Francisco in November and transferred to Philadelphia where he served in a guard company until he was discharged as a corporal on March 1, 1946.

Directors and Producers

Robert Altman. TV and film director, writer.

Born in Kansas City, Missouri, in February 20, 1925, and descended from Mayflower settlers, Altman joined the U.S. Army in 1943 at age 18. After basic and flight training, he was commissioned a lieutenant and sent to the Dutch East Indies where he served as a bomber pilot, flying 46 missions. Altman stated in an interview that it never occurred to him that he was killing people, and he doubted it would have bothered him if it had.

He was discharged from the army in 1947 and attended the University of Missouri while making industrial films for the Calvin Company. He went on to commercial success with the film *M*A*S*H** (1970), earning six Oscar nominations.

Mel Brooks. Oscar-winning comedian, film producer, writer.

Born Melvin Kaminsky in New York City on June 28, 1926, Brooks enlisted in the army while still a senior in high school. He was inducted at Ft. Dix, New Jersey, upon his graduation.

After basic training at historic Virginia Military Institute (VMI), where he learned mounted cavalry drills, Brooks was sent to combat engineering school at Ft. Sill, Oklahoma, where he was trained in how to deactivate land mines. Sent overseas to Europe, he first saw combat during the Battle of the Bulge in Belgium in December 1944.

Brooks, although not the model of a warrior at 115 pounds, was highly regarded by his comrades for his quick wit and entertaining stories. On one occasion after the battle at Bastogne, Brooks responded to German propaganda being broadcast by loudspeaker by setting up his own loudspeaker and belting out an Al Jolson imitation of "Toot Toot Tootsie."

Recognized for his ability to entertain, Brooks was transferred to special services, and by the end of the war, he was playing in shows in occupied Germany and later at Ft. Dix, New Jersey.

After his discharge in 1947, Brooks attended Brooklyn College, and began a career in film as an actor, writer and director of films like *Young Frankenstein* and *Blazing Saddles*. Brooks won an Oscar for Best Writer in 1968 for *The Producers.*

Frank Capra. Three-time Oscar-winning producer/director.

Born in Palermo, Sicily, on May 18, 1897, Capra graduated the California Institute of Technology in 1918, and enlisted in

Frank Capra, John Ford

the army during WWI. He was commissioned an artillery officer and taught math at Ft. Scott in San Francisco until the end of the war.

After Pearl Harbor, and upon completing the film *Arsenic and Old Lace*, Capra returned to the army with a major's commission and was initially assigned to the 834th Photographic Signal Detachment. The unit was under the command of Special Services rather than the Signal Corps' Army Pictorial Service, which made training films.

His mission was to educate a rapidly expanding wartime army

on the reasons for the war, and to counter enemy propaganda. He produced the documentary series *Why We Fight*, a collection of seven films. He also filmed a *Know Your Enemy* and *Know Your Ally* series. He spent three and a half years stateside and was discharged June 15, 1945, with the rank of colonel, a Legion of Merit and the Distinguished Service Medal.

John Ford. Five-time Oscar-winning director.

Born Sean Aloysius O'Feeney in Cape Elizabeth, Maine, on February 1, 1895, Ford hoped for a career in the navy and applied to Annapolis upon his graduation from high school in 1914, but was not selected. After a brief stay at the University of Maine, Ford followed his brother to Hollywood.

In 1917 Ford was working as an assistant director, but was not called for service during WWI because films were considered an "essential industry" to the war effort.

In September of 1934 Ford was commissioned a lieutenant commander in the U.S. Navy reserve. On several occasions in the late 1930s, he traveled to Mexico aboard his yacht *Arener*. Allegedly on a pleasure cruise, Ford was gathering information on the Japanese presence in Mexico for naval intelligence. He felt his reputation as a world famous movie director was the perfect cover.

In April 1940 Ford formed a naval reserve unit of filmmakers. Called the Naval Field Photographic, he recruited cinematographers Gregg Toland and Joe August, editor Bob Parish, and soundman Sol Halprin. In November the unit was reorganized and made official.

He won an Oscar for *Grapes of Wrath* in 1940, and was just completing *How Green Was My Valley* in September of 1941 when he was called to active duty, promoted to full commander, and ordered to Washington DC. Overnight, his salary went from $250,000 to $4,000 a year.

Ford and the Field Photographic were transferred to the direct command of the Office of Strategic Services (OSS) under

Colonel (later Major General) William Donovan. Ford and his unit would operate outside the navy chain of command, and his first assignment in November 1941 was to prepare a film report evaluating the condition of the Atlantic Fleet.

At this time the U.S. Navy was escorting convoys between the U.S. and Iceland in an undeclared war with German U-boats, and the OSS was charged with evaluating the readiness of army and navy commands. After Pearl Harbor Ford did a report on the condition of the Panama Canal defenses, and the film was shown to the President.

Ford was aboard the flagship cruiser USS *Salt Lake City* on April 14 when he learned that he had won his third Oscar for best director in *How Green Was My Valley*. The officers made a blue flag with a gold Oscar likeness that flew from the masthead throughout the mission. By May 1942 Ford was back in Washington but within days was en route back to the Pacific.

Ford and a team flew to Treasure Island where they boarded a destroyer to Hawaii, then flew in a patrol plane to Midway. The island was preparing for a battle, and days after his arrival, at dawn on June 4, 1942, the Japanese attacked. The prepared American defenders won a resounding victory, and Ford shot extensive footage of the battle and its aftermath. He was enough of a politician to include plenty of footage of marine Major James Roosevelt, the President's son.

After viewing the resulting film, *The Battle of Midway*, President Roosevelt, also a politician, remarked "I want every mother in America to see this picture," and the film was released at Radio City Music Hall in New York City.

By then Ford was en route to London to prepare Field Photographic units to cover the invasion of North Africa (Operation Torch). A combined task force of English and American troops would land at Oran, Algiers, and Casablanca simultaneously. Ford, working with Colonel Darryl Zanuck would film the invasion. He and his team had attended commando school in Scotland in preparation for the landing.

On November 8 troops landed and Ford's teams filmed all three landings, but Ford was forced to wait out the first phase in Gibralter. On November 14 Ford and a team left for Algiers, then commandeered a jeep and attached themselves to Company D, 13th Armored Regiment of the First Armored Division ("Old Ironsides"). He put ashore at Tunisia, and linked up with Zanuck who was driving a civilian Chevrolet coupe, and gathering footage for his own documentary, *At the Front*. Zanuck soon returned to the rear but Ford continued on.

On one occasion, Company D was attacked by a German JU-88 fighter. A German crewman bailed out after being shot down by a British Spitfire, and Ford and his crew took the crewman prisoner. After six weeks in the field, Ford and his team returned to the U.S. aboard the destroyer USS *Samuel Chase.*

From January to August of 1943 Ford worked on administrative matters for the Field Photographic Unit. During this period the U.S. Senate War Investigating Committee, led by Senator Harry S. Truman, was looking into the commissioning of "Hollywood Colonels," which caused Colonel Zanuck to return to inactive status. Ford was careful to document his unit's legitimate contribution to the var effort. Also during this period, in March 1943, Ford won his fourth Oscar for Best Documentary for *The Battle of Midway*.

In May of 1943 Ford was tasked with creating a film about the China-India-Burma theater of operations in hopes of improving Anglo-American relations. In August he and his team left Washington, arriving in New Delhi four days later. Ford made the rounds in British-ruled India, acting as an "advance man" for the OSS in India. He also taught camera techniques to the 14th Air Force in China.

Back in Washington by late January 1944, Ford was briefed by OSS Chief Donovan who revealed to him that the Allied invasion of Europe was planned for June. It was to be the largest invasion in history, and Ford was to be in charge of all Allied photography. On April 5, 1944, the newly promoted Captain Ford left Washington for London.

Ford prepared for two months, and by the night of June 5 the unit was ready. He had camera crews dispersed throughout the invasion fleet. Ford reported aboard the battleship USS *Augusta*, the invasion command ship. At 0800 hours on June 6, he observed the landing on Omaha Beach.

Ford spent that afternoon and the next five days aboard a PT boat commanded by Lt. Commander John Bulkeley. Bulkeley who had evacuated General MacArthur from the Philippines and had won the Medal of Honor, was in charge of a squadron of PT boats patrolling the coast of Normandy. Ford had been approached earlier to direct a movie called *They Were Expendable* about Bulkeley's action in the Philippines. After seeing combat with the man for five days, Ford decided to do it.

Ford returned to the U.S. and began plans to film *They Were Expendable*. Shooting began on February 1, 1945, Ford's fiftieth birthday. The Germans surrendered in May and Japan surrendered in August while the film was still in production. It was released on December 7, 1945, the fourth anniversary of Pearl Harbor, but did poorly in the box office because after four years, and a hard-won victory, America was tired of war.

On September 27 Ford was awarded the Legion of Merit by director Donovan. The next day the Field Photographic was disbanded and Captain John Ford, USNR, returned to civilian life and a career in Hollywood. Ford retired from the navy reserve with the rank of rear admiral.

In 1952 Ford won his fifth Oscar for *The Quiet Man* with John Wayne.

Howard Winchester Hawks. Producer, director, screenwriter.

Born in Goshen, Indiana, on May 30, 1896, Hawks graduated Cornell University with a degree in engineering. He was working in films as an assistant director with Mary Pickford when he enlisted in the army air service as a pilot in 1917.

He was discharged in 1920, and after working briefly as a civilian pilot, began working in motion pictures again. He pro-

duced many major films, but his only Academy Award nomination was for *Sergeant York* in 1941, which he lost to John Ford's
How Green Was My Valley.

John Huston. Writer, director.

Born on August 5, 1906, Huston was the son of actor Walter
Huston. After graduating Lincoln High School in Los Angeles,
he began boxing and won 23 of 25 bouts as a professional light-
weight. At 19 he went to Mexico and was commissioned a lieutenant in the Mexican cavalry, where he served for two years,
resigning at age 21.

Huston wrote short stories for *American Mercury* magazine
where he became a protege of H. L. Mencken who recognized
talent in the young author. Huston obtained work with Sam
Goldwyn in Hollywood and was working as a director at the
start of WWII.

In 1942 Huston enlisted in the army Signal Corps, and received his orders to report on March 20, 1942, but the studio
obtained a sixty-day deferment so he could finish directing the
film *Across the Pacific* with Mary Astor and Humphrey Bogart.

In May Huston was commissioned a lieutenant in the Signal
Corps, and was put to work making propaganda films. In September he was sent to the Aleutian Islands, which was the only
theater at the time where American troops were engaged in combat. For four months he flew on B-24s recording air combat over
the Japanese occupied islands of Attu and Kiska. On one occasion he manned the guns during an air attack.

Late in 1942 Huston returned to Astoria Studios in Long Island to begin editing the film that was to become *Report from the
Aleutians.* During this time he was promoted to captain.

Early in 1943 the film taken of the invasion of North Africa
was lost when the ship it was being transported on was sunk by
the Germans. Embarrassed, the army brass had Huston and
Major Frank Capra stage and film an "invasion" in the Mojave

Desert. The resulting "Mockumentary" titled *Tunisian Victory* was shown to the President.

In October of 1943 Huston was assigned to a joint project with English novelist Eric Ambler to film the Allied entry into Rome. They traveled from London to Morocco to Naples and followed the 143rd Infantry Regiment, recording a tank battle at the town of San Pietro in which 12 of 16 American tanks were destroyed. He returned to the States in May of 1944.

By August the film was ready. Although Huston believed that the film illustrated the "futility" of war, it was not warmly received by the generals. Huston was summoned to General Surrold's office and was told that his film could be interpreted as an anti-war film. Huston responded by saying, "If I ever make anything other than an anti-war film, I hope you take me out and shoot me." The film was scheduled to be suppressed until it was viewed by General George Marshall. Once it became clear that Marshall approved of the film, attitudes changed. Huston was awarded the Legion of Merit and promoted to major.

The resulting film, *The Battle of San Pietro*, has been called a masterpiece of on-the-spot war reporting. It was filmed "under fire" and accurately conveys the realities of war. However, Peter Maslowski in his book *Armed with Cameras: The American Military Photographers of WWII* suggests that much of the footage was exposed on the battlefield, and had to be restaged after the battle. Huston continued to maintain in his autobiography *An Open Book* that the film was "the first time real infantry combat conditions involving Americans had ever been seen on the screen."

The last combat of WWII that Huston participated in occurred at a Hollywood party at the home of David Selznick when he got in a fist fight with Errol Flynn over a woman's reputation.

Huston's last Signal Corps assignment was to make a film about the aftereffects of war. He filmed the treatment of psychologically disturbed veterans at a military hospital, but the resulting film, *Let There Be Light,* was deemed too depressing, was classified "top secret," and was suppressed until it was finally released to the public in December of 1980, largely through the influence of Vice President Mondale.

Before he died on August 28, 1987, Huston served as the writer of 19 films, director of 46 films and acted in 38 others.

Stanley Kramer. Film producer and director.

Born in New York City on September 29, 1913, Kramer's family was involved early in the distribution of motion pictures. He graduated Dewitt Clinton High School in New York, and earned a degree from New York University in 1933. He moved to Hollywood and worked a variety of jobs, learning how to write for, and edit movies. By the start of WWII, Kramer was working as an assistant producer.

During the war, Kramer served with the army Signal Corps, stationed in Astoria, New York. He was responsible for making orientation and training films. He was discharged as a first lieutenant at the end of the war.

Upon his release, he started his own production company in New York. Fifteen of his movies won Oscars, including *High Noon* (1952) and *Guess Who's Coming to Dinner* (1967).

Norman Milton Lear. TV producer.

Born in New Haven, Connecticut, on July 27, 1922, Lear enlisted at the start of WWII in early 1942. He entered the Army Air Corps and was trained as a radioman. Assigned to the 15th Air Force in Italy as a technical sergeant, he flew 57 missions aboard bombers, more than twice the required number. He was discharged at the end of the war.

Lear built a TV empire by producing sitcoms that challenged contemporary attitudes like *All in the Family* and *Maude*.

Joshua Logan. Playwright, director, producer.

Born in Texarkana, Texas, on October 5, 1908, Logan, the co-author of *Mister Roberts* and *South Pacific*, began his military career at the Culver Military Academy where his stepfather, Colonel Noble, served on the staff.

After studying drama at Princeton with James Stewart and Henry Fonda, he was working as a successful Broadway director when he was drafted in June 1942, just a month after the opening of *By Jupiter*. He had to enter the army as a private because the commission from Culver had expired. His first assignment was working with Irving Berlin in *This Is the Army*. Later he entered OCS, graduated at the head of 3000 classmates, and was commissioned as a second lieutenant. He attended air intelligence school in Harrisburg, Pennsylvania, with his roommates Bruce Cabot and Robert Preston.

He served in the Ninth Air Force as a public relations and intelligence officer for the 405th Fighter Group. He later served in Paris with Special Services. Logan was discharged as a captain at the war's end. He returned to Broadway to work again with Irving Berlin in *Annie Get Your Gun*.

Sidney Lumet. Film director.

Born in Philadelphia, Pennsylvania, on June 25, 1924, the director of films such as *Failsafe* and *The Pawnbroker* served as a radar repairman in the U.S. Army during WWII. Radar was a new and highly sensitive assignment.

Assigned to the China-India-Burma theater of operations, he served from 1942 to 1946 and returned to acting on Broadway.

Carl Reiner. Emmy-winning producer, writer, director, actor.

Born in New York City on March 20, 1922, Reiner was acting in local theaters when the U.S. entered WWII. He enlisted in the army and was briefly assigned to Georgetown University's School of Foreign Service where he studied French. He was transferred to Hawaii and assigned to the 3117th Signal Battalion. When his acting background became known to his superiors, he was transferred to special services, taking a reduction in rank from corporal to private because only slots for privates were open.

Reiner spent 18 months performing in GI revues all over the South Pacific. He was discharged as a sergeant in 1945. Reiner returned to acting after the war, earning numerous Emmys for *The Dick Van Dyke Show* (1961–66).

Aaron Spelling. TV and film producer.

Born in Dallas, Texas, on April 22, 1928, Spelling has been called television's most successful producer for shows like *Charlie's Angels*, *The Mod Squad*, and *Love Boat*.

Upon his graduation from high school in 1942, Spelling enlisted in the U.S. Army Air Corps, and saw combat in Europe where he earned a Bronze Star and Purple Heart.

After completion of his three-year tour of duty, Spelling worked in Europe as a civilian organizing special service tours, and working as a correspondent for *Stars and Stripes*. He returned to the U.S. and attended Southern Methodist University on the GI Bill.

Oliver Stone. Four-time Oscar-winning writer, director.

Born William Oliver Stone in New York City on September 15, 1946, Stone left Yale in his junior year to take a position teaching English at the Free Pacific Institute in Saigon. This was during the period of U.S. troop buildup in Vietnam. He returned to the U.S. as a merchant seaman after six months in Vietnam. Stone wrote about his experiences in the novel, *A Child's Night Dream*, but was unable to get it published, so he returned to Yale.

Stone again dropped out of Yale and enlisted in the U.S. Army in April 1967. After basic and advanced infantry training at Ft. Jackson, South Carolina, Stone volunteered for Vietnam. He remembers that at the time he was "gung ho" to fight communism. He left from Oakland for Vietnam on September 14, 1967.

Stone was assigned to 2nd Platoon, B Company, 3rd Battalion of the 25th Infantry Division (the "Tropic Lightning" Division), operating near the Cambodian border. He described the unit as "demoralized" and came to identify less with his privileged Republican background and more with the "poor and un-educated members of his unit."

On New Years Day 1968, the fire base where he was stationed was attacked by two full regiments, resulting in over 500 dead. Two weeks later Stone was wounded in the leg while rescuing two platoons pinned down in an ambush. He was in a hospital recovering during the Tet Offensive.

He was transferred to an auxiliary military police unit guarding installations in Saigon, but a fight with a rear echelon sergeant resulted in his choosing to return to combat rather than face charges.

Stone was sent to a LRRP (Long Range Reconnaissance Platoon) with the First Cavalry Division in April 1968. His mission was to operate behind enemy lines gathering intelligence. A photo of his squad appeared in *People* magazine. Stone was present at the three-day battle at South China Beach in August 1968. Bad intelligence caused his unit to confront a vastly superior enemy force. By this time, Stone recalls, he had witnessed many atrocities, and only cared about surviving Vietnam.

It was in Vietnam that Stone first began an interest in photography, which he used as a form of stress relief. By the end of his tour, he had earned a Bronze Star and two Purple Hearts.

Stone left the army in November 1968 and incorporated many of his combat experiences into the script for *Platoon—A Common Soldier's View of the War* and won Best Director and Best Picture for the film in 1986. He also won an Oscar for another Vietnam film, *Born on the Fourth of July*.

David Susskind. Movie producer.

Born in Brookline, Massachusetts, in December 1920, Susskind graduated cum laude from Harvard with a history degree in 1942, and immediately applied for a naval commission. He was called to active duty as an ensign, and assigned to the Port of New York as an insurance officer.

Susskind requested sea duty and was assigned as communications officer aboard an attack transport in the Pacific. He saw action at Iwo Jima and Okinawa, and was discharged in 1946 as a lieutenant.

William Wellman. Oscar-winning director.

Born in Brookline, Massachusetts, on February 29, 1896, Wellman went to France in April of 1917 as an ambulance driver. In June he enlisted in the French Foreign Legion where he served as a pilot with the Lafayette Flying Corps, a French aviation unit. He was shot down in combat and injured his back. By December 1917 Wellman was back in the States and was a first lieutenant in the U.S. Army Signal Corps' Aviation Section, serving at Rockwell Field, California, until the war ended. He was awarded the Croix de Guerre for his service to France.

Wellman earned fame as the director of films like *A Star Is Born, Public Enemy*, and *The Ox Bow Incident*. He was awarded the first Academy Award for Best Picture in 1927–28 for *Wings*, about aviators in WWI. He died in Los Angeles on December 9, 1975.

William Wilder. Six-time Oscar-winning director, producer.

"Billy" Wilder was born in Vienna, Austria, on June 22, 1906. The director of classic films such as *Some Like It Hot, The Seven Year Itch, Stalag 17*, and *Sunset Boulevard*, Wilder joined the U.S. Army Psychological Warfare Section late in WWII.

He was commissioned a colonel and sent overseas to Germany where he spent six months working with the denazification program in charge of restructuring German radio. He returned to Hollywood after the war.

William Wyler. Oscar-winning director/producer.

Born on July 1, 1902, Wyler was already a successful director with four Oscar nominations at the start of WWII. In 1941 he won his first Oscar for Best Director for *Mrs. Miniver*, which received five other nominations, including Best Picture.

Wyler enlisted in the U.S. Army Air Corps early in 1942. He was commissioned a major and assigned to the Motion Picture Unit of the 8th Air Force, attached to the 91st Bomber Group at Bassingbourne, England. He had already worked as a civilian on Major Frank Capra's *Why We Fight* series, and wanted to film the war rather than make films about its causes. He was assigned to make a film about heavy bomber operations over Europe. He and his crew attended gunner's school at Bovington, which included aircraft recognition classes. Army regulations prohibited anyone from flying on B-17s without gunnery training.

The resulting film, *Memphis Belle* (1944), has been called one of the best factual films of WWII. In order to get the necessary film footage, Wyler flew on five combat missions at great risk and against orders. He once asked the pilot to fly closer to the flak, so he could get a better shot. Flying at 20,000 feet at temperatures of 60 below zero made movement, not to mention operating a camera, extremely difficult.

Upon completing the film, he returned to the U.S., edited the film, and gave a private screening to President Roosevelt and General Arnold at the White House. Wyler was presented the Air Medal and was promoted to lieutenant colonel.

Although there was some mention of a Distinguished Service Cross, the handy application of a right hook to the doorman of a hotel who made an anti-semitic remark (Wyler was Jewish) resulted in Wyler being brought up on charges. He received a letter of reprimand for conduct unbecoming an officer, and no further mention of the medal was ever made.

Wyler returned to the Mediterranean to produce a documentary about the 57th Fighter-Bomber Group of the 12th Air Force. While riding in the waist of a bomber for 45 minutes to get aerial shots of Rome, Wyler suffered nerve damage to his ears, resulting in a partial loss of hearing for which he was awarded the Purple Heart. He was discharged from the Air Corps as a lieutenant colonel with a partial disability.

The film *Thunderbolt* (1945) was completed after the war, so the war department offered the 40-minute film free to theaters. It received a lukewarm reception from an American public tired after four years of war, which caused Wyler to feel that he sacrificed his ears for nothing.

Wyler was awarded the Legion of Merit for his wartime service, and returned to Hollywood. He owed Sam Goldwyn one more picture, so with Robert Sherwood he worked on a story treatment called *Glory to Me* about three returning veterans. It was released under the title *The Best Years of Our Lives*. (*Glory to Me* was originally a 434-page blank verse poem.)

Wyler won two more Oscars, one for *Best Years of Our Lives* (1946) and the other for *Ben Hur* (1958). President Roosevelt once remarked that Wyler's film, *Mrs. Miniver*, was instrumental in shaping American public opinion in favor of war with Germany. He died on July 27, 1981.

Darryl Francis Zanuck. Producer, screenwriter.

Born in Wahoo, Nebraska, in 1902, Zanuck lied about his age to enlist in the U.S. Army in 1916 at age 14. He was sent to Deming, New Mexico, for basic training. He dreamed of going off to fight Pancho Villa with General Pershing. What he got was six months of drilling, marching, and KP. He was saved when Congress declared war on Germany and America entered WWI. Sent to Ft. Dix, New Jersey, as part of the 34th U.S. National Guard Division, he was shipped to France aboard the *Baltic*, departing in August 1918. Upon arrival, his unit was absorbed into the 37th Division. He served as a messenger and runner, and represented the U.S. Army as a flyweight boxer at the Allied forces championships.

Throughout the summer of 1918 his division trained for combat in Belgium, and his unit moved to the front in November, arriving just in time for the signing of the armistice. His great ambition was to be in combat but he finished the war without ever facing the enemy.

He was mustered out as a private first class with two wounds (neither earned in combat) in 1919, just prior to his 17th birthday. The publication of his letters home in a local paper encouraged his resolve to become a writer.

In the years between the wars, Zanuck rose in the ranks at Warner Brothers Studios (1924–33) and 20th Century Fox (1933–71), which he helped organize. He produced *The Jazz Singer* (1927) which was the first popular film with sound, *Little Caesar* (1930), *Public Enemy* (1931), and *Grapes of Wrath* (1940) to name but a few.

In January of 1942 Zanuck was commissioned a lieutenant colonel in the U.S. Army Signal Corps. He was put in command of a film unit, and was initially sent to Astoria Studios in Long Island. Zanuck wanted to see combat, and made a personal request to Army Chief of Staff General George Marshall, who was impressed with Zanuck's enthusiasm. He arranged for Zanuck to be posted to London as chief liaison officer to the British Army film units.

While in London, Zanuck endured almost nightly blitz attacks by holding parties in his "quarters," a suite on the top floor of Claridges Hotel in Mayfair overlooking Hyde Park. His "Blitz Parties" became legendary for the food, booze, and beautiful women. Guests included Generals Eisenhower and Clark, Noel Coward, Laurence Olivier and others.

One guest, Lord Montbatten, was persuaded to take Zanuck along as a U.S. observer on a Royal Marine commando raid. They crossed the English Channel at St. Valery, where they successfully destroyed a German radar station. They withdrew under heavy fire, and Zanuck was judged a "good Yank" by the Brits.

Zanuck was next assigned to record the American force's invasion of North Africa, and he arrived in Algiers aboard General Clark's personal plane in the middle of a German air raid. They barely landed intact. Zanuck was joined by Commander John Ford, and a unit from the Field Photographic on a combined operation. The resulting film, *At the Front*, gave Zanuck credit as producer, but no mention was made of Ford, prompting Ford to return to the States and declare that he was going to "get that thieving bastard Zanuck, and shoot him where it will hurt him the most—and I don't mean the head."

In 1943 the Truman Committee began a congressional investigation into the favoritism and high ranks shown to some Hollywood studios. On the advice of General Marshall, Zanuck went to reserve status in May 1943. He was awarded the Legion of Merit for "exceptional courage under fire" in 1944. Since Zanuck made a legitimate contribution to the war effort, and was not one to back away from a fight, even with Congress, there is speculation that his resignation may have had something to do with his indiscretion with sensitive information he may have acquired from high-ranking contacts.

Zanuck was recalled to active duty during the Korean War at the direction of Secretary of Defense Louis Johnson. A review by the Department of Defense in 1969 restored Zanuck to the rank of colonel (retired).

Section 4

Poets, Authors, Artists and Journalists

Jack Northman Anderson. Columnist, investigative reporter.

Born on October 19, 1922, in Long Beach, California, Anderson was raised a Mormon in Utah and began his obligatory missionary work on December 7, 1941. Two years later, his mission complete, he enlisted in the U.S. Merchant Marine officer's course as a cadet midshipman. He served for seven months before being accredited as a foreign correspondent to China for a Mormon newspaper, *The Deseret News*.

In China Anderson ignored routine news stories in favor of stories that promised adventure. He visited secret OSS bases, and interviewed nationalist guerrillas. He was among the earliest to report of a pending civil war in China. Anderson was finally located by his draft board toward the end of 1945, and was drafted into the U.S. Army at Chunking. He served with the quartermasters corps working on newspapers and Armed Forces Radio. Upon his discharge in 1947, Anderson travelled to Washington DC and went to work for columnist Drew Pearson as a reporter. He won a Pulitzer Prize in 1972 for his column, "Washington Merry Go Round."

George Baker. Cartoonist, creator of "Sad Sack."

Born on May 22, 1915, in Lowell, Massachusetts, Baker was an artist at Walt Disney Studios and worked on *Pinocchio* (1940) and *Dumbo* (1941) before being drafted into the army in 1941. He was sent to Ft. Monmouth, New Jersey, where he worked as an animator on Signal Corps films.

In 1942 he was one of the original staff of *Yank Magazine*. Baker created the character "Sad Sack," an underdog enduring the army as a buck private. The comic was popular with over 10 million readers. Although Baker was discharged at the end of the war, "Sad Sack" remains in the army, still a private.

Saul Bellow. Writer, university professor.

Born in Lachine, Quebec, on July 10, 1915, Bellow earned a degree in anthro-sociology in 1937 and was working as an editor for Encyclopedia Britannica when he joined the U.S. Merchant Marine in 1943. While serving at sea he wrote his first published novel, *Dangling Man*. The book was an account of a non-combatant's experiences during WWII. He has won a Pulitzer Prize, and the Nobel Prize for Literature for *Humboldt's Gift*.

Benjamin C. Bradlee. Journalist, editor of the *Washington Post*.

Born in Boston on August 26, 1921, Bradlee was attending Harvard when America was attacked on December 7, 1941. He doubled his class load so he could graduate faster and enlist.

He earned his degree in August 1942, promptly joined the U.S. Navy, and was commissioned an ensign. He was assigned as a combat communications officer aboard a destroyer in the South Pacific. He was discharged as a lieutenant at the end of 1945, and took a job with the New York office of the ACLU. Bradlee was vice president and editor of the *Washington Post* from 1968 to 1991.

David McClure Brinkley. Journalist, TV reporter.

Born in New Hanover, North Carolina, on July 20, 1920, Brinkley saw brief service with the U.S. Army when he enlisted in the National Guard in September 1940. He foresaw the war in Europe spreading, and wanted to get his military requirements out of the way. He served as a supply sergeant for an infantry company at Ft. Jackson, South Carolina.

Brinkley was given a medical discharge and was mustered out as a staff sergeant. He spent WWII stateside as a reporter for United Press and NBC radio. In this he was fortunate. Brinkley's old unit, Company I, 120th Infantry took over 90% casualties at the Normandy invasion. Less than one dozen men survived.

Art Buchwald. Journalist, columnist, author.

Born in Mt. Vernon, New York, on October 20, 1925, Buchwald left Forest Hills High School in Queens at age 16 to

try to enlist in the military after Pearl Harbor. He recalls that he was as much motivated by the opportunity to escape boredom as a patriotic desire to serve God and Country. On December 8, Buchwald lied about his age and enlisted in the U.S. Army. On December 9, his father tore up the papers.

Undeterred, Buchwald ran away to Durham, North Carolina, and used a pint of stolen whiskey to persuade a local drunk to impersonate his father and sign the enlist-

Art Buckwald

ment papers. He joined the Marine Corps in October 1942 just after his 17th birthday.

After basic training at Parris Island, South Carolina, Private Buchwald was sent to Cherry Point, North Carolina, for aviation training, and Camp Lejeune for infantry training where he studied various types of ordnance. As a Northern Jew, Buchwald had difficulty adjusting to the South, and was once almost lynched for offering his seat on a bus to a black woman.

After advance training with VMF 113 at El Toro Naval Air Station where he was promoted to corporal, Buchwald was sent overseas in early 1943. He was attached to the 4th Marine Air Wing in the Pacific where he served for three and a half years. Most of this time he was stationed at Enewetak in the Marshall Islands. He edited the outfit's newspaper, sold bogus "war souvenirs" to newly arriving troops, and endured kamikaze attacks.

Buchwald returned to the U.S. to be trained at torpedo school in Jacksonville, Florida, when the war ended. He was discharged as a sergeant on November 12, 1945. Upon his return to civilian life, he attended the University of Southern California on the GI Bill, and has enjoyed a distinguished career in journalism. His column appears in over 500 newspapers.

William F. Buckley Jr. Editor, author, political theorist.

Born in New York City on November 24, 1925, Buckley was the sixth of ten children in an affluent family. Schooled in England and France, he graduated from the Milbrook School in 1943. After a brief time at the University of Mexico, he entered the U.S. Army in 1944.

He served in the infantry, rising to the rank of first lieutenant. He was discharged in 1946. He entered Yale and came to define an element of modern conservative thought in his magazine, *National Review*, which he began in November 1955. He served as its editor until 1988, and also served as host on Public TV's *Firing Line*. Buckley is known as a "voice" of the new political conservatism.

Edgar Rice Burroughs. Author, creator of "Tarzan."

Born in Chicago, Illinois, on September 1, 1875, Burroughs grew up in an affluent family and was educated in private academies. After leaving a military academy in Michigan, he enlisted in the U.S. Army.

Burroughs served with a cavalry troop until it was discovered that he was underage, whereupon he was promptly discharged. He worked as a cowboy, miner and railroad detective before beginning to write short stories. He published his first novel, *Tarzan of the Apes*, in 1914.

He did not participate in the First World War. Too old for military service during WWII, Burroughs worked as a civilian war correspondent with the U.S. Army in the Pacific.

John Chancellor. Journalist, TV newsman.

Born July 14, 1927, in Chicago, Chancellor entered the U.S. Army toward the end of WWII in 1945. He was assigned as a public relations specialist where he rose to the rank of technician 5th grade by the time of his discharge in 1947.

Upon his return to civilian life, Chancellor became involved in broadcast journalism and served as anchor of NBC *Nightly News* from 1970 to 1982.

Raymond Chandler. Author, screenwriter.

The author of crime fiction such as *The Big Sleep* and *Farewell My Lovely*, Chandler was born to Quaker parents in Chicago on July 23, 1888.

Like many Americans, he enlisted in the Canadian army at the start of WWI. He was sent overseas with the Canadian 7th Infantry Battalion and saw extensive combat, earning two medals for valor. Chandler was training as a pilot with the Royal Flying Corps when the armistice was signed.

Paddy Chayefsky. Oscar-winning playwright.

Born Sidney Chayefsky in the Bronx on January 29, 1923, Chayefsky was studying languages at Fordham University when he enlisted in the army reserve before WWII.

Called to active duty on September 1, 1942, after graduating with a degree in social science, Chayefsky was assigned to the 4th Platoon, Company I, 413th Regiment of the 104th Division (the "Timberwolves" Division). The division entered combat in Belgium in October 1944, capturing the cities of Stolberg and Eschweiler by the end of November. Holding the line during the Battle of the Bulge, it advanced to the Rohr River by February 1945, and crossed the Rhine in March, trapping the German troops in the Rurh pocket. The division met up with Russian troops on April 26, 1945.

Chayefsky served as a machine gunner in an infantry company. He was wounded by a land mine while on patrol, and was sent to a hospital in England to recover. While hospitalized, he wrote the musical comedy, *No T.O. for Love.*

He earned the nickname "Paddy" while in the army. He was trying to avoid KP and requested permission to attend mass. A skeptical lieutenant gave him the nickname. (Perhaps his skepticism was due to the fact that Chayefsky was Jewish.) After the war, Chayefsky was separated from the army at Ft. Dix, New Jersey, on February 27, 1946. He returned to his uncle's print shop but continued to write.

Chayefsky would write *Marty* which won Oscars for Best Actor, Director and Best Picture in 1956. He also won an Oscar for Best Writer for *The Hospital* (1971) and *Network* (1976).

Tom Clancy. Techno-military novelist.

Born in Baltimore, Maryland, in 1947, Clancy enrolled in ROTC (Reserve Officers Training Corps) while at Loyola College in Baltimore, but poor eyesight kept him from his desire of serving in Vietnam.

Samuel Langhorne Clemens. Author, "Mark Twain."

Born in Florida, Missouri, on November 30, 1835, Clemens served two weeks as a second lieutenant in the Confederate army before being mustered out for unmentioned "disabilities." His company of volunteers, the Marion Rangers, never met the enemy, and fell back at any rumor of a Union advance. In Clemen's own words, "I knew more about retreating than the man who invented retreating."

James Fenimore Cooper. Novelist.

Born in Burlington, New Jersey, on September 15, 1789, Cooper was the 11th of 12 children of a prosperous landowner and

Congressman who built a settlement, Cooperstown, on the edge of the wilderness.

He was an "indifferent" student, and left Yale in 1805 to go to sea in preparation for a naval career. He was sixteen at the time. After a year-long voyage to England, he returned to America to be commissioned a midshipman in the U.S. Navy in 1807.

He served aboard the warship *Vesuvius* in 1808, worked on the construction of a brig on Lake Ontario, served for a short time in command at Lake Champlain, and returned to sea duty in the Atlantic aboard the *Wasp* in 1809. In 1810 Cooper took a 12-month furlough from the navy. Upon the completion of his furlough, he resigned his commission and left the navy. He went on to write novels, including his famous *Last of the Mohicans*. He died on September 14, 1851.

Walter Cronkite. Journalist, broadcaster.

Called "the most trusted man in America," Cronkite was born in St. Joseph, Missouri, on November 14, 1916. After Pearl Harbor, he was one of the first journalists accredited to American forces. He was working for United Press at the time.

As a reporter, he was present at many of the most significant moments of the war. He witnessed the Battle of the North Atlantic (1942) and the Battle of the Bulge (1944). He flew on bombing raids over Germany, endured the blitz bombing of London, parachuted into the Netherlands, and waded ashore at Normandy on D-Day. He was the chief UP correspondent at the Nuremberg trials.

Cronkite stated in interviews that he was scared the whole time, and that the secret to his "courage" was that he knew he only had to do it once. Cronkite was the "anchor" at *CBS News* from 1962 to 1981.

Walt Disney. Cartoonist, film maker.

Born Walter Elias Disney in Chicago on December 5, 1901, Disney tried twice during WWI to enlist in the navy to join his brother Roy, but at 16 he was rejected as too young. Instead, he enlisted in a Red Cross ambulance unit under an assumed name, and used his real name only after his seventeenth birthday when he re-enlisted with his parent's permission.

The war ended before he could be sent overseas, but there was still need for trained personnel in Europe to tend the sick and wounded, and Disney was part of a 50-man unit that arrived in France on November 30, 1918. He recalls gun crews firing at unexploded mines on the cruise over.

Assigned to Evacuation Hospital #5 in Paris as a driver with the motor pool, Disney celebrated his 17th birthday on December 5. He spent his time driving VIPs during the day, and working various money-making schemes on his time off. His buddies would collect German helmets, which Disney would paint and "age" into "war souvenirs" to sell to newly arrived troops. He also camouflaged footlockers, and painted Croix de Guerre on leather jerkins.

Only on one occasion did Disney have trouble with his superiors. In December 1919 Disney and a helper were assigned to deliver a load of beans and sugar to a devastated area near Soissons. When the truck broke down, Disney stayed to guard the valuable cargo, and sent his helper by train to Paris for help. Instead, the helper went drinking. Disney stayed awake for two days and nights, but finally went into town for food. He was sleeping when they came and recovered the truck. Almost court-martialed, he was let off when the true story came out. He almost signed up for the battlefields of Albania, but returned instead to the U.S. He served overseas for 11 months, and saved enough money to help bankroll his cartoon career in later years

Will Eisner. Cartoonist, graphic artist.

Eisner's cartoon, "The Spirit," was already gaining popularity when he was drafted into the U.S. Army in 1942. He was assigned as an artist tasked with creating and producing a series of safety posters with the character of a soldier named "Joe Dope."

He was transferred to the Pentagon and assigned to the office of the Chief of Ordnance where he edited an army publication titled *Firepower*. Eisner developed a series of cartoon-type training manuals. He was discharged in 1946 with the rank of chief warrant officer.

William Faulkner. Nobel Prize-winning novelist.

Born in New Albany, Mississippi, on September 25, 1897, Faulkner enlisted in the Royal Air Force in Canada in June 1918. He hoped to go to Europe to participate in the "Great War," but was disappointed when the war ended before he finished training. In November 1918, after five months of service, Faulkner was discharged with the rank of cadet.

For a time after the war, he dressed in an English officer's uniform impersonating a wounded British aviator. Faulkner won the Nobel Prize for literature in 1949 and a Pulitzer Prize in 1962.

Jules Feiffer. Cartoonist.

Born in the Bronx, New York, on January 26, 1929, Feiffer was drafted into the army in 1951. He spent two years in the Signal Corps, assigned to an animation unit. While in the service, he created a cartoon called "Munro" about a four-year-old boy drafted into the army by mistake.

After his discharge, Feiffer began a career in cartooning, and as a satirist for *The Village Voice*, where he won a Pulitzer Prize in 1986.

F. Scott Fitzgerald. Author of *The Great Gatsby*.

Born Francis Scott Key Fitzgerald on September 24, 1896, in St. Paul, Minnesota, Fitzgerald enlisted in the U.S. Army in March 1918 during WWI. He was sent to Camp Taylor, Kentucky, with the 45th Infantry Regiment.

Later commissioned a second lieutenant, he served at Ft. Leavenworth as a training officer under Captain Dwight Eisenhower. In June he was promoted to first lieutenant and was sent to the 67th Infantry at Ft. Sheridan, Alabama. The unit was ordered to prepare for shipment overseas, but the orders were canceled with the armistice in November. Much to his disappointment, Fitzgerald was discharged in February 1919, having never seen combat.

In his works like *Tender Is the Night* and *The Great Gatsby*, Fitzgerald came to epitomize the Jazz Age.

Shelby Foote. Author, Civil War historian.

Born in Greenville, Mississippi, on November 11, 1916, Foote joined the Mississippi National Guard in 1939 after leaving the University of North Carolina at Chapel Hill.

With his unit's mobilization in 1940, Foote was promoted to sergeant in the Regular Army. Then with America's entry into WWII, he was sent to Europe as the battery commander of a field artillery unit. He was commissioned and rose to the rank of captain, but he went AWOL to visit a girlfriend in Belfast, Ireland, which led to a court-martial and his resignation and discharge. In 1944 he married the girl in Ireland, and returned to the United States.

He worked briefly as a reporter for the Associated Press before enlisting in the Marine Corps. Foote was assigned to a combat intelligence unit, but the war ended before he could be shipped overseas. He was discharged in November 1945.

He would write several novels before beginning his monumental three-volume work, *The Civil War: A Narrative*, which he would write from 1958 to 1974.

Theodor Seuss Geisel. "Dr. Seuss."

With over 48 children's books (sales of over 200 million), three Oscars, a Pulitzer citation "for his lifelong commitment to the education and entertainment of children," Dr. Seuss earned a worldwide following with characters like *The Cat In the Hat* and *The Grinch Who Stole Christmas*.

Born Theodor Seuss Geisel in Springfield, Massachusetts, on March 2, 1904, Geisel drew political cartoons opposing isolationism for several years before WWII. After Pearl Harbor, he drew a cartoon of a battered Uncle Sam Cat rising from a rocking chair with the caption, "End of the Nap."

Although at 38 he was too old for the draft, he applied for a commission in naval intelligence. While his application was being processed, he continued to draw cartoons for the treasury department and the war production board. His "liberal" tendencies delayed his commission long enough that he decided to accept a commission as captain in the U.S. Army Signal Corps unit commanded by Major Frank Capra. This unit also included Captain John Huston, Major Merideth Wilson (the composer), Private Irving Wallace, and civilian animators Chuck Jones and Fritz Freleng.

Commissioned a captain on January 7, 1943, he was sent to "Fort Fox" in Hollywood, where the only shots fired were on the small arms range located behind the Santa Anita racetrack. He divided his time between soldiering and producing films. He learned about the new art form of animation, and used it in the production of training films on hygiene and field sanitation. He collaborated with Chuck Jones on a series of training films featuring the character of "Private Snafu."

In March of 1944 Geisel was promoted to major. The Allies were winning the war, and an eventual victory in Europe was anticipated. Geisel was ordered to prepare a film explaining the army's mission in a postwar occupied Germany. It was titled *Your Job in Germany*. The film's production pace was accelerated after the liberation of Paris on August 24, 1944.

In November, Geisel was sent overseas to Europe carrying a top secret copy of the film for viewing by the theater's commanders. He traveled to London, Paris, Luxembourg and the Netherlands. He met with every major commander from General Eisenhower on down. He was accompanied by Robert Murphy of the State Department, and Major John Boettiger, FDR's son-in-law.

During the German counter-offensive in December 1944, Geisel was sent to the "quiet" sector of Bastogne. He arrived with a military police escort hours before the beginning of the Battle of the Bulge, the bloodiest battle since D-Day. He was separated with one M.P. behind German lines for three days before being rescued by English troops.

He returned to the U.S. in January 1945, and was discharged a year later as a lieutenant colonel on January 13, 1946. He was awarded the Legion of Merit for his wartime service. His film, *Your Job, in Germany* was released commercially as *Hitler Lives* and won an Oscar for Best Documentary in 1946.

John Howard Griffin. Author, activist.

Born in Dallas, Texas, on June 16, 1920, Griffin was living in France as a music student at the outbreak of WWII. He joined La Defense Passive, an organization that assisted German and Austrian Jewish refugees fleeing the Nazis. Griffin returned to the United States two steps ahead of the Gestapo, and joined the U.S. Army Air Corps.

Stationed in the South Pacific during the war, he was wounded twice, once with a severe head wound when his bomber exploded, and again when the hospital he was in was bombed.

He lost his sight in 1946, possibly a result of his war wounds, so Griffin became a writer. He wrote a book that was considered obscene, so he took the case all the way to the Supreme Court, and won. Ten years after losing his sight, he spontaneously regained it. He went on to write *Black Like Me*, an autobiographical account of his trips in the South in 1961 disguised as a black man.

Alex Haley. Author of *Roots*.

Born Alexander Murray Haley in Ithaca, New York, on August 11, 1921, Haley enlisted in the U.S. Coast Guard in 1939 as a messboy. During WWII he served as a cook aboard a ship in the South Pacific.

Haley spent the long hours at sea reading every book in the ship's library. He also began writing. After the war, the coast guard created the rating of journalist expressly for Haley. He retired after 20 years in the coast guard as a chief petty officer. After he retired, Haley wrote landmark bestsellers like *The Autobiography of Malcolm X* and *Roots*.

Hugh Hefner. Editor/publisher/creator of *Playboy* magazine.

Born Hugh Marston Hefner in Chicago, Illinois, on April 9, 1926, Hefner graduated Steinmetz High School in February 1944, and promptly enlisted in the U.S. Army. He was seventeen years old.

After taking infantry rifleman training in Texas, he was sent to Ft. Meade, Maryland, for shipment overseas. While at Ft. Meade, there was a need for typists, so Hefner spent the next two years as a clerk/typist at army induction centers in the United States. He occasionally did cartoons for military papers.

He was discharged in 1946, attended the University of Illinois, and married at age 23 in June of 1949. He started *Playboy* magazine in 1953 on a borrowed $600.

Robert Heinlein. Science fiction writer.

Robert Heinlein

Born in Butler, Missouri, on July 7, 1907, Heinlein graduated the Naval Academy in 1929, was commissioned an ensign and served for five years as a line officer aboard navy ships. He was discharged in 1934 with a medical disability.

During WWII Heinlein worked as a mechanical engineer at the Naval Air Material Center in Philadelphia. He won four Hugo Awards for his science fiction stories. His titles include *Stranger in a Strange Land* (1961) and *The Moon Is a Harsh Mistress* (1966). He died in Carmel, California, on May 8, 1988.

Ernest Hemingway. Nobel Prize-winning novelist.

Born Ernest Miller Hemingway in Oak Park, Illinois, on July 21, 1899, Hemingway enlisted in a Red Cross ambulance unit in 1917. He was commissioned a second lieutenant and served at the front in Italy. In July 1918 he was wounded in the leg by shrapnel, and was awarded Italy's Silver Medal of Military Valor.

Hemingway remained in Europe after the war, and reported from the battlefields of the Spanish Civil War for American newspapers. He wrote *Farewell to Arms* in 1929 based on his experiences in WWI.

Hemingway saw active service during WWII patrolling the waters around Cuba on anti-submarine duty aboard his yacht *Pilar*. Later in the war, he flew as an "observer" on missions with the U.S. Army Air Corps and the Royal Air Force. A formal investigation by the army to determine if his participation violated the Geneva Convention resulted in his being cleared of any wrongdoing. From the spring of 1944 on, Hemingway was a correspondent for *Colliers*, and was awarded a Bronze Star for meritorious service as a war correspondent in 1947. On the other hand, he almost lost his accreditation from the army for leading a Free French unit during the liberation of Paris.

He wrote *For Whom the Bell Tolls* in 1939, won a Pulitzer Prize in 1953, and the Nobel Prize in Literature in 1954 for *The Old Man and the Sea*. He died in Ketchum, Idaho, on July 2, 1961.

Tony Hillerman. Mystery and detective writer.

Born in the dust bowl at Sacred Heart, Oklahoma, on May 27, 1925, Hillerman grew up among Seminoles and Blackfeet Indians. On August 16, 1943, at age 18, he followed his older brother Barney and enlisted in the U.S. Army.

He trained as an infantryman and his unit was sent overseas

to Europe to spent two years on the front line. Of the original 212 men in his unit, only eight survived the war. His first published works were his letters home to his mother (his father died Christmas Day, 1941), published in the hometown newspaper.

Toward the end of the war, Hillerman stepped on a concussion mine while on patrol behind German lines. Both legs were broken, and he lost part of his sight from the blast. He was returned to the States, discharged as a private first class on October 16, 1945. He was awarded both the Silver and Bronze Stars and a Purple Heart. He entered the University of Oklahoma as a journalism major, graduating with a B.A. in three years. He writes novels on Indian culture such as *The Blessing Way* (1970) and *Sacred Clowns* (1993).

James Jones. Novelist.

Born in Robinson, Illinois, on November 6, 1921, Jones tried unsuccessfully to enlist in the Canadian army before enlisting in the U.S. Army Air Corps on November 10, 1939. In December of that year he was transferred from Ft. Slocum, New York, to Hickham Field, Hawaii.

In September 1940 he was transferred to Schofield Barracks near Honolulu, and was stationed there on December 7, 1941, when the Japanese attacked Pearl Harbor. He remained stationed in Hawaii for almost a year. He was promoted to corporal in May 1942.

In December 1942 Jones' unit, part of the 25th Infantry Division ("Tropic Lightning"), was shipped out to Guadalcanal where they landed on December 30.

Jones' unit went directly into combat at Guadalcanal, where Jones suffered a shrapnel wound to the head in January. He returned to duty after one week.

After killing a Japanese soldier in hand-to-hand combat, he was bothered emotionally, and after reinjuring an ankle, Jones was shipped home to Kennedy General Hospital in Tennessee in May 1943.

In November 1943 Jones elected to remain in the army rather than accept a medical discharge, on the condition he be classified "limited service." Despite this, he was transferred to a combat unit preparing to ship overseas. In December 1943 he was reduced in rank to private. He was promoted to sergeant in March 1944 but after episodes of AWOLs and arrests, he was reduced in rank and ordered to take a psychiatric evaluation. He was given a medical discharge and left the army at Camp Campbell, Kentucky, as a sergeant on July 6, 1944. He was awarded a Purple Heart for his wound on Guadalcanal.

In the postwar years Jones wrote his war trilogy, *From Here to Eternity* (1951), *The Thin Red Line* (1962), and *Whistle* (1975). (The latter was finished after Jones' death by his friend and fellow writer, Willie Morris).

Jack Kerouac. Counter-culture author and poet.

Born Jean Lois Lebris de Kerouac in Lowell, Massachusetts, on March 12, 1922, Kerouac spent the early part of WWII in the U.S. Merchant Marine before entering the U.S. Navy in 1942. He was given a psychiatric discharge after only three months for having "an indifferent character."

His work, *On the Road* (1957), helped define the "beat generation."

Hank Ketcham. Cartoonist, creator of "Dennis the Menace."

Born Henry King Ketcham in Seattle on March 14, 1920, Ketcham enlisted in the navy in 1942 and was assigned to the office of the Secretary of the Navy. He was assigned to draw cartoons for war bond campaigns and created the navy cartoon "Half Hitch." It was during this time that Ketcham sold his first cartoon to *The Saturday Evening Post*.

He romanced and married an admiral's secretary named Alice in June 1942. His son, Dennis, was born in 1946, the year Ketcham was honorably discharged from the navy. He began drawing the comic strip "Dennis the Menace" in 1952.

Joyce Kilmer. Poet.

Born Alfred Joyce Kilmer in New Brunswick, New Jersey, on December 6, 1886, Kilmer, the author of *Trees and Other Poems* (1913), enlisted in the army upon America's entry into WWI. His unit sailed to France early in 1918. Assigned to the 165th Infantry Regiment (better known as the "Fighting 69th") as a sergeant, Kilmer was killed in action during an attack along the Circq River on July 30, 1918, while serving as an adjutant to Major William "Wild Bill" Donovan. He was posthumously awarded the Croix de Guerre by the French government. He is portrayed in the film *The Fighting 69th*.

Eric Knight. Author of *Lassie Come Home*.

Born in Yorkshire, England, on April 10, 1897, Knight moved to the U.S. at age 15 and served briefly with the Canadian army during WWI. Two of his brothers were killed while serving with the 110th Pennsylvania Infantry Regiment of the U.S. Army.

On June 18, 1942, Knight again enlisted, this time in the U.S. Army, and was commissioned a captain in special services. Promoted, Major Knight was killed in action when the plane he was in crashed while en route to North Africa in 1943.

Louis L'Amour. Author of western novels.

Born in Jamestown, North Dakota, on March 22, 1908, L'Amour enlisted at age 33 in the U.S. Army during WWII and served as a tank crewman. He was promoted to first lieutenant by the war's end. During lulls on the battlefield, L'Amour would entertain his comrades with western stories. They suggested he put them down on paper.

After his discharge, L'Amour began to write, and published his first western, *Hondo*, in 1953. He has written over 101 western novels.

Beirne Lay. Novelist, combat pilot

Born Beirne Lay Jr. in Berkeley Springs, West Virginia, on September 1, 1909, Lay was an undergraduate at Yale University when he saw the movie *Wings* which "set the course of my life." He resolved to become a flier.

After graduating Yale in 1931, where he spent four years in the ROTC program, Lay enlisted in the U.S. Army Air Corps as an aviation cadet on July 3, 1932. He graduated on June 29, 1933, and was commissioned a second lieutenant in the reserve. He served until December 31, 1934, with the 20th Bombardment Squadron at Langley Field, Virginia, and from January 15, 1937, until April 12, 1939, learning to fly fighters with the 8th Pursuit Group. He also flew air mail routes (at the time the army had that responsibility). He wrote the semi-autobiographical novel, *I Wanted Wings*, late in 1935 and was hired as screenwriter when Paramount Pictures made the book into a movie in 1939. He made numerous Hollywood contacts in the process.

Called back to active duty in July 1941, he served briefly as a flight instructor before being assigned public relations duties in the office of Chief of Air Corps. In February 1942, Lay deployed overseas to England on the staff of Brigadier General Ira Eaker who took command of the 8th Bomber Command. He served as temporary chief of the 8th Air Force Film Unit, and assisted Major William Wyler in filming and producing *Memphis Belle*. Attached to the "Hard Luck" 100th Bomb Group for 30 days, he flew on the raid over Regensburg-Schweinfurt.

After returning to the U.S. for a transition course in flying B-24s, Lay served briefly as Deputy Group Commander of the 490th Bomber Group before taking command of the 487th Bomber Group 12 days before its deployment overseas in March 1944. Lay, now a lieutenant colonel, arrived with the group at Levenham, Suffolk, on April 5, 1944.

As commanding officer and group leader, Lay would fly in the lead plane on missions, exercising "personal leadership." On his third mission, on May 11, 1944, the B-24 Lay was piloting was crippled by flak, forcing a bail out over France. Lay, and 2Lt. Walter Duer hid with a French family until they were able to link up with the resistance. They were liberated by American troops on August 13, 1944, and Lay later wrote about the experience in "Down in Flames—Out by Underground" which appeared as a series of articles for *The Saturday Evening Post* in July 1945.

Lay was released from active duty on December 3, 1945, with the awards of the Distinguished Flying Cross, Air Medal and Purple Heart. He retired from the reserve as a colonel in July of 1963. He became a successful screenwriter after the war, writing screenplays for *Twelve O'Clock High* (1949), *Above and Beyond* (1952), *Strategic Air Command* (1955), and *The Gallant Hours* (1960).

Lay was twice nominated for Oscars. He died of cancer in Los Angeles on May 26, 1982.

Stan Lee. Comic book writer, editor of Marvel Comics.

Born in New York City on December 28, 1922, Lee was writing scripts for comics when he enlisted in the army in 1942 during WWII. After basic training, he was assigned as one of only nine men classified as "playwrights" in the army. He spent the war writing scripts for training films. Playwright William Saroyan was also in his unit.

In 1945 Lee was discharged from the army and returned to the comic industry. He joined Marvel Comics in 1961, and is credited with fathering a generation of characters with complex emotions and motivations, like "Spiderman" and "The Hulk."

Robert Ludlum. Political suspense novelist.

Born in New York City on May 25, 1927, Ludlum was working as a young actor at the start of WWII. He tried to enlist in the Royal Canadian Air Force in 1943, but was rejected because he was only 16 years old.

Towards the end of the war in 1945, Ludlum enlisted in the Marine Corps, and spent two years as an infantryman. After his discharge, he enrolled in Wesleyan University in Connecticut as a theater arts major, earning a B.A. with honors in 1951.

Ludlum has written numerous political intrigue novels, many of which were made into movies, like *The Scarletti Inheritance*,

The Osterman Weekend, and *The Rhineman Exchange.*

Archibald MacLeish. Poet, Assistant Secretary of State.

Born in Glencoe, Illinois, on May 7, 1892, MacLeish enlisted in the army after earning a law degree from Harvard, and served overseas in France during WWI. He served first with a hospital unit, then was transferred to the field artillery and promoted to captain. His brother Kenneth, an aviator, was killed in action.

MacLeish served as Assistant Secretary of State during WWII. He won three Pulitzer Prizes during his literary career for *Conquistador* (1932), *Collected Poems* (1953), and *J.B.* (1958).

Norman Mailer. Pulitzer Prize-winning writer.

Born in Long Branch, New York, on January 31, 1923, Mailer was drafted into the U.S. Army upon his graduation from Harvard in 1944. After basic training, he was sent to the Pacific theater. Trained as an artillery surveyor, he was transferred to the intelligence section of an infantry regiment upon his arrival in the Philippines. On his first night the regiment invaded Luzon, and Mailer typed combat reports and interpreted aerial photos.

With the novel he would later write in mind, he requested a transfer to a front line unit where he served as a rifleman with the 112th Cavalry Regiment (Special) at Luzon, attached to the 1st Cavalry Division ("The First Team"). After the end of WWII, he served with the occupation forces in Japan until 1946. He attained the rank of sergeant tech/4, but was demoted for discipline problems.

His experiences helped him in writing *The Naked and the Dead* (1948). Mailer and his wife, WAVES Lieutenant Beatrice Silverman, went to Europe where Mailer studied at the Sorbonne on the GI Bill. He won Pulitzer Prizes for *Armies of the Night* (1969) and *Executioner's Song* (1980).

Bill Mauldin. Cartoonist, creator of "Willie and Joe."

Bill Mauldin

Born William Henry Mauldin in Mountain Park, New Mexico, on October 29, 1921, Mauldin enlisted in the army at age 18 and was assigned to the 45th Infantry Division (the "Thunderbird" Division) after basic training. The division was made up of National Guard units from Colorado, Oklahoma and New Mexico.

On the staff of *Stars and Stripes*, Mauldin traveled throughout Italian and German areas of operations. He saw action at Casino and Anzio during the Italian campaign, and

"He's right, Joe. When we ain't fightin' we should ack like sojers."

was awarded a Purple Heart for wounds received at Salerno in the winter of 1943.

His cartoon of two lowly GIs, "Willie and Joe," were much loved by the troops, if not always by the "Brass." In June of 1945 Mauldin published *Up Front*, a collection of his wartime cartoons, and was discharged as a sergeant shortly thereafter.

Rod McKuen. Poet, composer, singer.

Born Rodney Marvin McKuen on April 23, 1933, in San Francisco, McKuen was already a radio personality in the San Francisco Bay Area when he was drafted into the army towards the end of the Korean War.

He was sent to Tokyo as a public information specialist, writing psychological warfare scripts. He also worked as a writer and director for special services, as well as appearing in five Japanese movies. In 1954 McKuen was sent to Korea as part of the Civil Assistance Command and was discharged in 1955.

James Michener. Novelist.

Born on February 3, 1907, in New York City, Michener entered the U.S. Navy as an enlisted man early in 1943. He was commissioned a lieutenant at age 36, and was sent to Washington DC as a publication editor for the Bureau of Aeronautics. It was an assignment he hated. In November 1943 he was transferred to the Philadelphia Aviation Depot.

In April of 1944 Michener sailed to the South Pacific, and was assigned as a liaison to the native populations of 49 different islands. He incorporated these experiences into his novel *Tales of the South Pacific* (1947). He served briefly as a naval historian, and was discharged at the end of 1945 with the rank of lieutenant commander.

Besides *South Pacific*, for which he won a Pulitzer Prize, Michener wrote numerous novels, among them *Hawaii* (1959), *The Source* (1965), *Chesapeake* (1978), *Space* (1982), and *Texas* (1985). He was awarded the Medal of Freedom by President Ford in 1977, and died in Austin, Texas, on October 16, 1997.

Leroy Neiman. Artist.

Born in St. Paul, Minnesota, on June 8, 1927, Neiman quit school at 15 to enlist in the army in 1942. He was sent overseas as a cook, but gained popularity for the murals he painted in mess halls and the officer's club, many of which were considered "sexually suggestive."

After the war, until his discharge from the army in 1946, Neiman was assigned to special services painting stage sets and backgrounds for Red Cross shows. Neiman credits the army for being the first to "validate" him as an artist. After his discharge, he attended the Art Institute of Chicago under the GI Bill. He is best known for his abstract paintings of athletes.

George Plimpton. Writer, editor.

Born in New York City on March 18, 1927, Plimpton served in the army as a tank driver stationed in Italy (1945–46). He enlisted as a private but rose to the rank of second lieutenant in the infantry by the time of his discharge in 1946.

Plimpton became famous for his participatory journalism when his book, *Paper Lion* (1966), was made into a movie starring Alan Alda.

Edgar Allen Poe. Author, poet.

Born in Boston on January 19, 1809, Poe falsely enlisted and served in the U.S. Army as Edgar E. Perry from 1827 through 1829. With the aid of his step-father, he was discharged. Later he was appointed to West Point, but was dismissed for academic reasons in 1831. He would serve in the military nevermore!

Poe is credited with being the father of the modern detective novel with *The Telltale Heart*.

Joseph Pulitzer. Journalist.

Born in Mako, Hungary, on April 10, 1847, Pulitzer came to the United States in 1864 by accepting passage from a Union army recruiter in exchange for enlisting in the Union army. He had previously been rejected by the Austrian, French, and English armies. Upon arrival in New York, Pulitzer was mustered into the 1st New York Cavalry which was comprised of primarily foreign-born Germans. He served in a few skirmishes and was mustered out on July 7, 1865.

He established the St. Louis *Post Dispatch* and died in Charleston, South Carolina, on October 29, 1911. He created the Pulitzer Prizes in 1903.

Joseph Pulitzer II. Editor, publisher.

Born in New York City on March 21, 1885, the son of Joseph Pulitzer (above), Pulitzer was accepted into naval aviation during WWI while still an undergraduate student. He was commissioned an ensign in November 1918, the month the war ended.

Pulitzer served as the editor/publisher of the St. Louis *Post Dispatch* from 1912 until 1955.

Norman Rockwell. Artist, illustrator.

Born in New York City on February 3, 1894, Rockwell was already a famous painter when war was declared in April 1917. Rockwell attempted to enlist in the navy at Pelham Bay in June, but was rejected for being 17 pounds underweight. Undeterred, he went to New York City where he hoped to slip by in the higher volumes of enlistees at the recruiting station.

In New York he recognized a medical yeoman as a former classmate. He was advised that the doctors could be persuaded to overlook ten pounds underweight. Rockwell stuffed himself with bananas, doughnuts and water, and amazingly, was able to gain enough weight to get his enlistment papers signed by the astonished doctors.

Sent to Charleston Naval Yard as a painter/varnisher 3rd class, Rockwell was assigned to the camp newspaper *Afloat and Ashore* where he did layouts and cartoons. In his spare time he earned extra money by drawing portraits of officers. He also continued his career as a commercial illustrator.

He obtained his discharge immediately after the armistice on the grounds of "inadaptability." He illustrated covers of *The Saturday Evening Post* from 1916 to 1963 and won the Presidential Medal of Freedom in 1977.

Will Rogers Jr. Publisher, author, actor.

The son of humorist Will Rogers, Rogers was born in New York City on October 28, 1911. He graduated Stanford University with a degree in journalism in 1935, months before his father died in a plane crash on August 15. He and his brother and sister bought the Beverly Hills *Citizen* and he served as publisher.

Rogers was a second lieutenant in a tank destroyer battalion at Ft. Hood, Texas, early in WWII, but left the army after he was elected to Congress in 1942. He resigned from Congress on May 24, 1944, to re-enter the army. He was attached to the 814th Tank Destroyer Battalion, attached to the 7th Armored Division (the "Lucky Seventh"), and fought in most of the major land campaigns in France and Germany. The 814th was comprised of M-10, and later M-36 tank destroyers, and was attached to the 7th Armored Division from August 13, 1944, until May 9, 1945. He was promoted to first lieutenant and awarded a Bronze Star for leading a patrol against a larger German force at St. Vith.

Rogers was wounded in the leg near Kassel, Germany, in April 1945 for which he was awarded the Purple Heart. Upon his discharge in November 1945, he returned to his newspaper, and served as a delegate for Truman in the 1948 election. He played his father in the 1950 film *The Story of Will Rogers*.

Andy Rooney. Columnist, author, commentator.

Born Andrew Aitken Rooney in Albany, New York, on January 14, 1919, Rooney was drafted into the U.S. Army as a private in July 1941. He was assigned to Battery C, 17th Field Artillery at Ft. Bragg, North Carolina, where he worked on the regimental newspaper. He applied for officer training but his request was denied. He also applied for a position as a reporter for *Stars and Stripes* (the army newspaper in Europe) which was accepted.

As a reporter, Rooney was semi-independent. He went on bombing missions with the 8th and 9th Air Forces, endured the bombing of London, was present at D-Day, the Liberation of Paris, and the liberation of concentration camps. He also visited India and China. He was discharged as a staff sergeant at the end of the war, winning the Air Medal and a Bronze Star.

William Safire. *New York Times* columnist.

Safire, a former Nixon speechwriter, was born in New York City on December 17, 1929. Drafted into the U.S. Army in 1952, Safire was assigned to public relations.

His most significant military accomplishment was getting NBC to televise a ceremony awarding military medals on the 4th of July, arranging for the ceremony to be held at the base of the Statue of Liberty. He was discharged in 1954 and returned to NBC radio.

Safire has written a column for the *New York Times* since 1973, and won a Pulitzer Prize in 1978.

Pierre Salinger. Reporter, presidential press secretary.

Born Emil George Pierre Salinger in San Francisco on June 14, 1925, Salinger joined the U.S. Navy in 1942 at the age of 17. He spent three years in the Pacific rising to the rank of full lieutenant and commander of a sub-chaser, making him one of the youngest men to command a naval warship in the history of the U.S. Navy. He was awarded the Navy and Marine Corps Medal for his actions during a typhoon off Okinawa in 1945 in which he put himself at risk while rescuing 15 men.

During the Kennedy administration, he became the youngest press secretary in U.S. history. He went to work for ABC News in 1983.

Arthur Schlesinger Jr. Historian.

Born in Columbus, Ohio, on October 15, 1917, the son of a noted historian, Schlesinger served with the Office of War Information for the first year of WWII, then transferred and served in the OSS (Office of Strategic Services). He was sent overseas in the spring of 1944. He was appointed deputy chief of the OSS reports board in the Paris station. This high position carried with it the rank of corporal. He was discharged in 1945. With the help of his wife and father, Schlesinger published *Age of Jackson* in 1945.

Schlesinger served as a special assistant to the President in both the Kennedy and Johnson administrations. He wrote *1,000 Days* in 1965.

Charles Schulz. Cartoonist, creator of "Peanuts."

Born in Minneapolis, Minnesota, on November 26, 1922, Schulz was drafted into the army in February 1943. He spent two years at Camp Campbell training with .30 and .50 caliber machine guns. He was assigned to the newly formed 20th Armored Division. "Charlie" was remembered as a quiet guy who entertained his buddies with his cartoons.

In February 1945 Schulz and his unit was sent overseas to Croisey sur Andelle in Northern France. The division went into combat in the middle of April. He was a sergeant in charge of a machine gun squad. His squad crossed the Rhine into Germany at Remagen and entered the Dachau concentration camp the day after its liberation. His unit was approaching Salzburg, Austria, when the war ended on May 5, 1945.

Schulz recalled that he wasn't that good a soldier, once refusing to throw a grenade at an enemy artillery emplacement because it would endanger a stray dog. His unit was scheduled for transfer to the Pacific, but was never sent. He was shipped back to California and was discharged as a staff sergeant in February 1946. He won an Emmy for a "Peanuts" cartoon in 1966.

Rod Serling. Author, TV screenwriter.

Born on Christmas Day, 1924, in Syracuse, New York, Serling, the son of a wholesale butcher, became president of his high school class and editor of the school newspaper. Upon his graduation from high school, he enlisted in the U.S. Army in January of 1943.

While at Ft. Niagara, New York, he saw some paratroopers and decided to volunteer for the paratroops. He was sent to Camp Toccoa in Georgia for screening, but was rejected because of his height (5' 5") and weight (115 pounds). He went to the commanding officer, and refused to leave until the officer changed his mind. Impressed by his determination, he was conditionally accepted pending successful completion of jump school.

After basic training at Camp McCall, North Carolina, and jump school at Ft. Benning, Georgia, Serling was awarded his paratrooper wings and was assigned to the 511th Parachute Regiment of the 11th Airborne Division. Serling was then sent back to Ft. McCall for advanced training. He was assigned to a demolitions unit at Ft. Polk, Louisiana. It was there that he first tried boxing, winning 17 of 18 amateur military matches.

Serling was sent to the Pacific in April of 1944, where he contracted malaria while in New Guinea. He was assigned to an intelligence company tasked with capturing prisoners and evaluating captured documents.

He landed at Leyte as part of the forces re-invading the Philippines. He spent 30 days in the jungle involved in small arms combat while being resupplied by airdrops. By January 1945 Serling was suffering from battle fatigue and was removed to Luzon.

In August his unit was preparing to invade Japan as part of a "floating reserve." The target was to be Kyushu and heavy casualties were expected. The bombing of Hiroshima and Nagasaki made an invasion unnecessary, and he served with the occupation forces in Japan until being returned stateside and discharged on January 13, 1946.

After the war, Serling attended college on the GI Bill where he began writing radio dramas. He would go on to win five Emmys and create the popular science fiction series *The Twilight Zone* in 1959, as well as write the script for *Planet of the Apes* in 1968. He also taught writing at Ithaca College in New York. He died in Rochester on June 28, 1975.

Max Shulman. Author, humorist.

Shulman was born in St. Paul, Minnesota, on March 14, 1919, and enlisted as a private in the U.S. Army Air Corps in June 1942. Certain that he would die in combat, Shulman spent the duration writing training manuals for the Air Corps. He was discharged in 1946 as a technical sergeant. He would go on to write *Rally Round the Flag* and *Dobie Gillis*.

Neil Simon. Playwright.

Born Marvin Neil Simon in New York City on July 4, 1927, Simon enlisted in the U.S. Army Air Corps reserve while an engineering student at New York University in 1943. By August of 1945 he was working as the editor of the base newspaper at Lowry Field, Colorado. He was discharged as a corporal in 1946.

Simon won four Tony Awards for his plays like *The Odd Couple* and *The Good Bye Girl*, as well as a Pulitzer Prize for *Lost in Yonkers*. His play, *Biloxi Blues*, is a semi-autobiographical account of his time in the army.

Mickey Spillane. Writer, author of the *Mike Hammer* series.

Born Frank Morrison Spillane in New York City on March 9, 1918, Spillane enlisted in the U.S. Army Air Corps on December 8, 1941, the day after Pearl Harbor. After flight training and a commission as a second lieutenant and pilot, Spillane volunteered for combat, but was assigned stateside as a cadet flight instructor in Florida and Mississippi until the end of the war. He was discharged with the rank of captain.

Leon Uris. Novelist.

Born in Baltimore, Maryland, on August 3, 1924, Uris enlisted in the Marine Corps after quitting his senior year of high school in 1942 at age 17. After basic training in San Diego, and transit to New Zealand and Hawaii, he was sent to the Pacific as a radio operator and participated in battles at Guadalcanal and Tarawa before catching malaria and being sent stateside. He volunteered for limited duty so that he could remain in the marines until the end of the war. He was stationed in San Francisco until he was given a medical discharge as a private first class in 1946. He married Sgt. Betty Beck whom he met while hospitalized.

Uris drew on his experiences as a marine in the Pacific in writing the novel, *Battle Cry*.

Gore Vidal. Novelist, historian.

Born Eugene Luthor Gore Vidal at the Cadet Hospital in West Point on October 3, 1925, Vidal was the son of Eugene Vidal, an aviation pioneer who was the U.S. Military Academy's first aviation instructor, as well as the football coach.

Early in 1942 Vidal volunteered for the Army Specialized Training Program (ASTP) which trained army engineers at the Virginia Military Institute (VMI). He flunked out after three months and was transferred to the Air Corps at Peterson Field. Vidal always considered this fortunate since the engineer program was subsequently canceled, and the majority of the students were sent to Europe as infantrymen arriving in time for the Battle of the Bulge where they suffered severe casualties.

He trained as a deck hand on army crash boats at Lake Pontchartrain in Louisiana, picking up "downed" aircrews in training. He was promoted to first mate, but his poor eyesight disqualified him from being commissioned as an officer. He was promoted to warrant officer junior grade, and was transferred to the transportation corps.

He was sent to the Aleutians as the first mate of freight ship #35 (FS-35), carrying cargo and troops on a circuit from Chernowski Bay to Unimak Island to Dutch Harbor, and navigating the worst seas on the planet.

Hypothermia and rheumatic fever caused his reassignment to Birmingham Military Hospital in Van Nuys, California. After recovering, he was transferred to the Air Corps detachment at Mitchell Field, Long Island, where he served on limited duty until his discharge in 1946.

His first novel, *Williwaw,* was based on his wartime experiences. He would go on to write *Burr* (1973), *1876* (1976), *Lincoln* (1984), and *Empire* (1987), as well as plays for Broadway and screenplays.

Kurt Vonnegut. Hugo Award-winning science fiction writer.

Born in Indianapolis, Indiana, on November 11, 1922, Vonnegut was studying biochemistry at Cornell University when he enlisted in the U.S. Army in late 1942. He was trained as a mechanical engineer at the Carnegie Institute, then sent to the University of Tennessee to train with 240 millimeter howitzers. Assigned as an infantry battalion scout, he returned home on leave for Mother's Day, 1944, to learn his mother had committed suicide the previous evening.

Sent overseas in August 1944, he was captured by the Germans at the Battle of the Bulge in December 1944. He was assigned to a POW work group in Dresden prior to its fire bombing. On February 13, 1945, the Allied high command ordered the saturation bombing of Dresden, even though there were no military targets. It resulted in the largest estimated loss of life of the war, greater than Hiroshima and Nagasaki combined.

Vonnegut survived with other prisoners and six German guards by taking shelter in the underground freezer of a slaughterhouse. In the aftermath of the raid, Vonnegut helped unearth some of the estimated 130,000 corpses buried in the rubble (necessary for sanitary reasons).

Liberated and repatriated by Soviet troops in April 1945, Vonnegut was discharged and returned to Chicago to work as a reporter. His war experiences were recounted in the novel, *Slaughterhouse Five* (1969).

Irving Wallace. Novelist.

Born in Chicago on March 19, 1916, Wallace enlisted in the U.S. Army Air Corps in October 1942. After basic training, he was assigned to the motion picture unit in Culver City making training and orientation films. He was transferred to the Signal

Corps Photographic Unit in Los Angeles where he served until the end of the war. He was discharged in February of 1946 as a staff sergeant.

Lewis "Lew" Wallace. Author, territorial governor, diplomat.

The author of *Ben Hur* was born in Brookville, Indiana, on April 10, 1827. In 1846, at the age of 19, he raised a company of volunteer infantry for the Mexican War, and was commissioned a second lieutenant in the 1st Indiana Infantry. He saw service in Mexico and returned to Indianapolis after the war.

He was working as a lawyer and state senator when the Civil War started in April 1861. He was first appointed state adjutant general, then colonel of the 11th Indiana Infantry. In September he was promoted to brigadier general of volunteers. He commanded a division under General Grant at the capture of Ft. Donelson on February 16, 1862.

Promoted to major general of volunteers in March, he was with Grant at Shiloh in April, and advanced to Cornith. In September Wallace took command of the defense of Cincinnati, helped contain Confederate General Kirby-Smith, and in early 1864 was given command of VIII Corps. He was defeated by General Jubal Early at Monocracy River in July 1864, and saw no further major action for the remainder of the war.

After the war, in May and June of 1865, he served as a member of the military court that tried the Lincoln conspirators, and presided over the war crimes trial of Captain Henry Wirz, the commandant of Andersonville Prison Camp. After brief service in Mexico he returned to Indiana and law practice.

In 1878 President Hayes appointed Wallace governor of the New Mexico territory during the Lincoln County War. Wallace almost pardoned Billy the Kid, and later served as minister to Turkey from 1881 to 1885. He wrote *Ben Hur* in 1880.

Mike Wallace. Journalist, TV commentator.

Born Myron Leon Wallace in Brookline, Massachusetts, on

May 9, 1918, Wallace was working in radio and narrating a navy recruiting program when he took his own advice and joined the U.S. Navy in December 1943 as an ensign.

He served as a shore communications officer in Hawaii and Australia and aboard a submarine tender. He was also officer in charge (OIC) of radio entertainment at the Great Lakes Naval Station before he was discharged in 1946 as a lieutenant (j.g.). After his discharge he returned to work as a radio announcer.

Wallace has co-hosted the weekly television news magazine *60 Minutes* since 1968 and was voted into the Television Hall of Fame in 1991.

Walt Whitman. Poet, author.

Born in West Hills, New York, on May 31, 1819, Whitman traveled to Virginia in 1862 to seek his brother who was wounded on a battlefield during the Civil War. He stayed on to serve as a battlefield nurse in Washington DC for the remainder of the war. He wrote *Leaves of Grass* in 1855.

Thornton Wilder. Playwright, 3-time Pulitzer Prize winner.

Born in Madison, Wisconsin, on April 17, 1897, Wilder left Oberlin College for military service during WWI with the U.S. Army Coast Artillery in Rhode Island. After the war he returned to college and graduated Yale in 1920. He won a Pulitzer Prize for *Bridges of San Luis Rey* in 1928 and for *Our Town* in 1938.

After Pearl Harbor, in 1942, Wilder was commissioned a captain in the U.S. Army Air Corps. Assigned to intelligence and sent overseas to Italy, he contributed to the strategic planning in the Italian theater of war (1942–45). He was discharged with the rank of lieutenant colonel.

Walter Winchell. Journalist, radio broadcaster.

Born Walter Winschel or Weinschel on April 7, 1897, in Harlem, New York, Winchell was a song-and-dance man in vaudeville from the age of 12. He enlisted in the U.S. Navy reserve on July 22, 1918, during WWI. In August he was assigned the duties of a yeoman, and in September was called to active duty. He patrolled New York harbor aboard the USS *Isis*.

He was assigned as a receptionist to Admiral Marbury Johnson at the New York City Customs House. It is prophetic perhaps that he once burned his nose on a candle while sealing a letter because he was too intent listening to a conversation in the admiral's office. He was released from active duty on December 5, 1918.

Winchell remained in the navy reserve, and in June 1940 was aboard the shake down cruise of the newly commissioned USS *North Carolina*. He requested active duty, but Winchell, now a prominent anti-isolation journalist, was too valuable to the Roosevelt administration. By the attack on Pearl Harbor, Winchell had attained the rank of lieutenant commander in the reserves.

Winchell was briefly called to active duty on December 1, 1942, when he was sent on a fact-finding tour of Brazil for the state and navy departments. He returned to the States on January 5, 1943, aboard a naval patrol boat on anti-submarine patrol, where he manned a gun. He reached Miami on January 8 and was soon returned to reserve status. His congressional enemies kept Winchell from returning to active duty, and he spent the remainder of the war volunteering his time five days a week at the 3rd Naval District Headquarters where he worked without pay or official position.

An advocate of FDR in the forties, and of Joseph McCarthy in the fifties, Winchell at one time had a weekly radio audience of 50 million, and his daily newspaper column was syndicated in over 2,000 newspapers. He is credited with coining the phrase "America, love it or leave it," referring to the German-American Bund, a pro-Nazi organization. He died in Los Angeles, California, on February 20, 1972.

Grant Wood. Artist, painted "American Gothic."

Born in Anamosa, Iowa, on February 13, 1892, Wood enlisted

in the army when America entered WWI. He served stateside in the camouflage division. He drew sketches of the troops to supplement his pay (25¢ for enlisted, $1 for officers). He served until his discharge after the armistice. He created his most famous painting, "American Gothic," in 1930.

Bob Woodward. Investigative reporter, author.

Born in Geneva, Illinois, on March 26, 1943, during WWII, Woodward grew up in Illinois and joined the naval ROTC while

Bob Woodward

a student at Yale to get the scholarship money. Four weeks after earning his B.A. in journalism, he began his four-year tour of duty.

After being commissioned an ensign, his first assignment was as a communications officer aboard a ship. To avoid the "deathtrap" of service in Vietnam, Woodward volunteered for duty aboard a guided missile frigate. His tour of duty was extended for one year in 1969, and he was reassigned to Washington DC where he served as a liaison officer between the Pentagon and the White House.

This experience would serve him well two years later when he was assigned to investigate the Democratic national headquarters break-in at the Watergate Hotel for the *Washington Post*. He wrote the best seller, *All the President's Men*, in 1974 about the Watergate cover-up.

Discharged from the navy in 1970, Woodward was awarded the Navy Commendation Medal.

Herman Wouk. Pulitzer Prize-winning novelist.

A script writer for Fred Allen before the war, the author of *The Winds of War* and *The Caine Mutiny* was born in New York City on May 27, 1915. He enlisted in the U.S. Navy after Pearl Harbor and served as an officer aboard the USS *Zane* (DMS-14) in the South Pacific. In 1943, while aboard ship, he wrote the novel *Aurora Dawn*.

Wouk won a Pulitzer Prize for *The Caine Mutiny* and it was made into a movie of the same name, starring Humphrey Bogart.

Section 5

Science and Medicine

Isaac Asimov. Scientist, science fiction writer.

Born on January 21, 1920, in Petrovichi, U.S.S.R., Asimov came to the U.S. at age three, and was already writing science fiction and working on his degree in chemistry at Columbia University at the start of WWII. He spent most of the war working as a civilian chemist at the Naval Experimental Station in Philadelphia.

In 1945 Asimov enlisted in the U.S. Army and served until 1946 when he was discharged with the rank of corporal. He returned to Columbia University to earn his doctorate in chemistry. He earned fame as a writer of both fiction and nonfiction. Among his well-known books are *I, Robot* and *The Foundation Trilogy*. He died in New York City on April 6, 1992.

Euell Gibbons. Naturalist, author.

Born in Clarksville, Texas, on September 8, 1911, Gibbons enlisted in the army in 1934 at age 23. He learned the trade of boatbuilder/carpenter, and was discharged in 1936 after two years of service. He wrote *Stalking the Good Life* in 1971. He died in Sunbury, Pennsylvania, on December 25, 1979.

Donald Herbert. Educator, "Mr. Wizard" on TV.

Born on July 10, 1917, in Waconia, Minnesota, Herbert attended a teacher's college hoping to teach drama. He majored in general science and English and graduated in 1940.

Upon the U.S. entry into WWII, Herbert enlisted as a private in the Army Air Corps. He later graduated from flight school, earned his pilot's wings, and a second lieutenant's commission.

Herbert flew B-24 bombers assigned to the 15th Air Force in the Mediterranean. He flew strategic bombing missions in central Europe from Foggia, Italy, won the Distinguished Flying Cross, and an Air Medal with three Oak Leaf Clusters. He was discharged as a captain in 1945, and accepted a job in radio in Chicago. He created the TV character "Mr. Wizard" on NBC in March 1951. *Mr. Wizard* was a science education show.

Edwin Hubble. Astronomer.

Born in Marshfield, Missouri, on November 20, 1889, Hubble worked as a lab assistant to Robert Millikan after graduating from the University of Chicago in 1910. He studied law as a Rhodes scholar at Queen's College, Oxford, before he enlisted in the army in 1917.

After taking officer's training at Camp Sheridan, Illinois, Hubble was commissioned a captain in the infantry and was assigned to the 86th Division. Promoted to major in December 1917, he was sent overseas to France in August 1918, and saw combat.

After the armistice, Hubble remained in Europe where he served as a judge advocate at courts-martial, and later as an administrator for American officers. He returned to San Francisco and was discharged in August 1919.

Hubble accepted the position of staff astronomer at the Mt. Wilson Observatory in Pasadena, California, and his study of nebulae helped scientists to better understand the nature of the universe. The Hubble Space Telescope and numerous celestial bodies are named in his honor.

Jack Kevorkian. Pathologist, "Dr. Death."

Born in Pontiac, Michigan, on May 26, 1928, Kevorkian served 15 months as an army medical officer in Korea during the Korean War in 1953. After the cease-fire, he was sent to Colorado where he finished his tour of duty. He was discharged as a captain in 1955. He returned to civilian medicine, and went on to head the controversy over physician-assisted suicides in the 1990s.

Robert Andrews Millikan. Physicist.

Born in Morrison, Illinois, on March 22, 1868, Millikan served as chief of the Science and Research Division of the U.S. Army Signal Corps during WWI. He was given a direct commission as lieutenant colonel. After his discharge in November 1919, Millikan returned to the University of Chicago.

Millikan's work in physics included the photo-electric effect, light polarization, and jet and rocket propulsion. He won the Nobel Prize in physics in 1923 and authored many books.

John Wesley Powell. Geologist, pioneer explorer, engineer.

Born in Mt. Morris (now part of New York City) on March 24, 1834, Powell was collecting materials for the Illinois State Natural History Society along the Mississippi and Ohio Rivers when the Civil War interrupted his studies.

Powell enlisted as a private with the 20th Illinois Infantry. He studied texts on military engineering and fortifications and was promoted to sergeant, and later to lieutenant. With his knowledge, Powell quickly came to the attention of General Grant who placed him in command of several forts along the Mississippi River.

After returning to duty from a furlough in Illinois where he married his cousin, Powell took command of a battery of artillery at the Battle of Pittsburgh Landing. His unit held the center of the line of what came to be known as the "Hornet's Nest" at the Battle of Shiloh in April 1862. He was wounded so severely that his right arm required amputation.

Upon recovering, the now one-armed Powell was present at the siege of Vicksburg where he took time to collect fossils in the trenches during lulls in the battle. He commanded the artillery at the Battle for Atlanta, and was with General Sherman on his "March to the Sea."

Powell was discharged with the rank of major, and took a position as professor of natural history at Illinois Wesleyan College. Ignoring warnings from the army, Powell went on to map the Colorado River despite the presence of hostile Indians. He spent the next 25 years performing geographical and geological studies of the Rocky Mountains.

Walter Reed. Surgeon.

Born in Belroi, Virginia, on September 13, 1851, Reed graduated from the University of Virginia and entered the U.S. Army Medical Corps in 1875. He served on the frontier for 15 years.

In 1893 he was appointed professor of bacteriology at the U.S. Army Medical School, with a promotion to major. In 1900 he was named head of the commission that was sent to Cuba to investigate the cause and mode of transmittal of yellow fever. Reed proved the disease was transmitted through the saliva of mosquitoes, and this knowledge made its control possible. Walter Reed Hospital in Washington DC is named in his honor.

B. F. Skinner. Behaviorist, psychologist.

Born Burrus Frederic Skinner on March 20, 1904, in Susquehanna, Pennsylvania, Dr. Skinner (as a civilian) was given a $25,000 grant during WWII to teach pigeons to serve as the guidance system for missiles and/or bombs (no kidding)! Amazingly, preliminary test results showed that it was feasible.

Dr. Benjamin Spock. Pediatrician, author, anti-war activist.

Born Benjamin McLane Spock in New Haven, Connecticut, on May 2, 1903, Spock's ancestors included John Hooper of Somersetshire, a religious reformer burned at the stake in 1555, Samuel Wardell, executed for witchcraft in 1692, and William Hooper of North Carolina, a signer of the Declaration of Independence. Spock himself rowed crew with the Yale team in the 1924 Olympics.

Called to active duty in 1944, at the age of 41, Spock entered the navy as a lieutenant commander during WWII. After training at Bethesda Naval Medical Center, he was assigned the duties of a psychiatrist evaluating sailors facing discharge for being unfit (there was little call for the services of a pediatrician in the wartime navy).

Spock served at Bethesda until late in 1945 when he was transferred to the West Coast in preparation for duty overseas. The war ended, so Spock spent the rest of his time at various hospitals until his discharge on May 7, 1946.

Section 6

Adventurers and Explorers

Neil Armstrong. Astronaut, first man on the moon.

Born in August of 1930, Armstrong earned his pilot's license at the age of 16. In 1947 he entered Purdue" University as a naval aviation midshipman.

Neil Armstrong

He was called to active duty in 1949. As a naval aviator, he flew 78 combat missions in Korea from the carrier USS *Essex*, where he earned three Air Medals. During one low level strafing run over North Korea, Armstrong's F9F Panther severely damaged its wing when it struck a tree. He was able to nurse the plane back to a South Korean base, but the plane was so damaged he was unable to land and was forced to eject. After his discharge, he accepted a position as a civilian test pilot.

In 1962 he was accepted by NASA for the astronaut program. On March 16, 1966, Armstrong entered space for the first time aboard *Gemini-8* with Major David Scott.

On July 16, 1969, Armstrong, along with Edwin Aldrin and Michael Collins, left Earth aboard *Apollo XI* on the first lunar landing mission. On July 20 at 10:56:22 p.m., Armstrong became the first man to step on the surface of the moon, with the now historic words, "That's one small step for a man; one giant leap for mankind." He resigned from NASA in 1971 to take a position as professor of engineering at the University of Cincinnati.

Daniel Boone. Frontiersman and explorer.

Born in Berks County, Pennsylvania, in 1734, Boone's military service was primarily in the militia. In 1755 he was in British General Braddock's expedition against the French at Ft. Duquesne. He also saw service during the French and Indian War.

In 1775 he led a party through the Cumberland Gap to the Kentucky River where he founded the settlement of Boonesboro, one of the first in Kentucky. He was captured by Indians and later adopted by the tribe, but escaped in 1778 to warn the fort of an impending attack. Boone organized the defense against a much larger force of Indians for which he was promoted to major. Later, after moving to what is now West Virginia, he was appointed lieutenant colonel of the Kanawha County militia. He was later elected to the Virginia assembly, and served as a magistrate in Missouri before his death in 1820.

Frank Borman. Test pilot, astronaut, businessman.

Born in Gary, Indiana, on March 14, 1928, Borman moved with his family to Phoenix, Arizona, at an early age because of his respiratory problems. The dry climate allowed him to excel in sports. He went to the state championships as quarterback of his high school football team.

Borman entered West Point in 1946, and graduated 8th in a class of 670 in 1950. He was commissioned a second lieutenant in the U.S. Air Force, and took flight training at Williams AFB. He earned his pilot's wings in 1951.

He served as a fighter pilot with the 44th Fighter-Bomber Squadron in the Philippines (1951–53), then returned stateside to serve as a pilot-instructor until 1956.

Borman earned his master's degree in aeronautical engineering from the California Institute of Technology in 1957, then served as an instructor of thermodynamics at West Point (1957–60). In 1960 he was transferred to Edwards Air Force Base for test pilot training. Upon graduation he served as an instructor.

Borman was among the second group of astronauts, selected in 1962. In 1965 he was promoted to colonel, and in December of that year he and fellow astronaut James Lovell were sent into space aboard *Gemini 7* where they joined and linked up with *Gemini 6* (Schirra and Stafford).

Borman was part of the team that investigated the Apollo lab fire of December 21, 1968. He circumnavigated the moon aboard *Apollo 8* with Lovell and Anders in 1968. His landing on December 27, 1968 was only 45 seconds behind schedule.

In 1969 he was named deputy director of flight operations for NASA. In 1970 Borman retired from both NASA and the air force, and 1975 he accepted a position as vice president, later president, of Eastern Airlines.

Kit Carson. Trapper, scout, explorer, Indian agent.

Born Christopher Carson on Christmas Eve, 1809, in Madison County, Kentucky, Carson spent his early years hunting, trapping, and learning the territory. At 16 he ran away to join the Santa Fe Expedition in 1826, and was along on the California Expedition (1829–31).

In 1842, while in St. Louis, he met Lt. John C. Fremont and thus began an association wherein he served as a guide in three subsequent expeditions (1842, 1843, and 1845) and shared fame with the "Pathfinder," as Fremont was called.

Carson was in California during the War with Mexico. He traveled with Fremont and 150 men by ship to San Diego, then overland to Los Angeles as part of Commodore Stockton's "Navy Battalion of Mounted Riflemen." The Mexicans under General Castro fled, and Fremont captured the settlement.

On October 6, 1846, while carrying dispatches to Washington DC with an escort of 15 men, he encountered General Kearney on his march to California, and was ordered to act as a guide for Kearney, while the others continued on.

At the Battle of San Pasqual on December 6, Carson, along with navy Lieutenant Beale crawled through Mexican lines to travel to San Diego and summon a relief force under Commodore Stockton to relieve General Kearney's surrounded command. He was present at the Battle of San Gabriel on January 8, 1847, and the Battle of Los Angeles on January 9 and 10. He was again sent to Washington with dispatches, this time with Lt. Beale.

After a stay in the Capital, he was appointed a lieutenant of rifles in the U.S. Army by President Polk, and sent back to California with instructions for Stockton and Kearney. Upon his return he was assigned to guarding Tejon Pass in command of a detachment of the 1st Dragoons, under the command of Captain (later Major General) Andrew Jackson Smith.

Upon his trip back to Washington, he learned that the U.S. Senate had never confirmed his commission. Disappointed, he nonetheless completed the mission.

After eight years of service as Indian Agent to the Ute Indians (1853–61), Carson raised and commanded the 1st New Mexico Volunteers. He fought Indians in the Southwest Territories during the Civil War, rising to the rank of brevet brigadier general. He died in Fort Lyon, Colorado, on May 23, 1868.

John Fremont. U.S. Senator, presidential candidate, explorer.

Born in Savannah, Georgia, on January 21, 1813, Fremont was assigned topographical duties as an army officer as early in his career as 1838. By the time of the Mexican War, which Fremont fought in California, he was a captain. He resigned from the army over a dispute with his superiors but continued to explore in the West, and was elected U.S. Senator from the new state of California.

Fremont ran for President as the first candidate of the newly formed Republican Party in 1856. With the outbreak of the Civil War, he served as a major general in the Regular Army (1861–62). He resigned rather than serve under General Pope. He later served as Governor of Arizona. Although he acquired great wealth during his lifetime, he died in poverty in New York City on July 13, 1890.

John Glenn. Astronaut, first American to orbit the earth, U.S. Senator.

Born in Cambridge, Ohio, on July 18, 1921, Glenn enlisted in the naval aviation program in March 1942. He was commissioned

John Glenn

a second lieutenant in the U.S. Marine Corps reserve as a pilot in March 1943. Promoted to first lieutenant in October, and assigned to the 155th Fighter Squadron of the 4th Marine Aircraft Wing, Glenn flew 59 combat missions in the Pacific (1944–45) in F4U Corsair fighters. He won two Distinguished Flying Crosses and 19 Air Medals. Promoted to captain in July 1945, he was integrated into the Regular Marine Corps in March 1946, and was assigned to the 9th Marine Aircraft Wing at Cherry Point, North Carolina.

Sent overseas in 1947, Glenn spent two years patrolling North China as part of Marine Fighter Squadron #218, of the 1st Marine Airwing. After a stint as a flight instructor in 1952, Glenn, by now a major, was sent to Korea where he flew 90 more missions while assigned to the 25th Fighter Squadron, an Air Force unit. He downed a total of three MIG-15 fighters. He earned two additional DFCs and eight more Air Medals.

In 1959 he was promoted to lieutenant colonel and was selected as one of the original seven astronauts of Project Mercury. At 40 Glenn was the oldest, and the only marine. On February 20, 1962, aboard *Friendship 7*, he became the first American to orbit the earth. He resigned from NASA in 1964 and retired from the marines as a colonel on January 1, 1965. He successfully ran for the U.S. Senate from Ohio in 1974.

Meriwether Lewis. Scientist, explorer.

Born in Albemarle County, Virginia, on August 18, 1774, Lewis was commissioned an ensign in the Regular Army in 1795 at age 21. By 1800 he was a captain and was serving as a secretary to President Jefferson.

In 1803, along with Captain William Clark, Lewis was sent on an expedition to the Pacific which was completed in 1806. He died mysteriously while en route to Washington in 1809.

Charles Lindbergh. World famous aviator, airline executive.

Born in Detroit, Michigan, on February 4, 1902, Lindbergh grew up in Little Falls, Minnesota, the son of a Congressman. He applied for admission to the army's flying cadet program on March 19, 1924 and on March 15 passed the exams at Brooks Field, Texas. He entered the U.S. Army as a cadet four days later. On March 14, 1925, Lindbergh was among the 18 out of a class of 104 that graduated. He was commissioned as a second lieutenant. He then resigned from active duty and automatically became a member of the Reserve Corps.

Lindbergh's famous trans-Atlantic flight in his plane, *The Spirit of St. Louis*, in May 1927 made him a world hero. He was awarded the Distinguished Flying Cross and promoted to colonel in the reserves. Congress voted to award him the Medal of Honor in 1927.

During the 1930s Lindbergh observed European air forces and reported to Washington. His admiration of national socialism in Germany caused him political problems at home and put him in direct opposition to many of FDR's policies. Lindbergh visited Berlin three times and was decorated with the Service Cross of the German Eagle, a high Nazi award to civilians. When war began in 1939 Lindbergh exerted tremendous energy to persuade the American public to remain neutral. He became a prominent member of America First, a non-interventionist pressure group. The political feud between a President committed to lend-lease for Britain and Lindbergh, a highly visible public figure, led to Lindbergh's resignation from the Army Air Corps on April 25, 1941. Denied the opportunity for active service after Pearl Harbor, Lindbergh went to work for Henry Ford, another FDR opponent, and served as a civilian advisor to the War Department at $66 a week (which he refused). He went to the Pacific in the spring of 1944 to evaluate B-24 bombers. He "unofficially" flew several combat missions, and shot down an enemy fighter on July 28, 1944. In 1954 President Eisenhower restored Lindbergh's commission in the reserves and promoted him to brigadier general in the U.S. Air Force. After the war, he and his wife, Ann Morrow, and their four children moved to Hana on the island of Maui, where he died and was buried in 1974.

Zebulon Montgomery Pike. Explorer.

Born in Trenton, New Jersey, on January 5, 1779, Pike began his military career as a cadet in his father's regiment in 1794. In 1800 Pike, now a lieutenant, explored the sources of the Mississippi and Arkansas Rivers. He was promoted to major in 1808, and to colonel in 1812. He served as a brigadier general in the War of 1812, but died from wounds received during the action against York (Toronto) in 1813. Pike's Peak in Colorado is named after him.

Francis Gary Powers. U-2 pilot, intelligence agent.

Born the son of a coal miner on August 17, 1929, in Burdine, Kentucky, Powers enlisted in the U.S. Air Force as an airman in

1950 after he graduated college. After basic training he was assigned to flight training. Upon his graduation, he was commissioned a second lieutenant and awarded his pilot's wings. He was promoted to first lieutenant in 1952, and was stationed at Turner Air Force Base outside Albany, Georgia.

In 1955 Powers and other military pilots were recruited by the CIA and began training to fly the U-2 reconnaissance plane. Powers resigned from the air force, and went to work as "Francis G. Palmer" of the Lockheed Aircraft Corporation. For three years Powers flew military missions over the Soviet Union from Incirlik Air Force Base in Turkey.

On May 1, 1960, U-2 plane #360 was shot down by surface-to-air missiles over Soviet territory. The pilot, Powers, was tried for espionage and was convicted. He was swapped for Soviet agent Rudolph Abel on February 10, 1962. In 1970 Powers authored the book *Operation Overflight* about his experiences in the CIA.

Powers died piloting a helicopter while covering Santa Barbara, California, brushfires for KNBC television on August 1, 1977. He is buried in Arlington National Cemetery.

Alan B. Shepard. Astronaut, first American in space.

Born in East Derry, New Hampshire, on November 18, 1923, Shepard was one of the original seven Project Mercury astronauts. He entered the Naval Academy at Annapolis in 1940 and graduated in 1944.

After service in the Pacific aboard the destroyer USS *Cogswell* (DD-651) during WWII, Shepard was accepted for flight training where he qualified as a pilot in March 1947. He served in a fighter squadron until he was accepted for test pilot training at Patuxent River, Maryland, in 1950.

After another tour of duty with a fighter squadron (1953–55), Shepard returned to Patuxent as a test pilot and part-time instructor.

After graduating the Naval War College in 1958, Shepard served on the staff of the Atlantic Fleet Commander. In April 1959 Lt. Commander Shepard was selected as one of the original seven Project Mercury astronauts. After two years of intensive training, he took a 15-minute suborbital flight in *Freedom 7* on May 5, 1961, attaining the never-before-reached altitude of 115 miles. This made him the first American in space.

In 1963 an ear equilibrium problem resulted in Shepard, now a full commander, being removed from active status as an astronaut. He served as the chief of the Astronaut Section of NASA, and was promoted to captain in 1967.

With the surgical correction of his ear problem, Shepard was returned to active status. On January 31, 1971, he commanded the Apollo XIV mission (with Roosa and Mitchell) and piloted the lunar landing module to within 60 feet of its lunar target site. He became the fifth man on the moon (and the first to "tee off" a golf shot on the moon).

Promoted to rear admiral in August 1971, Shepard served as a delegate to the United Nations before retiring from the navy and NASA in August 1974 to pursue private interests.

Walter Marty Schirra Jr. Project Mercury astronaut.

Born in Hackensack, New Jersey, on March 12, 1923, Schirra entered the U.S. Naval Academy in 1942. He graduated and was commissioned an ensign toward the end of WWII, late in 1945. In 1948 he was accepted for flight training as a pilot.

During the Korean War, Schirra flew 90 combat missions with the 154th Fighter-Bomber Squadron. He worked to help develop the *Sidewinder* air-to-air missile, and did a tour of duty aboard the aircraft carrier USS *Lexington* before being accepted for test pilot training at Patuxent River Test Station in 1958.

In April 1959 Schirra was among the first seven astronauts selected for Project Mercury under NASA. He piloted *Sigma 7* on October 3, 1962. Promoted to naval captain in 1965, Schirra piloted *Gemini 6* with copilot Tom Stafford into the first rendezvous in space with the already orbiting *Gemini 7* (Borman and Lovell) on December 15, 1965.

On October 11, 1968, Schirra re-entered space for the third time aboard *Apollo 7* (with Don Eisele and Walter Cunningham). This, the first of the Apollo series, would pave the way for the moon landing the following year. Schirra resigned from NASA in 1969.

Henry Morton Stanley. Explorer, journalist.

Born in Denbigh, Wales, on January 31, 1841, Stanley was known as John Rowlands until he was informally adopted by Henry Morton Stanley, a New Orleans merchant in 1859, and assumed his benifactor's name. He came to America as a cabin boy aboard a sailing ship after escaping from a workhouse in England at the age of 16.

He was working as a storekeeper in Arkansas when the Civil War broke out. He enlisted in the "Dixie Greys" and fought with the Confederate army until his capture at the Battle of Shiloh. He was interned at Camp Douglas near Chicago where he wrote vividly about the hardships endured by Confederate prisoners. (Over 26,000 Confederate prisoners died in Union POW camps during the war.) After two months in prison, Stanley was released in exchange for enlisting in the Union army and thus became what was known as a "Galvanized Yankee." But his captivity had so destroyed his health that he was medically discharged within a month of his enlistment.

He returned home to England but came back to America in 1863. The year 1864 found him in the Union navy. He was present aboard a warship when a combined army-navy attack captured the Confederacy's last major port at Wilmington, North Carolina, at the Battle of Fort Fisher on the 13th and 14th of January 1865.

After the war, Stanley turned his talents to journalism. He visited Asia Minor, explored the American frontier, accompanied General Hancock against the Indians on the American frontier, and was with the British forces in Abyssinia in 1868. In 1869 Stanley was commissioned by James Gordon Bennett of the *New York Herald* to travel to Africa and locate David Livingstone. He traveled into the interior of Africa, finally locating a frail, white-haired Livingstone in the village of Ujiji on November 10, 1871, speaking the greeting that has passed into immortality, "Dr. Livingstone, I presume?"

For the rest of his life he explored Africa, lectured in Europe and America, and wrote of his experiences. He retired to England, married, was knighted, and was elected a member of Parliament in 1895. He died in London on May 10, 1904.

Edward H. White II. Astronaut, second man to walk in space.

Born in San Antonio, Texas, on November 14, 1930, White grew up the son of a retired major general and pioneer balloonist. He attended West Point from 1948 to 1952, and after graduating, took a commission in the U.S. Air Force. White took flight training and flew F-86s and F-100s before being accepted as a test pilot at Edwards Air Force Base.

In the mid-60s White was accepted into the Gemini Project in the second group of astronauts. During the *Gemini 4* mission, he was the first American to exit an orbiting spacecraft and "walk" in space.

Section 7

Sports and Athletes

George Allen. Football coach.

Born on April 29, 1922, in the Grosse Point Woods district of Detroit, Allen enrolled in the navy's wartime V-12 program while attending college during WWII. He played football at Marquette University.

Upon graduation, Allen was commissioned an ensign and assigned to the navy basic training program at Farragut, Idaho, as athletic adjutant. He was discharged in 1946, and continued his schooling at the University of Michigan. During the 1970s and 1980s he was the head coach of the Los Angeles Rams and Washington Redskins. He died in Rancho Palos Verdes, California, on December 31, 1990.

Ernie Banks. Hall of Fame baseball player.

Born on January 31, 1931, in Dallas, Texas, Banks was playing for the Kansas City Monarchs in the American Negro League when he was drafted into the U.S. Army in March 1951. He served as a private in Europe until his discharge in 1953. He went on to become the first black ballplayer on the Chicago Cubs and was voted MVP in 1958 and 1959.

Lawrence "Yogi" Berra. Hall of Fam baseball player.

Born in 1925, Berra was 18 when he was offered a position with the Yankee's farm club in Kansas City. Instead, he enlisted in the U.S. Navy, and was sent to Norfolk Naval Station in Virginia for basic training. He had hoped to play baseball for the navy, but changed his mind, and volunteered for rocket boats which provided off-shore fire power support during amphibious landings.

He trained in Glasgow, Scotland, as a gunner's mate, and was aboard the USS *Bayfield* (APA-33) as a gunner aboard an LCI (R) (Landing Craft Rocket) at the Normandy landing on June 6, 1944. He provided anti-aircraft cover, and was under continuous fire for 15 days. In the confusion of the battle, he remembers only one confirmed hit. Unfortunately, it was an American plane. Berra recalls that "the pilot was mad as hell," and that "you could hear him (the pilot) swearing as he floated down" to be picked up by another LCI (R).

After service overseas, he was sent to New London, Connecticut, where he was assigned to the welfare and recreation section until his discharge in May 1945.

Howard Cosell. Sportscaster, attorney, author.

Certainly one of the best known sportscaster to ever call a play over the air, Howard Cosell became one of the most loved and most reviled men in broadcasting for "telling it like it is." Born Howard Cohen in Winston-Salem, North Carolina, on March 25, 1920, Cosell was a good student. He entered New York University School of Law, edited the law review, and passed the bar by the age of 21.

Cosell enlisted in the U.S. Army as a private shortly after WWII began, and took basic training in Brooklyn. He rose to the rank of technical sergeant before applying for OCS (Officers Candidate School).

He was accepted, and sent to Transportation Corps School at Mississippi State University. Upon graduation, he was commissioned a second lieutenant and was assigned to the Port of New York as a transportation planner. He was rapidly promoted to captain, then shortly after to major, making him possibly the youngest major in the U.S. Army.

The New York Port of Embarkation was the largest stateside

port shipping out personnel and material. Major Cosell negotiated contracts with the International Longshoreman's Union, and exercised supervision of over 50,000 civilian employees. It was at the port that Cosell met and married Mary Edith Adams, a WAC stationed under his command. Because she was enlisted, written permission was required for the two of them to date.

After his discharge at war's end, he opened a law office in Manhattan but became less interested in law, finally switching to sports broadcasting, taking a job with ABC in 1956. He covered the Mexico City Olympics in 1968, the Munich Olympics in 1972, and had a long career on *Monday Night Football* from its inception in 1970. In a business dominated by former athletes, Cosell brought flair and intelligence to sports commentary.

Jay Hanna "Dizzy" Dean. Baseball pitching great.

Born in Lucas, Arkansas, on January 16, 1911, Dean lied about his age and enlisted in the army in 1927 to escape the life of a migrant cotton picker. He was only 16 years old at the time. He was sent to Fort Sam Houston and assigned to the 12th Field Artillery, where he served for three years.

Introduced to the game of baseball while in the army, he enjoyed such success on the company baseball team that he decided to join a semi-pro team upon his discharge in 1930. He entered the Major Leagues with the St. Louis Cardinals in 1932, and was elected to the Baseball Hall of Fame in 1953. He was the first of only two men to pitch a 30-game winning season.

Jack Dempsey. Heavyweight boxing champion.

Born William Harrison Dempsey in Manassa, Colorado, on June 24, 1895, Dempsey became the World Heavyweight Boxing Champion in 1919 at age 24 when he defeated Jess Willard in four rounds. Dempsey tried to enlist in the army after Pearl Harbor, but was rejected for being too old at 47 years of age, despite the fact that he was in excellent condition.

Early in 1942 he accepted a commission as a full commander

in the U.S. Coast Guard where he was named director of physical training, stationed at Sheepshead Bay, New York.

In July of 1945 Dempsey was sent to the Central Pacific theater as a morale officer, where he landed with the assault troops at the invasion of Okinawa. He ended his service with a war bond tour before being discharged in November 1945.

Joe DiMaggio. Baseball great.

Born in Martinez, California, on November 25, 1914, DiMaggio was playing ball for the New York Yankees when WWII started. Although he was classified 3-A for being married and over 28 years of age, "Joltin Joe" voluntarily gave up his deferment and $43,500-a-year salary to enlist in the U.S. Army Air Corps in 1943 as a private at $50 a month.

DiMaggio spent 31 months in the military, serving as a PT (Physical Training) instructor in programs stateside and in Hawaii. He spent considerable time in military hospitals with a stomach ulcer, and was discharged as a staff sergeant in 1945. He returned to the Yankees.

DiMaggio played in ten World Series, set the longest hitting streak in major league baseball (56 games), married Marilyn Monroe in 1954, and was voted into the Baseball Hall of Fame in 1955.

Abner Doubleday. Credited with creating baseball.

Born in Ballston Spa, New York, on June 26, 1819, Doubleday graduated from West Point in 1842, and hoped for a career as a civil engineer. He was assigned instead to the artillery, where he served in the Mexican and Seminole Wars rising to the rank of first lieutenant in 1847 and captain in 1855.

Doubleday was stationed at Ft. Sumter when it was fired upon by Confederate troops on April 12, 1861. He returned fire, the first Union shot of the war. In May he was transferred to the 17th Infantry as its major. He saw service in the lower Shenandoah Valley and in the defense of Washington.

Promoted to brigadier general of volunteers in 1862, he led a brigade into combat at Rappahannock, Second Bull Run, South Mountain, Antietam and Fredericksburg.

By July 1863 Doubleday was a major general of volunteers, and commanded the 1st Corps at the Battle of Gettysburg after the death of General John Reynolds on the field. He was passed over for permanent command of the corps, and spent the rest of the war assigned to administrative duties in Washington DC. His meritorious service at Gettysburg has only recently been acknowledged. He retired from active service in 1873.

He is credited with creating the modern game of baseball while attending school at Cooperstown, New York. He died in Mendham, New Jersey on January 26, 1893.

Whitey Ford. Pitcher, New York Yankees.

Born Edward Charles Ford in Manhattan, New York, on October 21, 1928, Ford was playing ball for the Yankee ballclub when he was inducted into the army in 1951.

He was assigned to Ft. Monmouth, New Jersey, after basic training as a lineman in the Signal Corps. His fall from a telephone pole caused his reassignment to a desk job as a radar operator. He was discharged in 1953 and returned to the Yankees.

Curt Gowdy. Sportscaster.

Born in Green River, Wyoming, in 1919, Gowdy was commissioned and called to active duty after graduating from the University of Wyoming in 1942.

He requested assignment to the Air Corps but injured his back while doing calisthenics prior to beginning flight training. After four months in an army hospital, he was given a medical discharge for a ruptured disc in 1943 after eight months of service.

He went on to a career in radio and television as a popular play-by-play sportscaster.

Roosevelt "Rosey" Grier. Football lineman.

Born on a farm in Cuthbert, Alabama, on July 24, 1932, Grier was playing pro football for the New York Giants when he was inducted into the army, completely missing the 1957 season. He was discharged in 1958, and returned to the Giants ballclub, winning All-Pro twice. He was a bodyguard for Senator Robert Kennedy during his campaign for President in 1968 when Kennedy was shot by Sirhan Sirhan at the Ambassador Hotel in Los Angeles.

Woody Hayes. Legendary football coach.

Called the "General Patton of college football," Wayne Woodrow Hayes was born in Clifton, Ohio, on February 14, 1913. He earned a master's degree in education from Ohio State in 1939. He joined the U.S. Navy in 1941 and earned a commission as an ensign. He served as athletic director in charge of exercise programs at Norfolk. Toward the end of the war, he served aboard a destroyer escort in the Pacific.

Hayes was discharged as a lieutenant commander in 1946, and took a position as coach at Dennison University. He went on to unprecedented success for over two decades as head coach of Ohio State's football team, winning two national championships. He died in Upper Arlington, Ohio, on March 12, 1987.

Gil Hodges. Baseball Hall of Famer.

Born Gilbert Raymond Hodges in Princeton, Indiana, on April 4, 1924, Hodges was called up into the marines in September 1943 and was sent to the South Pacific as part of the 16th Anti-Aircraft Battalion. He saw action at Tinian and Okinawa and was discharged as a sergeant in February 1945 after 18 months of active service. He returned to baseball, and played in seven World Series and six All-Star games for the New York Dodgers (later Los Angeles Dodgers). He died in West Palm Beach, Florida, on April 2, 1972.

Ralph George Houk. Yankee manager, catcher.

Born on August 9, 1919, on a 160-acre farm near Lawrence, Kansas, Houk was the fourth of five children. He grew up in a family of semi-professional ballplayers and made "all-state" on his high school baseball team. He began his baseball career as a catcher with a Yankees minor league franchise in 1939.

At the beginning of WWII, Houk and his brother Harold enlisted as privates in the army in 1942. Houk's first assignment was to "whip into shape" the Ft. Leavenworth baseball team. He was rapidly accepted into officer's training.

Sent to Ft. Knox for armor officer training, he was commissioned a second lieutenant after graduation, and sent overseas to England with the 89th Cavalry Reconnaissance Squadron of the 9th Armored Division. (Although the division didn't have an "official" nickname, it was called the "Remagen" Division.) Brought into the line in September 1944, the division saw its first major action at the Battle of the Bulge, holding two crital roads against intense German attacks for 48 hours, allowing the 101st Airborne (the "Screaming Eagles") to enter and hold Bastogne. In January the division crossed the Roer River and drove to the Rhine. It earned its nickname by capturing the Remagen Bridge over the Rhine intact on March 7, 1945, which considerably shortened the European war. Elements of the division fought in the Ruhr pocket, and others captured Frankfurt. In April the entire division encircled Leipzig, and were in Czechoslovakia when the war ended.

From the Normandy invasion, and across France, Houk's unit scouted in advance of the division's eastward thrust. On one occasion in the Ardennes Forest, his unit was isolated from the rest of his battalion in a Luxembourg town when they were confronted by six enemy tanks. Houk slipped through enemy lines, retrieved a tank destroyer, and returned to engage and destroy the tanks for which he was awarded the Silver Star.

On another occasion, a sniper's bullet narrowly missed its mark, passing through his helmet, but leaving him untouched.

He was mustered out at the end of the war as a major, and additionally won the Bronze Star and Purple Heart. Houk returned to baseball, getting to "The Bigs" in 1947. He replaced the legendary Yankee manager Casey Stengel on October 20, 1960. He won three pennants and two World Series as manager.

Tom Landry. Superbowl-winning football coach.

Born Thomas W. Landry in Mission, Texas, on September 11, 1924, Landry was a freshman on a football scholarship at the University of Texas in the fall of 1942. When he learned that his brother Robert, an army pilot in Europe, was missing in action, Landry enlisted into the U.S. Army Air Corps as a private in Austin, Texas, on December 12, 1942.

After ground school at Sheppard Field in Texas, and pilot training in Missouri and Oklahoma, Landry graduated and was commissioned a second lieutenant and pilot. He took multi-engine training at Sioux City, Iowa, where he learned to fly B-17s, and by the fall of 1944 Landry was en route to England as part of the 862nd Bomber Squadron, 493rd Bombardment Group ("Helton's Hellcats") assigned to the 8th Air Force at Debach, England. It was the last 8th Air Force group to go operational.

Landry flew 30 missions over Germany and Occupied Europe and was shot down once. After the war, First Lieutenant Landry was discharged in Sioux City, Iowa, on November 15, 1945. He earned the Air Medal with four Oak Leaf Clusters.

As head coach of the Dallas Cowboys football team (1960–88), Landry won two Superbowls and was voted into the Football Hall of Fame in 1990.

Joe Louis. Heavyweight boxing champion.

Born Joseph Louis Barrow in a shack outside Lexington, Alabama, on May 13, 1914, Louis won the heavyweight boxing championship after defeating James Braddock on June 22, 1937, successfully defended the title 25 times, and retired as champion in 1949.

Joe Louis, middle; Sugar Ray Robinson, right

During WWII, Louis served as a sergeant in special services, fighting in exhibition matches stateside and overseas for the troops. He donated his winnings from two title fights to the Army-Navy Relief Fund.

Rocky Marciano. Heavyweight boxing champion.

Born Rocco Francis Marchegiano in Brockton, Massachusetts, on September 1, 1923, Marciano won the heavyweight championship by defeating Jersey Joe Walcott for the title on September 23, 1952.

Drafted into the U.S. Army in 1943, Marciano was assigned to the 150th Combat Engineers. He was stationed in Wales where he was involved in operations on the English Channel. The 150th was awarded service stars for Normandy, Northern France, Rheineland, Ardennes-Asace and Central Europe.

It was in the army that Marciano first boxed, starting with unofficial bouts, and working up to junior amateur by the time of his discharge in 1947. After failing a tryout for catcher with the Chicago Cubs baseball team, Marciano returned to boxing. His record was 49 wins, no losses.

Willie Mays. Baseball Hall of Famer.

Born Willie Howard Mays Jr. in Fairfield, Alabama, on May 6, 1931, Mays was already playing semi-pro baseball for the Birmingham Black Barons of the American Negro League at the age of 14.

After his team, the New York Giants, lost the 1951 World Series, and after he won the vote for the National League's Rookie of the Year, Mays was drafted into the army in May 1952. He served stateside at Ft. Eustis, Virginia, until his discharge in March 1954.

After basic training, which was easy for Mays because of his physical conditioning, he was assigned to the physical training section as a ballplayer/instructor. He spent his two years playing ball, hitting .480 and .389. He holds third place for the number of home runs after Hank Aaron and Babe Ruth.

Jim McKay. Sportscaster.

Born James Kenneth McManus in Philadelphia, Pennsylvania, on September 24, 1921, McKay earned a bachelor's degree in 1943 and promptly enlisted in the U.S. Navy. He was commissioned an ensign and served for three years aboard a minesweeper in the Pacific theater. He was discharged in 1946 with the rank of full lieutenant. He was the first sportscaster to win an Emmy award.

Stan Musial. Baseball Hall of Famer.

Born Stanley Frank Musial on November 21, 1920, in Donora, Pennsylvania, Musial spent the majority of WWII breaking record after record in the National League, playing in All-Star games, and being voted Most Valuable Player. In 1944 Musial was called up and entered the U.S. Navy.

Assigned to the Bainbridge Training Center in Maryland as a seaman first class, then later at Pearl Harbor, Musial spent his spare time improving his batting technique. He was discharged in 1946 after 13 months of service. He returned to the St. Louis Cardinals in time to play in the 1946 World Series. He retired from baseball in 1964 and was voted into the Hall of Fame in 1969.

Arnold Palmer. Golf champion.

Born in Youngstown, Pennsylvania, on September 10, 1929, Palmer served for three years in the U.S. Coast Guard (1951–54). He was stationed in New Jersey, Connecticut and Ohio. It is unknown if he played golf during that time.

Palmer won four Master's Tournaments and was the first golfer to earn over a million dollars in one year.

Edward "Eddie" Rickenbacker. Race car champion, aviator.

Born Edward Vernon Rickenbacker on October 8, 1890, in Columbus, Ohio, he was already famous as America's highest paid race car driver ($40,000 a year) when the U.S. entered WWI. Rickenbacker promptly enlisted in the army, and hoped to get into the Air Corps, but was disqualified because of his height and 7th grade education. He was assigned as a driver to Colonel William "Billy" Mitchell on General Pershing's staff where he rose to the rank of sergeant.

Despite the fact that at 27 Rickenbacker was two years too old for aviator school, Colonel Mitchell used his influence to get Rickenbacker admitted to the primary flying school at Tours, France. He was commissioned a lieutenant and pilot upon graduation. He was assigned to the 94th Aero Squadron, the first American aviation unit in France.

Rickenbacker downed 22 planes and four balloons, and was promoted to captain and commanding officer of the 94th in September 1918. In one action on September 25, 1918, he single-handedly attacked seven planes, downing two, which earned him the Medal of Honor. Rickenbacker also earned the Distinguished Service Cross with nine oak leaves, and the Croix de Guerre. He was 28 when the war ended but he continued to have an interest in aviation for the rest of his life.

During WWII, while on an inspection tour for Secretary of War Stimson in October 1942, his plane was downed 500 miles north of Samoa. Rickenbacker and seven others endured exposure in a life raft for 23 days before being rescued. Two weeks later, Rickenbacker was back at work, en route to Guadalcanal.

He served as the head of Eastern Airlines from 1938 to 1963 and died in Zurich, Switzerland, on July 23, 1973.

Branch Rickey. Baseball executive, co-owner of the Brooklyn Dodgers.

Born in Stockdale, Ohio, in 1881, Rickey is best remembered as the man who integrated major league baseball by signing Jackie Robinson to a contract with the Brooklyn Dodgers.

Rickey was with the St. Louis Cardinals ballclub when the U.S. entered WWI. With the War Department's "Work or Fight" order issued on Labor Day 1918, Rickey enlisted in the army at age 36. He was commissioned into the newly formed Chemical Warfare Corps, and was a major by the time of his discharge shortly after the war ended.

His baseball career included manager of the St. Louis Cardinals, leading them to six pennants and four World Series titles. In 1945 he became co-owner of the Brooklyn Dodgers and served as general manager and president. He died on December 9, 1965, suffering a heart attack while delivering a speech at his induction into the Missouri Sports Hall of Fame. He was inducted into the Baseball Hall of Fame in 1967.

Robert Larimore "Bobby" Riggs. Tennis champion.

Born in Los Angeles on February 25, 1918, Riggs took basic training at Great Lakes Naval Training Center after enlisting in the navy during WWII. He served as an athletic specialist in

Hawaii and Guam, playing tennis at navy bases across the Pacific until his discharge in November 1945.

Riggs won Wimbledon and was on a winning Davis Cup team but is best remembered for his "match of the century" against Billie Jean King in 1973 (which he lost).

Brooks Robinson. Baseball player, Baltimore Orioles.

Born Brooks Calbert Robinson Jr. in Little Rock, Arkansas, on May 18, 1937, Robinson served six months active duty with the Arkansas National Guard from October 1958 to April 1959.

Jack Roosevelt "Jackie" Robinson. First black major league ballplayer.

Born in Cairo, Georgia, on January 31, 1919, Robinson became the first black ballplayer to play in the major leagues when he joined the Brooklyn Dodgers in 1947. He earned Rookie of the Year the same year and had a lifetime batting average of .311.

Because blacks were not allowed to play professional football in the States, Robinson was playing for the semi-professional Honolulu Bears in 1941. He was returning to the U.S. aboard a ship when Pearl Harbor was attacked on December 7. After receiving his induction notice in March of 1942, he entered the army on April 3, 1942.

After taking basic training at Ft. MacArthur in Los Angeles, Robinson was sent to Ft. Riley, Kansas, and was assigned to a cavalry unit. He spent his days tending the horses and cleaning the stables. He applied for OCS (Officers Candidate School) but was turned down because of his race. It was through the influence of boxing champion Joe Louis, who was serving as a sergeant at Ft. Riley, and his high profile connections, that the ban was lifted and a small group of blacks, including Robinson, was enrolled in a class.

Robinson was commissioned a second lieutenant of cavalry and was assigned as morale officer to the black troops. This assignment involved dealing with racism and the preferential treatment of white troops. In one instance Robinson complained to the base provost marshal about the segregation of the base canteen. Black troops were restricted to using the canteen only during certain hours, and those were the hours they were on duty, effectively keeping them out of the canteen. The provost marshal answered by asking, "Well, would you want your wife to have to sit next to a nigger?" Robinson added that to his list of grievances and went to the base commander.

Robinson's questioning of discriminatory practices at Ft. Riley earned him a transfer to a tank battalion at Ft. Hood in Texas, and orders to prepare for service overseas. It was at Ft. Hood that his football ankle injury was first documented.

In April 1943, Lt. Robinson was transferred to the 761st Tank Battalion as a platoon leader in Company B. The 761st was an all-black armor unit nicknamed the "Black Panthers." It too had recently been transferred to Ft. Hood. Previously stationed at Ft. Claiborne, Louisiana, the unit was transferred after the mistreatment of black troops in nearby towns got so bad that the unit armed their weapons and tanks and headed for town. A violent confrontation was only narrowly avoided.

On July 6, 1944, Robinson's refusal to move to the back of a civilian bus operating on base, despite the fact that discrimination was prohibited by regulation on army facilities, caused him to be brought up on three charges.

Charged with insubordination and conduct unbecoming an officer, Robinson demanded a court-martial, and was acquitted on all charges. He was granted a medical discharge in November of 1944, but was "honorably relieved from active duty by reason of physical disqualification" rather than honorably discharged, and so was ineligible for veteran's benefits. He was officially discharged as a first lieutenant on November 28, 1944.

This "injury" did not keep Robinson from accepting a position on the Kansas City Monarch baseball team of the Negro American League. In 1947 Brooklyn Dodger owner Branch Rickey broke the color barrier by signing Jackie Robinson as the first black in major league baseball.

Sugar Ray Robinson. Boxing champion. (See photo, p. 245)

Born Walter Smith Jr. in Detroit on May 3, 1921, Robinson won the Golden Gloves for featherweights in 1939 and the lightweights in 1940. In 1951 he won the middleweight title from Jake Lamotta.

After being drafted on February 27, 1943, Robinson was sent to basic training at Ft. Dix, New Jersey, and then was assigned to the Air Corps at Mitchell Field in Long Island, outside New York City. He spent his time coaching the boxing team and guarding airplanes. He married Edna May Holly on May 29, 1943, and continued to box professionally when on leave.

Robinson was promoted to corporal late in 1943, and was sent on a boxing tour of army and Air Corps bases with Sgt. Joe Louis. At Keesler Field in Mississippi, Robinson refused to box because the black troops (the army was still segregated in 1943) were not allowed to attend. He faced down a general officer and won. Robinson was promoted to sergeant, and scheduled to go overseas to Europe to entertain the troops. Prior to departing, he was required to attend advanced infantry training at Camp Seibert, Alabama.

While there, he and Louis got into a fight with white military policemen at a segregated bus stop, and were arrested. The charges were quietly dropped.

On March 29, 1944, at Ft. Hamilton, Robinson tripped down some stairs and suffered amnesia for three days. After neurological tests at Halloran General Hospital, Robinson was given a medical discharge as a sergeant on June 3, 1944. He returned to boxing, retiring in December 1965.

After his retirement, Robinson devoted himself to the Sugar Ray Robinson Youth Foundation. In his 25-year professional career he had 174 victories (110 knockouts) and was elected to the

Boxing Hall of Fame in 1967. He died in Culver City, California, on April 12, 1989.

Duke Snider. Baseball Hall of Famer.

Born Edward Donald Snider in Los Angeles on September 19, 1926, Snider enlisted in the U.S. Navy in December of 1944 at age 18. He spent 11 months in the Pacific aboard the USS *Sperry*, a submarine tender. He was discharged as a fireman second class in May 1945. Snider is the only man to hit four home runs in a World Series, twice (1952 and 1955). He played for the Brooklyn Dodgers (later Los Angeles Dodgers).

Warren Edward Spahn. Baseball record holder.

Born April 23, 1921, in Buffalo, New York, Spahn was drafted into the army late in 1942. He was assigned to the 276th Combat Engineers and saw combat at Remagen Bridge on the Rhine where he was wounded by shrapnel and earned a battlefield commission.

By the time of his discharge in 1946, Spahn was a lieutenant with a Bronze Star and Purple Heart. He is the only major league ballplayer to earn a battlefield commission. He returned to baseball and won his 300th game while pitching for the Milwaukee Braves on August 11, 1961. He was inducted into the Baseball Hall of Fame in 1973.

Roger Staubach. Superbowl-winning quarterback.

Born in Cincinnati, Ohio, on February 5, 1942, Staubach had his choice of football scholarships after high school, but chose the U.S. Naval Academy after being rejected by Notre Dame. Notre Dame later reversed itself but by then it was too late.

At his pre-entry physical at Fitzsimmons Army Hospital, an inattentive corpsman failed to notice that Staubach was partially colorblind. This would have disqualified him from the Naval Academy. When it was discovered later, he was restricted from flight training.

Roger Staubach

While at the Academy, Staubach was chosen as a future draft choice by both Kansas City and Dallas. He settled on Dallas which offered a $10,000 signing bonus and $500 a month while on active duty. While at Annapolis, Staubach made All-American and won the Heisman Trophy.

After graduating in 1965, Staubach did three years active duty with the navy, one year of it as a freight terminal officer at Chu Lai in Vietnam.

In 1968, while still in the navy, Staubach attended the Dallas Cowboys' training camp with the intention of staying in the navy if he didn't make the cut. He made the team and joined them after his discharge from the navy as a full lieutenant in January 1969. He played in five Superbowls with the Dallas Cowboys, winning two. He was voted into the Football Hall of Fame in 1985.

James Francis "Jim" Thorpe. All-American athlete.

Born of Sac and Fox Indian descent in Indian Territory (Oklahoma) on May 28, 1888, Thorpe had a career as an Olympic track star, and professional baseball and football player. He won Gold Medals in the pentathlon and decathlon at the Stockholm Olympics in 1912, and played major league baseball (1913–19) and professional football (1915–29).

Too old for service in the military during WWII, Thorpe signed up with the merchant marine in 1945, and sailed aboard ammunition ships in the Atlantic until the end of the war. In 1950 the Associated Press sportswriters named Thorpe the greatest athlete of the first half of the 20th Century. He died in Los Angeles on March 28, 1953.

Lee Trevino. Golf champion.

Born in Dallas, Texas, on December 1, 1939, Trevino was working as a caddie when he enlisted in the U.S. Marine Corps at 17 in 1956. By the second year of his second enlistment, he was assigned to the 3rd Marine Division's golf team. He won tournaments in Japan, Taiwan, and the Philippines.

He was discharged from the marines in 1961, and continued his golf career, becoming the first player to win all three Open tournaments (U.S., British, and Canadian).

Gene Tunney. Heavyweight boxing champion.

Born James Joseph Tunney in New York City on May 25, 1898, Tunney enlisted in the army after being turned down by the marines. By June 1918 he was en route to France aboard a troop-ship.

Tunney boxed as a member of the American Expeditionary Force as a light heavyweight, and won the championship in Paris in 1918. He was discharged in 1919 and continued to box. He won the World Heavyweight Championship from Jack Dempsey in 1926, and retired undefeated in 1928.

He directed the athletic and physical fitness programs for the U.S. Navy during WWII and died in Greenwich, Connecticut, on November 7, 1978.

Ted Williams. Baseball Hall of Famer.

Williams was duck hunting on the morning of December 7, 1941, and by his own admission was too involved with baseball to take much notice of world affairs in Europe and Asia.

In January 1941 Williams had been classified 1-A, but appealed stating that he was his mother's sole support. He was reclassified 3-A. In 1942 he signed a $30,000 contract with the Red Sox, but his popularity declined with a public whose sons and husbands were in uniform, so he and five other ballplayers enlisted in naval aviation at the end of the 1942 season.

Called to active duty in November, he was sent to ground school at Amherst College, but a hernia while participating in physical training earned him a two-month stay in Chelsea Naval Hospital. Williams rejoined his unit at Chapel Hill, North Carolina, for preflight training.

Williams took basic and advanced flight training, and was commissioned a marine second lieutenant and pilot upon graduation. He was assigned as a flight instructor. He next took combat training where he set a student gunnery record.

He was in San Francisco awaiting orders overseas when the war ended. He was discharged in time to play in the 1946 World Series, his only Series appearance. Despite being 34, Williams was called up from the inactive reserves in 1952 for service in the Korean War. He was commissioned a captain, and took an eight-week refresher course at Pensacola, Florida. He volunteered for jet pilot training, and after completing operational and cold weather training, he shipped out for Japan and Korea.

Williams was assigned to the 223rd Squadron of the 3rd Marine Air Wing flying F9F Panther jets. On one mission, he was attacking enemy troop positions above the 38th parallel when his jet was damaged by small arms fire, causing his plane to catch fire. He ascended to 10,000 feet where the air was thinner. Despite hydraulic system failure, he was able to return to base, but his plane exploded just prior to landing. Williams got out just in time.

Despite inner ear problems, Williams flew 39 missions before being sent to hospitals in Tokyo, Hawaii, and ultimately Bethesda Hospital in Maryland, where he was mustered out of the marines. Many feel that the five seasons of baseball that Williams missed because of his service in two wars, kept him from breaking Babe Ruth's home run record.

John Robert Wooden. Basketball coach.

Born on October 14, 1910, Wooden was an All-American at Purdue University, and played on the All-State basketball team three times. His first coaching job was at Dayton High School in Kentucky for the 1933–34 season. It was his only losing season.

During WWII Wooden was assigned as a PT (physical training) instructor for the U.S. Navy. Ensign Wooden had already received his orders assigning him to the USS *Franklin* (CV-13), an aircraft carrier in the Pacific, when a burst appendix may have saved his life. While recuperating in the hospital, he was replaced aboard the *Franklin* by another officer who was subsequently killed in a kamikaze attack. After his discharge from the navy as a lieutenant, Wooden took a coaching position at Indiana State Teacher's College. He was head coach at UCLA from 1949 to 1975, winning ten NCAA Championships. He was voted into the Basketball Hall of Fame as both a player and a coach, the only man to be so honored.

Section 8

Business and Industry

Wally Amos. Famous Amos cookies.

Born in Tallahassee, Florida, on July 1, 1936, Amos served in the air force from 1953 to 1957. He enlisted because he liked the uniform, and took training in radio/radar repair. While in the air force, he earned his high school diploma.

Roone Pinckney Arledge Jr. TV executive and producer.

Born in Forest Hills, New York, on July 8, 1931, Arledge earned a B.A. from Columbia University in 1952. He was drafted into the army shortly afterward, and spent two years at the Aberdeen Proving Ground in Maryland assigned as a public affairs officer where he produced and directed public relations radio spots promoting nuclear power.

As president of ABC Sports, Arledge introduced such television innovations as stop-action and split screens. He later served as president of ABC News.

John Jacob Astor. Capitalist, inventor.

Born in Rhinebeck, New York, in 1864, the great-grandson of fur trader John Jacob Astor (1763–1848), Astor graduated Harvard in 1888. He built the Astoria Hotel adjoining his cousin's Waldorf Hotel in 1897 creating the Waldorf-Astoria Hotel.

Commissioned a lieutenant colonel of volunteers in May 1898, Astor served in Cuba during the Spanish-American War. He campaigned actively and was present at the surrender of Santiago. He died in 1912, a passenger on the maiden voyage of the *Ti-*

tanic. He was the wealthiest man in America at the time of his death.

Bill Blass. Fashion designer.

Born in Ft. Wayne, Indiana, on June 22, 1922, Blass enlisted in the army at the start of WWII. For the next three and a half years, Blass was assigned to the 603rd Engineer Camouflage Battalion as a camouflage worker creating just the right color combinations.

Blass saw service in Germany, Holland, France and England, and was discharged after the war with the rank of corporal. He went on to become one of the most noted fashion designers in the world.

Adolphus Busch. Brewer, businessman.

Born in Mainz, Germany, on July 10, 1839, Busch and his brother Ulrich married two sisters, Lilly and Anna Anhueser, in St. Louis and started the Anhueser-Busch Brewery with their father-in-law.

During the Civil War, Adolphus took time away from the business to enlist in a Missouri militia company where he rose to the rank of corporal by the end of the war. He is fondly remembered as the man who developed the process for bottling beer. He died in Germany in 1913.

Oleg Cassini. Costume and fashion designer.

Born in Paris on April 11, 1913, Cassini was designing costumes for the movies when WWII erupted. Upon obtaining his U.S. citizenship in July 1942, Cassini joined the U.S. Coast Guard with Victor Mature and Ray Stark and patrolled the California coast in Mature's yacht, *The Bar Bill*, where he was assigned as cook. He would patrol during the day, and occasionally attend premieres in the evening, working 48 hours on, 48 hours off.

Because of a naval tradition of allowing only "native-borns" to be officers, Cassini's mother used her influence to get an act of Congress passed, permitting him to transfer to the U.S. Army cavalry, and in November of 1942, he reported to Ft. Riley, Kansas, for basic training. He was in the last cavalry class trained with horses, and his polo experience quickly earned him a promotion to corporal.

After surviving stampedes and tornadoes, he was accepted for OCS, graduated, and was commissioned a second lieutenant. He was an unusual officer, wearing pajamas on maneuvers, and being disciplined for a food fight in the officer's club.

In October of 1942 he was transferred to military intelligence because of his fluency in French and Italian. Selected for a mission, he was transferred to Camp Patrick Henry, Virginia, pending orders, but the birth of his handicapped daughter caused him to request reassignment to the cavalry.

Early in 1945 he was transferred to Hollywood and assigned to the 9th Service Command where his primary duty seems to have been locating starlets to date his commanding officer. After brief service guarding relocation camps near Gila, Arizona, Cassini was given a medical discharge (for asthma) with the rank of first lieutenant. He returned to costume design in Hollywood. He was the exclusive designer for First Lady Jacqueline Kennedy.

Marshall Field III. Publisher, banker, philanthropist.

Born in Chicago on September 28, 1893, the grandson of Marshall Field, founder of the Chicago department store, Field enlisted as a private in the U.S. Army ten days after America's entry into WWI.

He served in the 1st Illinois Cavalry, a National Guard unit, which was changed to the 122nd Field Artillery, at Camp Logan, Texas. In March 1918 he was sent overseas, saw action at St. Mihiel and the Meuse-Argonne, was decorated for bravery, and was discharged as a captain in January of 1919. Field founded the *Chicago Sun* newspaper in 1941.

Marshall Field IV. Publisher, newsman.

Born in New York City on September 4, 1917, the great-grandson of Marshall Field, Field was born into one of the wealthiest of American families. After Harvard, and law school at the University of Virginia where he was class president and editor of the law review, he was set to clerk for Supreme Court Justice J. Stanley Reed when Pearl Harbor interrupted his plans. He promptly joined the navy.

He resigned his initial commission as an ensign to attend a 120-day midshipman's school at Northwestern University in Illinois because he wanted an assignment aboard ship. He was recommissioned an ensign in June 1942 and was sent to the Pacific theater. Assigned as a gunnery officer aboard the USS *Enterprise* (CV-6), an aircraft carrier, he saw action in 12 major naval engagements.

He was wounded twice at the Battle of Santa Cruz (Oct. 26, 1942) which earned him a Silver Star and a Purple Heart. He was discharged as a lieutenant commander in 1945.

Harvey Samuel Firestone Jr. Businessman, inventor.

Born in Chicago on April 20, 1898, Firestone enlisted in the U.S. Navy during WWI and served in the Naval Aviation Corps.

He served as CEO and chairman of Firestone Tire and Rubber Company until 1963, seeing it grow to 121 plants in 29 countries. He died on June 1, 1973.

Malcolm Forbes. Publisher, sportsman.

Millionaire, publisher, art collector, politician, and balloonist, Forbes was born in Brooklyn on August 19, 1919. He founded his first newspaper, the *Lancaster Tribune*, after graduating from Princeton, where he founded an undergraduate magazine.

Inducted into the army as a pri-

Malcolm Forbes

vate at the start of WWII, Forbes was assigned to a heavy machine gun section in the 334th Infantry, 84th Infantry Division. He served in France, Belgium, Holland and Germany. Wounded in the thigh in combat just prior to the Battle of the Bulge, he spent ten months recovering in military hospitals before being discharged in August 1945 with the rank of staff sergeant. He was awarded of the Bronze Star and Purple Heart.

He went on to set the record for the first coast-to-coast hot air balloon flight. He was the publisher of *Forbes* magazine from 1957 until his death on February 24, 1990.

Henry Ford II. Industrialist.

Born in Detroit on September 4, 1917, the grandson of automobile pioneer Henry Ford, Ford left Yale in June of 1940 without graduating when it was discovered that his senior thesis was ghostwritten. This wasn't a serious setback since he was already a director of the Ford Motor Company since 1938.

When it appeared that Ford was going to be drafted into the army in 1941, he joined the U.S. Navy, and spent two years on shore duty rising from ensign to lieutenant. Ford requested sea duty in 1943 but the death of his father necessitated that he leave the navy to assume control of Ford Motor Company. This was at the encouragement of Secretary of the Navy Frank Knox, who felt that stable leadership at Ford was more vital to the war effort. Ford successfully revitalized the Ford Motor Company.

Fred W. Friendly. Radio/television executive.

Born Ferdinand Friendly Wachenheimer in New York City on October 30, 1915, Friendly was a business major at Nichols Junior College, Massachusetts, in 1937 when he began working at radio station WEAN in Providence, Rhode Island.

With the outbreak of WWII, Friendly enlisted in the U.S. Army. Because he was familiar with radio, he was assigned as an instructor with the Signal Corps. He served in both Europe and the Pacific as a correspondent for *CBI Round-Up*, the military newspaper for the China-Burma-India theater.

Friendly rose to the rank of master sergeant and was awarded the Legion of Merit for valor. He was also awarded the Soldier's Medal for his actions in rescuing survivors of a dock explosion in Bombay, at great risk to his own life.

Friendly was discharged in 1945 and returned to radio. In 1948 he met and became partners with Edward R. Murrow, beginning a collaboration that would become a legend in broadcasting history.

R. Buckminster Fuller. Inventor, engineer.

Born Richard Buckminster Fuller on July 12, 1895, in Milton, Massachusetts, Fuller was commissioned an ensign in the U.S. Navy in 1917, during WWI. After a three-month training course at Annapolis, he received training as an aviator. He served as a commander of crash boats at the Navy Flying School at Newport News, Virginia, and was discharged in 1919 as a lieutenant (j.g.) at the end of the war.

It was during his navy service that he developed his first two practical inventions: a seaplane rescue mast, and a jet stilt for vertical take-off aircraft. He later invented geodesic domes. He died in Los Angeles on July 1, 1983. Fuller often stated that he got the idea for his book *Manual for Spaceship Earth* from his experiences as a naval officer, comparing a planet traveling through space to a ship at sea.

James Gadsden. Railroad president, minister to Mexico.

Born in Charleston, South Carolina, on May 15, 1788, the man responsible for the Gadsden purchase from Mexico was a lieutenant of engineers during the war of 1812. Promoted to captain, he served defending the Gulf frontier in 1818, and was promoted to colonel as Inspector General for the Southern Division of the U.S. Army in 1820. In August 1821 Gadsden was appointed Adjutant General of the Army, but resigned eight months later when the U.S. Senate refused to ratify his appointment. He arranged the Gadsden Purchase in 1853.

John W. Gardner. Founder of Common Cause, cabinet secretary.

Born in 1912 Gardner had two intelligence assignments during WWII. In 1942–43 he was in charge of the Latin American section of the foreign broadcast intelligence service of the FCC which was responsible for monitoring Axis radio propaganda broadcasts in South America.

In 1943 he was commissioned a lieutenant in the U.S. Marine Corps and served first at Harvard University developing criteria and training for new agents of the OSS, and later in Europe and the Mediterranean as part of the OSS. He participated in "Operation Sunrise," facilitating the secret surrender of German forces in northern Italy. He was stationed in Austria at the time of his discharge in 1946, and left the service with the rank of captain.

Upon his discharge, he took a position with the Carnegie Foundation. He helped found Common Cause, a public interest lobby concerned with government reform and accountability, and served as Secretary of Health, Education and Welfare under President Johnson (1965–68).

Daniel Frank Gerber. Baby food manufacturer.

Born on May 6, 1898, in Fremont, Michigan, Gerber enlisted in the U.S. Army after graduating St. John's Military Academy in 1916.

Gerber served as an officer in Europe during WWI and earned the Croix de Guerre for valor. He was discharged in 1919. He founded a company that continues to produce baby food to this day. His slogan, "Babies are our business, our only business" accurately described his business. He died in Fremont, California, on March 16, 1974.

George Franklin Getty II. Corporate executive.

The firstborn son of J. Paul Getty, one of the richest men in the world, Getty was born on July 9, 1924, in Los Angeles, California. He left Princeton in 1942 to enlist in the army reserves and was called to active duty in February of 1943.

Commissioned a second lieutenant in the infantry in 1944, he went on to serve as a war crimes investigator to the legal section of the supreme command for Allied powers. He served 16 months in the Philippines, Malaya, and Japan. He was discharged from the army in 1947.

Berry Gordy. Founder of Motown Records, songwriter.

Born in Detroit in 1929, Gordy was drafted into the army in June of 1951 during the conflict in Korea. Sent for basic training to Camp Chafee, Arkansas, Gordy tried answering incorrectly on the tests at the induction center at Ft. Custer. He applied for special services but was rejected for not having enough experience in entertainment.

Gordy earned a GED degree, and was sent to leadership school before being assigned to an artillery unit. He went overseas to Korea and was sent to Panmunjom near the front lines. He volunteered for an assignment as a chaplain's assistant to avoid combat. He was accepted because of his musical ability. His duties involved driving a jeep, playing the organ, and accompanying the chaplain for services at the front. He learned that the quicker he set up, the quicker they could leave.

After his discharge, Gordy went on to found Motown Records in 1959 and built a record empire with sales of over $50,000,000. He has written countless hit songs.

Harry F. Guggenheim. Businessman, foundation executive.

Probably the best known philanthropist in the world, Guggenheim was born in West End, New Jersey, on Auguest 23, 1890. He served as a naval aviator in WWI which sparked a lifelong interest in flying. He served overseas in England, France, and Italy, and left active service in December 1918 with the rank of lieutenant commander.

Recalled to active service in 1942, he served as commanding

officer of Mercer Naval Field in New Jersey where combat planes were tested before being shipped overseas. Promoted to full commander in 1943, Guggenheim was aboard the aircraft carrier USS *Nehenta Bay* (CVE-74) during the Battles of Okinawa and Sakishima Islands. He was discharged as a captain in 1945 with two naval commendations.

After the war he returned to directing the family foundations and was appointed chairman of the New York Airport Authority. Other members were James Doolittle and Lawrence Rockefeller. He died in Sands Point, New York, on January 22, 1971.

Lou Harris. Public opinion analyst.

Harris was born in New Haven, Connecticut, on January 6, 1921. After graduating with a degree in economics from the University of North Carolina in 1942, he enlisted in the navy during WWII.

Harris rose from apprentice seaman to be commissioned an ensign in command of a patrol boat in the North Atlantic. He also served as the captain of a naval tugboat.

After the war Harris, now promoted to lieutenant (j.g.), was sent to Boston Naval Receiving Station where he gained his first experience in polling. He was assigned by the navy to get the opinions of sailors awaiting demobilization, and the results pleased neither the U.S. Navy nor Boston. He was discharged in 1946.

Conrad Hilton. Hotelier, businessman.

Born Christmas Day 1887 in San Antonio, New Mexico, Conrad Nicholson Hilton was the second of eight children of a prosperous lodgekeeper.

Not surprisingly, Hilton was assigned to the Quartermaster Corps upon joining the U.S. Army in August 1917. Commissioned a second lieutenant, he first was assigned to training officer candidates at the Presidio in San Francisco, and was then sent overseas to France in March 1918 and assigned to the 304th Labor Battalion for service at the front. He helped coordinate the feeding and quartering of the troops. He was discharged in February 1919.

Hilton began buying, and later building, hotels—first in Texas and later throughout the West. He formed the Hilton Hotel Corporation in 1946 and served as its first president. He died in Santa Monica, California, on January 3, 1979.

Jay C. Hormel. Meatpacker, creator of Spam.

Born the son of Hormel Meats founder, George Hormel, in Austin, Minnesota, on September 11, 1892, Hormel was inducted into the army on September 5, 1917. He reported to Camp Dodge, Iowa, as part of the 351st Infantry of the 88th Division. Assigned to Company G, he was promoted to corporal after nine days. Eleven days later he was promoted to regimental sergeant major, and was commissioned a second lieutenant 14 days after that.

Early in 1918 it was discovered that Hormel was knowledgeable in refrigeration, so he was transferred to the quartermaster corps and put in charge of Ice Plant Company #301 which was sent overseas to France for war service.

While there, he developed the process of boning beef before shipping, thereby reducing its bulk by 40%, an important logistical consideration during the war. Hormel was promoted to first lieutenant before being shipped stateside and was discharged in December 1918.

His major contribution to the war effort during WWII was the development of Spam, beloved lunchmeat of GIs on all fronts.

Howard Deering Johnson. Restaurant businessman.

Born in Boston in 1896, the founder of the large restaurant chain enlisted in the army during WWI, and served as a soldier with the AEF (American Expeditionary Force) in France.

He opened his first restaurant in 1929 and the chain grew to over 700 restaurants by 1970. He died in New York City on June 20, 1972.

Robert Wood Johnson. Executive of Johnson & Johnson.

Born in New Brunswick, New Jersey, on April 4, 1893, Johnson was already a vice president in the family business by age 25 in 1918. He was not drafted during WWI and chose to not enlist. At the beginning of WWII he was appointed the rationing administrator for New Jersey. He resigned that position in April of 1942 to take a position with the U.S. Army Ordnance Department, and was commissioned a colonel on May 29. He was placed in charge of the New York Ordnance District.

In January 1943, over the protest of Senator Harry S. Truman who feared creating a business monopoly, Johnson was appointed chairman of the SWPC (Small War Plants Corporation) and vice-chairman of the War Production Board.

Political considerations caused Johnson, now a brigadier general, to resign his commission in August 1943 to return to private industry and plan for the transition to a peacetime, postwar economy. He served as chief executive of Johnson & Johnson (1932–63) and died on January 30, 1968.

Lane Kirkland. Labor union leader, AFL-CIO.

Born Joseph Lane Kirkland in Camden, South Carolina, on March 12, 1922, Kirkland attempted to join the Canadian army when war broke out in Europe in 1939. Unsuccessful, he returned to the States to study at Newberry College, but in 1940 joined the merchant marine as a deck cadet aboard the SS *Liberator*.

In 1941 he attended the newly opened U.S. Merchant Marine Academy at King's Point, Long Island. Upon graduation in 1942, he was appointed a chief mate aboard merchant ships carrying war material to Europe. He served until the end of the war.

Upon completing his masters license, he was required to join Local 688 of the International Organization of Masters, Mates, and Pilots. This would be his only experience as a rank-and-file member of a union. After the war he attended Georgetown University's School of Foreign Service, and took a job as staff researcher for the AFL in 1948 where he rapidly rose in the ranks. He has served as the president of the AFL-CIO since 1979.

Raymond Albert Kroc. McDonald's founder.

Born in Chicago on October 5, 1902, Kroc left high school in Oak Park, Illinois, to enlist as an ambulance driver at the start of WWI. He was only 15 but lied about his age and was accepted into the Red Cross ambulance corps. Sent overseas to France, Kroc served in the same ambulance company as Walt Disney, then aged 16.

Kroc started McDonald's Corporation in 1955, and owned the San Diego Padres from 1974 to 1984.

Paul Mellon. Businessman, philanthropist.

Born in Pittsburgh on June 11, 1907, the son of Andrew Mellon (1855–1937; Secretary of the Treasury, Ambassador to England), Mellon earned his master's degree at Cambridge in 1938. He returned to the United States to attend St. John's College at Annapolis where he enlisted in the army in July 1941.

As a volunteer, Mellon chose the cavalry as his branch of service, and applied for officer candidate school. After nine months as a private, Mellon was commissioned a second lieutenant, and assigned as a horsemanship instructor at Fort Riley, Kansas, where he remained until 1944.

Mellon was sent overseas to England, transferred to the OSS, and finished the war with the rank of major. Since his discharge in 1945, he has spent his time giving large amounts of money to a variety of foundations. His father, Andrew, acquired the family fortune through banking and by investing in Gulf Oil and United States Steel.

Arthur Charles Nielsen. Market research engineer.

Born in Chicago on September 5, 1897, Nielsen, the father of market research, entered the naval reserve upon his graduation from the University of Wisconsin School of Engineering. He served overseas aboard the USS *Manchuria* as an ensign during WWI. He founded his market research firm in 1923.

William S. Paley. Founder of CBS.

Born in Chicago on September 28, 1901, Paley bought United Independent Broadcasting (later CBS) in 1928. In 1943 he turned over the administration of CBS to Paul Westen to accept a position as a civilian advisor to the Office of War Information. He was sent overseas to North Africa to reorganize radio operations.

In April 1945 Paley was commissioned a colonel in the U.S. Army and spent seven months on Eisenhower's staff as deputy chief of the Psychological Warfare Division. After the war in Europe ended in May, Paley helped organize press operations in occupied Germany. He was awarded both the Medal of Merit and the Legion of Merit, as well as the French Croix de Guerre with Palm, and the Order of the Crown from Italy. He was demobilized in November 1945 and returned to reorganize CBS.

H. Ross Perot. Industrialist, presidential candidate.

Born in Texarkana, Texas, on June 27, 1930, Perot broke horses from the age of six, and had his own distribution deal with the Texarkana *Gazette* by age 12. He was an Eagle Scout and was accepted to the U.S. Naval Academy at Annapolis in 1949.

He graduated 454th in a class of 925 but was voted all-around best midshipman. He was commissioned an ensign in June 1953 and was en route to Korea aboard the destroyer USS *Sigourney* (DD-643) when the war ended. His next assignment was as assistant navigator on the aircraft carrier USS *Leyte* (CV-32).

H. Ross Perot

Perot was dissatisfied with the navy's system of promoting by seniority rather than by merit, so he declined to remain in the navy, and was discharged as a full lieutenant in 1957. He went to work for IBM, selling computers.

David Rockefeller. Banker, economist, philanthropist.

Born in New York City on June 12, 1915, Rockefeller enlisted in the army as a private in 1942, shortly after earning his doctorate in economics from the University of Chicago. He was accepted for officer's training and was commissioned a second lieutenant after his graduation.

He was sent overseas to North Africa and later to France. He earned a Legion of Merit and the French Legion of Honor before being discharged as a captain in 1945.

Harland Sanders. Kentucky Colonel Sanders.

Born on a farm in Henryville, Indiana, on September 9, 1890, Sanders served for one year in the U.S. Army in Cuba in 1906. It is doubtful that the title "Colonel" resulted from his military service. He founded Kentucky Fried Chicken in 1956.

David Sarnoff. Chairman RCA and RKO, businessman.

Born outside Minsk, Russia, on February 27, 1891, Sarnoff came to the United States at an early age and is credited with being the first telegraph operator to respond to the distress call of the *Titanic* on April 14, 1912.

Sarnoff was working for RCA (Radio Corporation of America), a division of General Electric, at the outbreak of WWI. Wireless communication was a recent innovation and had never been utilized in wartime. During WWI all wireless facilities were placed under the control of the Navy Department. Sarnoff spent the war as a civilian negotiating contracts and advising Congress on communications issues.

Sarnoff was commissioned a lieutenant colonel in the Signal Corps of the army reserve in 1924. He attended the War College in 1926, and was promoted to full colonel in 1931.

Called back to active duty during WWII, Colonel Sarnoff was sent to London to serve on General Eisenhower's staff. He worked out of SHAEF headquarters (Supreme Headquarters Allied Expeditionary Forces) as a special assistant for communications. He coordinated all communications between SHAEF and the Normandy invasion forces on D-Day in June of 1944. He met with Churchill and organized Anglo-American broadcasting facilities. He also helped restore communications in liberated France.

Promoted, Brigadier General Sarnoff was discharged in December 1945. He returned to RCA where he preferred to be addressed as "General."

Robert W. Sarnoff. Radio/television executive.

Born in New York City on July 2, 1918, the son of David Sarnoff, Sarnoff graduated Harvard and attended law school at Columbia University. Upon graduation, he went to work for Bill Donovan in the Office of the Coordinator of Information (later the OSS) in Washington DC.

Commissioned an ensign in the navy in March 1942, he was assigned as a communications officer for the Chief of Naval Operations, Admiral Halsey. He spent two years in the Pacific setting up a radio network. In December of 1944, he returned to the U.S. to serve as liaison with the broadcasting industry in Los Angeles. He was discharged late in 1945 as a full lieutenant. Sarnoff returned to broadcasting to rise to president of NBC in 1955.

George M. Steinbrenner. Shipbuilder, baseball executive.

Born in Rocky River, Ohio, on July 4, 1930, Steinbrenner enlisted in the U.S. Air Force in 1952 after graduating Williams College. He served as an aide to the commanding general at Lockbourne AFB in Ohio. He was responsible for setting up athletic programs and sporting events.

Steinbrenner made his fortune in shipbuilding and bought the New York Yankees in 1973.

Dave Thomas. Founder/CEO of Wendy's Restaurants.

Born R. David Thomas in Atlantic City on July 2, 1932, Thomas dropped out of high school during the Korean War and volunteered for the army to avoid the draft and have some choice in assignments.

Thomas chose Cook and Bakers School at Ft. Benning, Georgia. He was sent overseas to Germany as a mess sergeant and was responsible for feeding 2000 soldiers daily. He attributes this experience in mass feedings to his success in fast food. He was discharged in 1953 as a staff sergeant.

Ted Turner. Broadcasting executive, sportsman.

Born in Cincinnati, Ohio, on November 19, 1938, Turner enlisted in the coast guard at his father's insistence after he was suspended from Brown University for "rowdy behavior" at a nearby women's college. He served on active duty for six months.

He returned to Brown but was asked to leave after breaking the rules regarding female guests. This resulted in a return to the coast guard for a summer cruise. The nautical training served Turner well when he won the America's Cup in 1977. He has used his talent with money to acquire the Atlanta Braves baseball team and the CNN Network. He is married to actress Jane Fonda.

Jack Valenti. President of Motion Picture Association of America.

Born in Houston, Texas, on September 5, 1921, Valenti served as a bomber pilot with the 12th Air Force during WWII. He served in Europe from 1942 to 1945 and flew 51 missions. He earned the Distinguished Flying Cross, the Air Medal with four clusters, and four Battle Stars. He served as assistant advisor on media to LBJ, leaving to take the position of president of the MPAA in 1966.

Cornelius Vanderbilt Jr. Publisher, financier.

Born in New York City on April 30, 1898, to one of the richest families in the world, Vanderbilt volunteered for the army at the outbreak of WWI, against his mother's wishes. He served in France as a driver and saw limited combat.

He returned to the U.S. in 1919 and attended the War College where he was commissioned a lieutenant in the reserves upon graduation in 1920. He served until 1923 when he was commissioned a captain in the National Guard. He served there until he returned to the army reserve in 1927 as a major. Called to active duty in 1942, Vanderbilt served as an intelligence officer stateside during WWII. He died in Miami, Florida, on July 7, 1974.

Charles Walgreen. Founder of Walgreen's Drug Stores.

Born in Knox County, Illinois, on October 9, 1873, Walgreen began as an apprentice druggist, moving to Chicago to learn pharmacology. After the start of the Spanish-American War, Walgreen enlisted with the 1st Illinois Volunteer Cavalry.

While serving in Cuba, he contracted malaria and yellow fever, which continued to plague him the rest of his life. After his discharge, he returned to Chicago and built a chain of pharmacies, starting in 1902.

George Westinghouse. Inventor, businessman.

Born in Central Bridge, New York, on October 6, 1846, Westinghouse enlisted in the Union army at 17 and served from 1862 to 1863, when he transferred to the Union navy as an engineer. He was discharged in 1865.

He founded the Westinghouse Electric Company in 1886 and was responsible for over 400 patents in his lifetime, including the railroad air brake (1869). He died in New York City on March 12, 1914.

Robert Elkington Wood. Sears founder and chairman.

Born in Kansas City, Missouri, in 1879, Woods graduated West Point in 1900 ranked 13th in a class of 54. Commissioned, he served in the army in the Philippines, and in the West, before volunteering for duty in Panama in 1905. He was responsible for purchasing supplies to feed and shelter the 50,000 workers employed constructing the Panama Canal.

Woods was allowed to take early retirement from the army by a special act of Congress in 1915. He retired with the rank of major, but re-entered the army during WWI and was commissioned a colonel. He was sent to Europe to prepare and organize the arrival of American troops. He was appointed Quartermaster General of the entire American Expeditionary Force with the rank of brigadier general. He was awarded the Distinguished Service Medal and released from active duty in 1919.

Wood went on to take a position with the mail-order company of Montgomery Ward, and opened the first Sears store, rising to chairman in 1939. Although he was a founder of America First, a group of isolationists committed to preventing America's entry into WWII, once the U.S. entered the war, Wood was quick to volunteer. He was rejected for being too old, so he served as a civilian advisor to the War Department.

Section 9

Academics, Clergy, and Idealists

Ralph David Abernathy. Civil rights leader.

Born the grandson of a slave in Linden, Alabama, on March 1, 1926, Abernathy served overseas with the U.S. Army during the closing months of WWII.

After the war, Abernathy was ordained a Baptist minister in 1948, and along with Dr. Martin Luther King, helped formulate a policy of non-violent confrontation of racism and segregation in the South. He took over as president of the Southern Christian Leadership Conference following Dr. King's assassination in April 1968 until 1977. He died in Atlanta on April 17, 1990.

Phillip Francis Berrigan. Peace activist, former Jesuit priest.

Born in Two Harbors, Minnesota, on October 5, 1923, one of six boys, Berrigan was drafted into the army in January 1943, during WWII. He considered applying for an exemption to become a priest, but decided that "action beat contemplation."

After basic training at Ft. Gordon, Georgia, Berrigan was sent to Ft. Blanding, Florida, and Ft. Bragg, North Carolina, for advanced training with howitzers and 8 inch field guns. Within one year Berrigan was promoted to sergeant.

By July 1944 Berrigan was in London, assigned to search the bombed-out ruins for salvage. Sent across the channel, Berrigan was present at the Battle of the Bulge in December 1944. His unit advanced through the Netherlands, and by early 1945 Berrigan was assigned to guarding German POWs.

Berrigan volunteered for OCS, 90 days later was commissioned a second lieutenant, and was assigned to the 8th Infantry Division (the "Pathfinder" Division) at Westphalia, Germany. He was in the city of Munster on V-E Day. His unit was returned to Ft. Leonard Wood, Missouri, for training in preparation for the invasion of Japan (Operation Coronet) but the dropping of the atomic bombs on Hiroshima and Nagasaki made an invasion unnecessary.

It was while he was stationed in the south that Berrigan first observed the poverty and discrimination that blacks were forced to endure, and this helped form his lifelong quest for social justice. After the war he returned to college, earning a B.A. at Holy Cross College in Worcester, Massachusetts.

In 1970 Berrigan became the first Roman Catholic clergyman to be sentenced to jail in the U.S. for political crimes when he was arrested for burning draft board records during raids on draft board offices in Baltimore in 1968 and 1969. He served 38 months in jail.

John Birch. Missionary, anti-communist.

There is an irony that the ultra-conservative, anti-communist John Birch Society selected John Morrison Birch to symbolize their philosophy, since it is unlikely that Birch himself would have approved of their agenda.

Birch was born in India to American missionary parents. He was raised in rural Georgia, and was working as a Baptist missionary in China when the United States declared war on Japan in December 1941. The Japanese in control of the Chinese provinces retaliated by burning missions, and interning the missionaries. Birch became a hunted man.

Birch fled to eastern China, where he encountered Captain James Doolittle in the Chekiang Province. Doolittle and his crew were hiding out from the Japanese after their bombing raid on Tokyo. Birch helped lead them, and other aircrews, to friendly territory. When he learned of Japanese reprisals on the Chinese population, with over 20,000 men, women and children killed, Birch volunteered for the army.

Because of his knowledge of the Chinese language, customs and culture, Birch was recruited by Major General Claire Lee Chennault, the commander of American Volunteer Group in China, to form a radio intelligence network to provide information on enemy troop movements. He was inducted into the China Air Task Force, later the 14th Air Force, as a second lieutenant on July 4, 1942.

Birch lived continuously in the bush for three years, infiltrating Japanese lines, leading missions and gathering intelligence. The war in the Pacific ended on August 14, 1945, but China continued to experience violence as warring factions fought for control of postwar China.

On August 25, 1945, Birch, now a captain, was leading a force of American, Chinese and Korean troops on a mission to liberate Allied POWs from a Japanese camp near Soochow when they encountered a party of Chinese Communist troops. The leader of the guerrillas demanded Birch surrender his revolver. When he refused, he and another soldier were shot dead, and the rest of the party interned. They were released a short time later.

Birch expressed his hope for the future in a poem he wrote four months before his death. "I want to reach the sunset of life sound in body and mind, flanked by strong sons and grandsons, enjoying the friendship and respect of neighbors and retaining my boyhood faith in Him who promised a life to come."

Cesar Chavez. Labor leader, civil rights activist.

Born in Yuma, Arizona, on March 31, 1927, Chavez enlisted in the navy in 1944 at age 17 to escape work in the fields. He described the navy as the worst two years of his life. After basic training in San Diego, Chavez was sent to the South Pacific where he served as a coxswain apprentice on small boats. At Saipan he assisted in ferrying ship's pilots in and out of the harbor, but he never saw combat. He was then transferred to Guam where he worked as a painter.

While on leave in Delano, California, Chavez successfully challenged a rule requiring minorities to sit in a segregated section of a movie theater. He was discharged from the Navy in 1946, and returned to his family and work in the fields of Delano.

Chavez helped organize the United Farm Workers, a farm labor union, in 1967. He led the union until his death on April 23, 1993.

Desmond Thomas Doss. Conscientious objector.

Born on February 7, 1919, Doss was a conscientious objector at the start of WWII, but turned down a shipyard deferment because he wanted to serve in the army but not carry a weapon. Doss was a Seventh-Day Adventist, a denomination which "advocates noncombatant service for their members since the time of the Civil War as a way of combining duty to country with a literalist interpretation of the sixth commandant, "Thou Shalt Not Kill." He enlisted on April 1, 1942, and after basic training at Camp Lee, Virginia, was assigned as a medic to the 307th Infantry Regiment, 77th Infantry Division. He was so unpopular because of his beliefs that his captain tried to have him discharged.

Doss was present at Okinawa as a corpsman from April 29 to May 21, 1945. During the battle, his unit was forced to retreat while scaling the Maeda Escarpment, leaving 75 wounded men exposed to enemy fire. Unarmed, Doss repeatedly crawled forward under heavy fire to pull each man to the edge of the cliff and lower him to safety. One by one, he rescued all 75 men, including the same captain who requested his discharge. His acts of heroism in exposing himself to enemy fire in rescuing his comrades earned Doss the Medal of Honor, becoming the first conscientious objector to win the award. He spent six years in hospitals recovering from his wounds.

Doss was discharged from the army as a corporal on July 17, 1946. He was also awarded two Bronze Stars, three Purple Hearts and a Good Conduct Medal. After his experiences, Doss stated that there was nobody who appreciated peace more.

Francis Patrick Duffy. Clergyman.

Born in Cobourg, Ontario, on May 2, 1871, Duffy earned a B.A. from the University of Toronto, and a master's degree, before entering the priesthood in 1895.

As the chaplain of the "Fighting 69th" Infantry Regiment, a unit of the New York National Guard, Duffy was commissioned a second lieutenant in 1898, two years after being ordained a Catholic priest.

He saw service with his regiment, both in the Spanish-American War (where he contracted typhoid fever) and during the hostilities on the Mexican border in 1916.

During the First World War, Duffy accompanied the regiment, redesignated as the 165th Infantry Regiment, overseas to France. The unit, commanded by Frank McCoy and later Bill Donovan, was present in the Luneville and Baccarat sectors. They saw action at the Argonne, and later at Remagen on the Rhine. He was decorated by both the French and American governments, winning the Distinguished Service Cross, the Distinguished Service Medal, the Legion of Honor, and the French Croix de Guerre with Palms.

After the war, Duffy returned to the church, and remained a simple parish priest until his death in 1932. He was given a military funeral at St. Patrick's in New York City with Governor Franklin Roosevelt and 25,000 in attendance. He was portrayed by Pat O'Brien in the 1940 film *The Fighting 69th*.

Daniel Ellsberg. Political scientist, economist.

Born in Chicago on April 7, 1931, Ellsberg waived his student deferment while attending Harvard graduate school and enlisted in the marines in April 1954. He was commissioned a first lieutenant and was eager to go to Korea, but was sent to the Middle East instead. He voluntarily extended his tour during the Suez Crisis in 1956. He saw no action.

After his release from active duty, Ellsberg returned to Harvard where he earned his Ph.D. He served as a military policy advisor to Senator John F. Kennedy.

He is best remembered for leaking sensitive documents concerning covert U.S. policy in Southeast Asia (the "Pentagon Papers") to the press in 1971. He wrote *Papers on the War* in 1972.

Howell Forgy. Navy chaplain.

Born in Philadelphia, Pennsylvania, on January 18, 1908, Forgy graduated from Princeton Theological Seminary and was fluent in both French and Spanish. He entered the navy on October 18, 1940, and was commissioned a lieutenant (j.g.) in the Chaplain Corps.

Stationed aboard the USS *New Orleans* at Pearl Harbor on December 7, 1941, Forgy is credited with the phrase, "Praise the Lord and pass the ammunition," while helping to fight off the Japanese attack. He served as chaplain and athletic officer aboard the *New Orleans* until April 7, 1943, when he was transferred to Treasure Island, California, where he was promoted to lieutenant commander. After a brief tour of duty at the Naval Technical Center in Norman, Oklahoma, Forgy returned to sea as chaplain/welfare officer aboard the USS *Bunker Hill*. He was discharged from the navy as a lieutenant commander on May 1, 1946. He died in Glendora, California, on January 20, 1972.

Benjamin Lawson Hooks. Lawyer, minister, executive director of NAACP.

Born in Memphis, Tennessee, on January 31, 1925, Hooks was the fifth of seven children. He was attending Le Moyne College when he was drafted into the U.S. Army in 1943.

His most vivid memory of the war was when he was assigned to guard Italian POWs in Georgia. The Italians would be served at "Whites Only" restaurants that Hooks was prohibited from entering because they were "off limits" to blacks.

After his discharge as a staff sergeant at the end of the war, he attended law school at De Paul University in Chicago. This was because there wasn't a law school in Tennessee that would admit blacks. Ordained a Baptist minister, he went on to become the national director of the NAACP.

Daniel P. Moynihan. Ambassador, sociologist, educator.

Born on March 16, 1927, in Tulsa, Oklahoma, Moynihan enlisted in the U.S. Navy in 1944 when he was 17. He was accepted into the V-12 officer training program at Middlebury College in Vermont. He earned a B.S. degree and a commission as an ensign. He served for one year as a communications officer aboard the USS *Quirinus* (ARL-39) before being discharged in 1947.

Ralph Nader. Consumer advocate, lawyer.

Born in Winsted, Connecticut, on February 27, 1934, Nader graduated Harvard law school in 1958 and enlisted for a six-month tour of active duty in the army to avoid the draft.

After basic training at Ft. Dix, New Jersey, Nader was sent to Cook and Bakers School. His proudest military moment was when he single-handedly prepared banana bread for 2000 troops. He was discharged in 1958 and served five years in the inactive reserve.

Pat Robertson. Televangelist, presidential candidate.

Born Marion Gordon Robertson in Lexington, Virginia, on March 22, 1930, Robertson was the son of a U.S. Senator whose ancestors include Presidents William H. and Benjamin Harrison and Winston Churchill. Upon completing naval ROTC during college, he took a commission in the Marine Corps.

After training at Quantico and Camp Pendleton, Robertson shipped out from San Diego for Korea and combat in January 1951 aboard the USS *General J.C. Breckinridge* (AP-176). He and some other officers disembarked at Kobe, Japan. This led to charges during Robertson's presidential campaign that he used his father's influence to avoid combat. He successfully sued Congressman Pete McCloskey for libel.

In any event, Robertson was subsequently transferred to Korea where he served as an assistant adjutant at the First Marine Division headquarters. His duties consisted of transporting classified codes and other intelligence between Korea and Japan. He was discharged as a first lieutenant.

Abram Joseph Ryan. Poet, priest.

Born in Hagerstown, Maryland, on February 5, 1838, the man known as "Father Ryan" was commissioned a chaplain in the Confederate army on September 1, 1862, shortly after his ordination as a Catholic priest. He served as a chaplain in military hospitals and also among the troops. His patriotic pro-Southern poetry made him well-known and popular among Southerners after the war.

Section 10

Notorious

John Wilkes Booth. Actor, assassin.

Born near Belair, Maryland, on May 10, 1838, Booth was from the prominent Booth family of actors. He was already a popular and successful actor at the beginning of the Civil War.

He borrowed a musket and was part of the Virginia militia company, the Richmond Greys, under Colonel Robert E. Lee when they battled the abolitionists under John Brown who had seized the arsenal at Harper's Ferry on October 18, 1859. He was also present when Brown was hanged on December 2nd.

Although he never again served in the military, Booth's pro-Southern sympathies caused him to smuggle morphine and other medicines into the South. He was involved in a plan to kidnap Lincoln in 1864 from the Soldier's Home, but it was never executed. The plot evolved into a conspiracy to assassinate the entire Lincoln administration.

On April 14, 1865, five days after Lee surrendered the Army of North Virginia, Lincoln attended a comedy, *Our American Cousin*, at Ford Theater in the Capital. Booth gained access to the presidential box, shot Lincoln in the back of the head, stabbed Lincoln's guest, Major Rathbone, in the arm, and leapt 12 feet onto the stage shouting "Sic semper tyrannis" ("Thus be it ever to tyrants").

After a nationwide manhunt, Booth was trapped in a barn near Port Royal, Virginia, on April 26, 1865. When he refused to surrender, the barn was set afire and Booth was fatally shot by

Sgt. Boston Corbett. Booth's body was returned to Washington, identified, and buried secretly beneath the floor of a prison.

John Dillinger. Bank robber.

Born on June 28, 1902, Dillinger enlisted in the U.S. Navy to get over a failed romance. Military life must not have agreed with him because he deserted five months later. He was subsequently given a dishonorable discharge.

Dillinger went on to success, earning the top position on the FBI's Most Wanted List for bank robbery.

Mildred E. Gillars. First woman convicted of wartime treason; known as "Axis Sally."

Born in Portland, Maine, in 1900, Gillars spent five years at Ohio Wesleyan University but never graduated. She was teaching English in Berlin when WWII began. Encouraged by her German lover, she began broadcasting Nazi propaganda to Allied troops in 1940.

Known as "Axis Sally," she became the highest paid broadcaster in Nazi Germany. Her broadcasts, like those of "Tokyo Rose," actually raised the morale of Allied troops. In 1946 Gillars was found by U.S. forces living in a bombed out basement in Frankfurt-am-main. She was arrested and returned to the United States where she was tried for treason in 1948. She was found guilty on March 10, 1949, and was sentenced to thirty years in prison. She served twelve years before being released in 1961.

She moved to Columbus, Ohio, where she went to college, earned a degree, taught kindergarten, and lived quietly until her death in June of 1968.

Oliver North. Marine lieutenant colonel, national security advisor.

Born in San Antonio, Texas, on October 7, 1943, North was the oldest of four children. His father, Oliver Clay North, was a

Oliver North

lieutenant colonel with Patton's Third Army during WWII. His brother John was a senior army officer and Vietnam vet. His brother Timothy was a naval officer. North joined the marine reserve while attending the State University of New York. He transferred to the U.S. Naval Academy in 1963. A car accident nearly cost North his life, and the months spent in bed recovering forced him to repeat his plebe year.

He was a welterweight boxing champion, and spent his summers attending jump school and survival training. In his senior year, North was one of 36 company commanders, and graduated 468th in a class of 835. He was so eager for duty in Vietnam that he passed up summer leave to attend marine basic training at Quantico, Virginia. On December 3, 1968, Lt. North assumed command of 2nd Platoon, Company K, 3rd Battalion, 3rd Marine Division in the Quang Tri Province, Vietnam. His gung-ho platoon called themselves "Blue's Bastards" in honor of their leader's code name. Their mission was to cut off the southward advance of North Vietnamese troops. North was wounded twice, once during a night patrol, and once when he was knocked off the turret of a tank. In both cases he continued to command his troops. By the end of his tour, North had earned the Silver Star, the Bronze Star, two Purple Hearts and a promotion to first lieutenant.

From November 1969 to July 1974, North taught guerrilla tactics at the marine basic school at Quantico. He was promoted to captain in 1971, and assumed command of the jungle warfare school at Okinawa in July 1974. In December, he was assigned as a plan-and-policy analyst at marine headquarters in Washington. After a tour of duty as a battalion operations officer, North was promoted to major and sent to the Naval War College in 1980.

In 1981 North was assigned to the staff of the National Security Council where he was involved in the sale of AWACS (surveillance planes) to Saudi Arabia, the invasion of Grenada (1983), and the *Achille Laro* incident (1985).

North was fired from the National Security Council on November 25, 1986. On March 16, 1988, he was indicted for his involvement with the Iran-Contra Affair. He put in for his retirement just two days later. He was found guilty on three counts (obstructing Congress, destroying documents, and accepting an illegal gratuity). On July 20, 1990, the U.S. Court of Appeals reversed one charge and vacated the remaining two. Then on November 27, 1990, the Marine Corps restored his pension.

North later ran unsuccessfully for the U.S. Senate in Virginia.

Lee Harvey Oswald. Assassin of John F. Kennedy.

Born in New Orleans on October 18, 1939, Oswald never knew his father who died two months before his birth. In October 1956 he enlisted in the marines at age 17. After ten weeks of basic training at San Diego, Oswald was still unable to qualify on the rifle range. In January of 1957 he took infantry training at Camp Pendleton, where he trained in amphibious assaults, squad tactics, and hand-to-hand combat.

In March he was sent to the Naval Air Technical Training Center in Jacksonville, Florida, where he trained as a radar controller, and was promoted to private first class upon his graduation. In August he was assigned to the Marine Air Control Squadron (MACS-1) of the 1st Marine Air Wing in Atsugi, Japan.

Nicknamed "Ozzie the Rabbit," Oswald is remembered as being shy and meek. He passed the test for corporal, but a series of mishaps involving a self-inflicted gunshot wound and insubordination resulted in a court-martial and 28 days of brig time. It was at this time that Oswald began studying Russian with the expressed intention of defecting to the U.S.S.R.

In September his unit was involved in assisting the Nationalist Chinese in Taiwan but the mission was "compromised" when the communists gained access to secret information. His unit, code named "Coffee Mill," was also involved with the U-2 aircraft which was capable of flying above anti-aircraft guns, missiles, and other aircraft.

A second shooting incident while on guard duty resulted in his return to Japan, and rotation stateside to MACS-9 in Santa Ana. He was granted a dependency discharge in September of 1959. It has been alleged that he offered to sell secret information to the Soviets, but it is questionable if he ever had access to secret information to sell.

Oswald is infamous as the accused assassin of JFK in Dallas on November 22, 1963. He himself was assassinated two days later by Jack Ruby, a stripclub owner, giving rise to numerous conspiracy theories.

Jack Ruby. Assassin of Lee Harvey Oswald.

Born in 1911, Ruby spent the months prior to America's entry into WWII breaking up meetings of the German-American Bund, a pro-Nazi group. Drafted into the Army Air Corps in May 1943, he spent the war assigned to bases in the South, and was by all accounts a good soldier.

Discharged as a private first class in February 1946, Ruby was awarded the Good Conduct Medal. He went on to acquire two strip clubs in Dallas, a petty criminal record, and immortality as the man who killed Lee Harvey Oswald in the basement of the Dallas Police Department on November 24, 1963, two days after Kennedy's assassination.

Cole Younger. Frontier outlaw.

Born in Lee Summit, Missouri, in 1844, Younger was the son of Henry Younger of Kentucky, a man of Union sympathies.

When the border war between Kansas and Missouri erupted in 1858, Cole Younger sided with the South.

Younger was 17 at the start of the Civil War, and enlisted in the Missouri State Guard as a private. He served under General Sterling Price at the Battle of Carthage (Missouri) on July 5, 1861. He then joined Quantrill's band of guerrillas in October, and was present at the raid on Lawrence, Kansas, where he killed his first man.

After his father was robbed and murdered by Unionist guerrillas, Younger enlisted in the Confederate army as a first lieutenant in Colonel Upton Hay's regiment under General Joe Shelby. At the Battle of Lone Jack in August of 1862, Younger displayed such courage, risking fire from Union troops less than 150 yards away to distribute ammo by horseback, that he was cheered by the Federal line.

When some southern girls (including two of Younger's cousins) died when the building they were confined in collapsed, Younger accompanied Quantrill, Bloody Bill Anderson, and Frank James on a return visit to Lawrence, where they murdered 183 men and boys.

After Quantrill disbanded his force, Younger went to Texas in the fall of 1863, and joined General McCulloch as a captain. In November he was sent to Louisiana to prevent cotton growers from selling to Union forces. By the winter of 1863–64, Younger was back in Texas where he was introduced to Myra Belle Shirley, known as Belle Starr.

He served under Colonel George Jackson, disrupting the telegraph line between Colorado and San Francisco, and was en route from Mexico, via California, to Canada to pick up and crew a warship when General Lee surrendered at Appomattox.

After the war he turned to robbing banks with the James Gang. Finally captured after an aborted bank robbery in Northfield, Minnesota, on September 7, 1876, he spent one third of his life in prison, was paroled in 1903, and died peacefully in his sleep with 14 bullets in him (from previous wounds) in 1916.

Section 11

Interesting or Unusual

Paul Mark Baron. Musician, marine, author's father.

Born in Chicago on September 11, 1924, Baron enlisted in the Marine Corps reserve on November 6, 1939, at age 15, by changing his birthday to 1921 and forging his mother's signature on the permission slip. He enlisted as a private/bandsman. When he was finally located by his parents, a letter to Major General Vandergrift secured an honorable discharge on November 7, 1940.

On January 14, 1942, six weeks after Pearl Harbor, Baron, now 17, again enlisted in the marines, this time with his parents' permission. Since he was employed in a dance band at the time, he was classified as a bandsman.

After basic training at San Diego, he was assigned to the 2nd Marine Division, Headquarters Company. He was promoted to private first class on June 5, 1942, and corporal in February 1943. The division was sent to New Zealand, and on August 7, 1942, he fought in the Battle of the Solomon Islands. In November 1943, Baron sailed to the Gilbert Islands where he participated in the Battle for Tarawa (November 25–28).

His unit sailed from Hawaii on May 25, 1944, for the Marianas Islands and participated in operations at Saipan from June 15 to July 8, 1944. He was wounded in action and evacuated to Hawaii, and then to a military hospital in Banning, California. He played in marine bands before being discharged at Quantico,

Virginia, on September 14, 1945. He was awarded the Bronze Star, Purple Heart, and three Presidential Unit Citations.

Samuel Powhatan Carter. Army general, navy admiral.

Born in Elizabethtown, Tennessee, on August 6, 1819, Samuel P. Carter is the only American to attain the rank of both general

in the army, and admiral in the navy. He entered the navy in 1840 and served with both the Great Lakes and Atlantic Fleets. After he graduated the Naval Academy in 1846, Carter saw service in the Mexican-American War, as an instructor at Annapolis, and at the Naval Observatory. He was promoted to full lieutenant in 1855. With the approach of the Civil War, he wrote a letter stating his intent to remain loyal should war come. The letter caught the attention of the

Samuel Carter

Governor of Tennessee, Andrew Johnson (later President), who arranged with the War Department in May 1862 for Carter to be commissioned a brigadier general of volunteers. He was assigned to recruiting and training the Tennessee State Militia.

During the war, Carter led cavalry raids, supported General Rosecrans at Murfreesboro, and was promoted to major general in 1865. Upon his release from the army in 1866, he returned to the navy with the rank of commander. Promoted to captain in 1870, he was captain of the USS *Monocracy* until he was appointed commandant of the Naval Academy. In 1878 he was promoted to commodore, and a year after his retirement in 1882, he was promoted to rear admiral. He died in Washington DC in 1891.

William "Buffalo Bill" Cody. Showman, frontier scout.

Born William Frederick Cody on February 26, 1846, in Scott

County, Iowa, Cody took a job as a Pony Express rider at age 14 in 1860. During the Civil War, Cody rode with the anti-slavery "Jayhawkers" in Kansas before he served as a scout for the 9th Kansas Cavalry in engagements against the Kiowa and Comanches in 1863. In February 1864 Cody enlisted in the Union army and served as a trooper with General A. J. Smith in Tennessee and General Price in Missouri against the Confederates.

After the war, Cody supplied the Union Pacific construction crews with buffalo meat, killing over 4,000 by his own count. He served as a scout for the 5th U.S. Cavalry in various Indian engagements between 1868 and 1872. His exploits were the subject of a series of "Ned Buntline" dime novels where he was dubbed "Buffalo Bill."

While serving as Chief of Scouts for Colonel Wesley Merritt and the 5th Cavalry on July 17, 1876, at the Battle of War Bonnet Creek, Cody is reputed to have had a duel with Cheyenne leader Yellow Hand. Cody finished his years as the legendary showman and owner of "Buffalo Bill's Wild West Show" which featured Annie Oakley and Sitting Bull, and enjoyed success for over thirty years. He died suddenly in Denver in 1917. Cody was awarded a Medal of Honor for his services as a scout with the frontier army during the 1870s. The medal was recalled in the Medal of Honor "purge" of 1916–17. It was restored (along with four other scout's medals) by an act of Congress in 1989.

Benjamin O. Davis Sr. First black general officer.

The grandson of a slave who bought his freedom in 1800, Davis was born in Washington DC on July 1, 1877, and attended Howard University. He left school in July 1898 to enlist in the army during the war with Spain.

Davis was commissioned a first lieutenant with the 8th U.S. Volunteer Infantry, an all-black unit. The following March, Davis was mustered out, but re-enlisted as a private in the 9th Cavalry, Regular Army. He served in the Philippines and rose to the rank of sergeant-major.

In 1901 Davis was commissioned a second lieutenant of cavalry and served as a professor of military science at Wilberforce University in Ohio (1905–09). He earned a promotion to first lieutenant. Davis served as a military attaché to Liberia, and in 1915 patrolled the Mexican border as a captain.

During WWI Davis rose to the rank of temporary lieutenant colonel while serving in the Philippines. In 1920 he reverted to the rank of major, but was promptly promoted to lieutenant colonel in the Regular Army. He served as an instructor at various posts, and was promoted to colonel in 1930. He retired in June 1941 with the rank of temporary brigadier general.

Benjamin O. Davis Sr.

Davis was recalled to active duty after Pearl Harbor and served with the Inspector General's Corps in Europe, assigned to Eisenhower's staff. He retired at the end of the war as a brigadier general. He died in North Chicago on November 26, 1970.

Benjamin O. Davis Jr. First black Air Force general.

Born in Washington DC on December 18, 1912, Davis attended West Point (1932–36) and endured hazing by silence to become the first black to graduate the military academy in 50 years. He was commissioned a second lieutenant in June 1936 and was assigned as a company officer with the 24th Infantry at Ft. Benning. Upon his graduation from infantry officers school, Davis was assigned as a tactics instructor at Tuskegee, and promoted to captain.

Davis took flight training in May 1941 and was placed in command of the all-black 99th Fighter Squadron at Tuskegee in March 1942. He was promoted to major, then lieutenant colonel. The 99th was sent overseas in 1943, and the unit won numerous awards during actions in North Africa, Sicily and Italy. On his return to the U.S. in October 1943, Davis assumed command of the 332nd Fighter Group in Michigan. He was in charge of directing their training prior to deployment overseas.

In January 1944 the 332nd was sent to the Mediterranean as part of the 12th Fighter Command. They flew escort for bombers at Cassino, Anzio, and all over Italy. Davis was promoted to full colonel in May 1944. In September he was presented the Distinguished Flying Cross by his father, Gen. Benjamin O. Davis Sr. By the war's end, the 332nd had flown over 200 missions without losing a single bomber. Davis was awarded the Silver Star, the Croix de Guerre and an Air Medal with four clusters.

In June 1945 Davis returned to Kentucky to assume command of the 477th Composite Group, but the war ended and he was sent instead to the War College. He was promoted to brigadier general by President Eisenhower in October 1954. Davis was the air force's first black general, and only the second black ever to attain general rank (the other was his father). He finished his career with a succession of increasingly responsible commands at air force headquarters, retiring with the rank of lieutenant general.

William Patrick Hitler. Dictator's nephew.

Born in Liverpool, England, on March 12, 1911, Hitler was the son of Alois Hitler Jr., Adolf Hitler's older half-brother. He met his Uncle Adolf when he was one and a half years old, when the older Hitler visited his brother in Liverpool.

William Patrick served with the U.S. Navy during WWII. His brother Heinz fought with the German Wehrmacht in Russia, was captured by the Russians at Stalingrad, and died as a POW.

Joseph P. Kennedy Jr. Older brother of John F. Kennedy.

Born on July 28, 1915, in Nantasket, Massachusetts, Joe Jr. was the oldest of the nine children of Ambassador Joseph Kennedy Sr. The elder Kennedy served as ambassador to England prior to WWII, but his admiration of the National Socialists in Germany, and his support of isolationism, came into conflict with the Roosevelt administration, and he was recalled.

Kennedy Jr. visited Nazi Germany in the late 1930s with his younger brother John, but they differed in their perception of Nazi Germany, with Joe Jr. taking his father's position. He served as a Roosevelt delegate at the 1940 Democratic Convention.

Joe Jr. had finished his second year at Harvard law school when he entered the naval cadet aviation program in May of 1940. After basic pre-flight training at Squantum Naval Air Facility outside Boston, he took ground school in Jacksonville in July, then operational training at Banana River in Florida. He earned his wings on May 6, 1942, and Ambassador Kennedy spoke at the graduation. Joe Jr. graduated in the top three of his class.

He learned to fly B-24 Liberator bombers, and went overseas with VB 110 to England in September 1943. Now a full lieutenant, he flew with the RAF. His mission was anti-submarine operations in the English Channel and the coast of occupied France. He flew 30 missions, then volunteered for an additional 10 missions. His crew also volunteered to the man.

Perhaps in reaction to his brother Jack's medal for *PT-109*, Joe Jr. remained in England and volunteered for the top secret "Operation Anvil." The plan was to load a PB4Y plane with high explosives and fly it over a target in Calais, France. The pilots would then aim the plane like a bomb, bail out, and the plane would then be controlled remotely by accompanying aircraft.

On August 12, 1944, Kennedy took off with his co-pilot Wilford Willy, escorted by two B-17s and 16 P-51 Mustangs. Also along on the mission was Lt. Colonel Elliott Roosevelt, the

President's son. He was in a British Mosquito fighter specially equipped for photo reconnaissance.

They took off from Fersfield Aerodrome at 1800 hours, but Kennedy's plane blew up 20 minutes into the mission. The irony was that the target site, a production point for the V-3 rocket/ bomb, had already been abandoned. He was posthumously awarded the Navy Cross.

Evel Knievel. Daredevil stuntmaster.

Born Robert Craig Knievel in Butte, Montana, on October 17, 1938, Knievel has made a career by risking death to perform spectacular stunts.

After basic training at Ft. Ord, California, Knievel served on active duty in the army at Ft. Lewis, Washington, where he distinguished himself by pole-vaulting a record 14 feet, six inches. He served from May 31 to November 30, 1957, and was discharged as a private.

David "Mickey" Marcus. Mercenary, soldier of fortune.

Born in 1902, Marcus graduated from West Point in 1924. Commissioned a second lieutenant, he attended law school while still in the army. Upon leaving the army in the 1930s, Marcus worked at a variety of civil service jobs, including Commissioner of Corrections for New York City. Marcus retained a reserve commission in the army, and in 1940, when war appeared imminent, he requested and was granted a return to active duty. Because of his law degree, he was assigned as judge advocate of the 27th Infantry Division (the "New York" Division), with the rank of lieutenant colonel.

Promoted to colonel after Pearl Harbor, Marcus was assigned command of the Jungle Warfare School in Hawaii. He requested a combat command but was transferred to a staff position at the Pentagon in 1943. Although a staff officer, and 42 years of age, Marcus jumped into Normandy on D-Day with the 101st Airborne ("Screaming Eagles"), despite the fact that he had never previously made a parachute jump. When his superiors learned of his adventures, he was promptly ordered back to Washington. After the war, he helped organize the government for Occupied Germany, and assisted at the Nuremberg war trials.

Resigning from the army in 1947, Marcus, a Jew, went to Palestine which became the State of Israel in 1948. He was a military advisor who helped organize and train the new nation's armed forces. He also used his knowledge of tactics and strategy to correctly predict and anticipate the actions of the Arab armies.

During the 1948 Arab-Israeli war, Marcus, using the pseudonym "Brigadier General Stone" was assigned command of the Jerusalem front. He helped relieve parts of the city under siege. He was accidentally killed on June 10, 1948, by his own sentries. Because he did not speak Hebrew, he didn't understand the sentry's challenge.

His body was returned to the United States and buried at the U.S. Military Academy at West Point. He is the only person buried there who died fighting under a foreign flag.

Zeppo Marx. Comedian, businessman.

Known as the "fourth Marx Brother," Zeppo Marx was a businessman who owned several businesses including a company that designed and manufactured clamping devices. It was his company that designed the special clamps that held "Little Boy" and "Fatman," the two A-bombs, on their way to Hiroshima and Nagasaki.

Wilmer McLean. Civil War landlord, grocer.

It can be said that the Civil War both began and ended on property owned by McLean. In 1854, after retiring from the U.S. Army with the rank of major, McLean moved his family to Prince George County, Virginia. He opened a store at Bull Run, near Manassas Junction. Because it was located close to the rail lines and the junction of several major roads, McLean's wholesale grocery business prospered.

It was for these same reasons that General P.G.T. Beauregard chose to occupy the area in May 1861. He was there to prevent the "invasion" of Federal troops. The three-day battle that occurred there between July 18 and 21 was called the First Battle of Bull Run by the North, and First Manassas by the South.

During the battle, Beauregard used the McLean home as his headquarters and the McLean barn as a field hospital. Federal artillery finally forced the Confederate withdrawal. Disgusted, McLean moved his family after the battle.

The McLeans lived peacefully for the next three years in the quiet little village of Appomattox Courthouse. On Sunday, April 9, 1865, McLean was approached by Colonel Charles Wallace, an aide to General Lee. Wallace was seeking a suitable location for Lee to meet with General Grant, the Federal commander. After declining an unfinished building as unsuitable, Wallace convinced McLean to allow them to use the parlor of the McLean home. Reluctantly, McLean agreed. After General Lee surrendered the Army of Northern Virginia to Grant, McLean's home was looted and ransacked by Federal troops (and officers) seeking souvenirs.

Sadao Munemori. Japanese Medal of Honor winner in WWII.

Born to immigrant Japanese parents in Los Angeles, California, in 1923, Munemori tried to enlist in the army after Pearl Harbor but was rejected because of his race. His family was relocated and interned in the Manzanar Camp in southeast California. They lost everything they owned.

Later, when Japanese Americans were permitted to volunteer, Munemori enlisted in the army and was assigned to an intelligence unit at Camp Savage where he rose to the rank of technical sergeant. He requested combat duty and took a reduction in rank to private to join the 100th Infantry Regiment, a unit comprised of Japanese Americans. This unit was later absorbed as the 1st Battalion, 442nd Combat Regiment.

After seeing extensive action across Italy and France, Private First Class Munemori was assistant squad leader in Company A. On April 5, 1945, Munemori's unit was pinned down by enemy fire near Seraveza. With the squad leader wounded, Munemori assumed command. He collected grenades from the squad members, and frontally assaulted two machine gun positions, destroying both. Withdrawing to his position under fire, he jumped on a German grenade, absorbing the explosion with his body. His actions saved the lives of two squad members.

He was posthumously awarded the Medal of Honor after the war, the only Japanese American to be so honored despite other noteworthy examples of valor. His mother was presented the medal while still interned at Manzanar.

Jeanette Rankin. First woman in Congress, anti-war activist.

Born in Missoula, Montana, on June 1, 1880, Rankin was elected to the U.S. House of Representatives in 1916. (While some states had passed legislation to allow women voters, most American women wouldn't receive the right to vote until the passing of the 19th Amendment on August 26, 1920.) She thus became the first woman elected to Congress.

A confirmed pacifist, she voted against America's entry into WWI. As a result, she was defeated in her bid for re-election in 1919. During the 1920s and 1930s she continued to advocate anti-war causes.

She was re-elected to Congress in 1941, but was the only legislator to vote against America's entry into WWII when Congress voted on December 8, 1941 (the day after Pearl Harbor). She was again defeated for re-election in 1943. She returned to her anti-war activities and led a march to Washington DC to protest U.S. involvement in the Vietnam War. She died in Carmel, California, on May 18, 1973.

Paul Revere. Silversmith, Revolutionary War hero.

Born the son of a silversmith in Boston on January 1, 1735, Revere grew up a silversmith, but also took great interest in local politics. He was a leader of the "Sons of Liberty," and partici-pated in the Boston Tea Party which was a response to the Tea Act of 1773.

His appointment as a messenger for the Massachusetts Pro-vincial Assembly in 1774 made him an insider to events. He car-ried news and issued warnings. In December 1774, Revere warned patriot leaders in Portsmouth, New Hampshire, of Gen-eral Thomas Gage's plan to capture the military stores at Fort William and Mary.

On April 18, 1775, Revere made the famous midnight ride immortalized in Longfellow's "Paul Revere's Ride." He rode to Lexington and warned patriot leaders Adams and Hancock of the British approach. Revere then rowed across the Charles River to Charleston. He was riding to Concord with William Dawes and Dr. Sam Prescott when they were stopped and detained by British troops. Only Prescott, who claimed a medical emergency, was allowed to proceed, and he gave the warning.

Revere served as the commander of Castle William, a for-tress protecting Boston harbor, as a commissioned lieutenant colonel of artillery. He accompanied expeditions to Rhode Is-land under General Sullivan in 1778, and Penobscot Bay under General Lovell in 1779. At Penobscot Bay, the expedition failed so badly that his reputation was tarnished for years. Revere con-tinued to wear his Revolutionary War uniform daily until his death in Boston on May 10, 1818.

Robert Leroy Ripley. Cartoonist, author.

Ripley never served in the military, either during war or dur-ing peacetime..... Believe it or not!

George Lincoln Rockwell. American Nazi Party leader.

Born in Bloomington, Illinois, on March 9, 1918, Rockwell expressed a prejudice against Blacks and Jews as early as high school. Barely graduating, he left Brown University at the start of WWII to be commissioned and trained as a navy fighter pilot. He saw service in the Pacific.

Recalled back into the navy during Korea, Rockwell served in Iceland, and later San Diego, rising to the rank of full commander. It was in San Diego that Rockwell discovered the works of Gerald L. K. Smith and other racist writers. In 1958, while still serving in the navy, he founded the American Nazi Party.

Because of his efforts as a proponent of fascism, Rockwell was honorably discharged by the navy in February 1960. Following a series of demonstrations and arrests, Rockwell was shot to death by a disgruntled former member of the American Nazi Party on August 25, 1967.

Walt Disney Studios.

During WWII, the studios went to work producing films, cartoons, and other media to support the war effort. They also designed artwork for hundreds of aircraft and military units. The insignia of the Flying Tigers was designed by Disney animator Roy Williams who would earn later fame as "Roy" of *The Mickey Mouse Club*.

The studio itself served as home to a 250-man army antiaircraft detachment, located on the back lot in Burbank. It must have been an effective deterrent, because Disney Studios was not attacked once during the war.

301

Photo Index and Credits

About the Author

Scott Baron. Author, investigator, police officer.

Born in Santa Monica, California, on September 3, 1954, Baron grew up in the San Fernando Valley, the youngest of three

children. After graduating North Hollywood High, he enlisted in the U.S. Army where he spent an undistinguished two years serving stateside and in Panama during the Vietnam War. He served in the infantry and as a military policeman.

His interest in law enforcement continued upon his return to civilian life, and he worked in the field for over a decade as a border patrolman, railroad special agent, and police officer. He has taught criminal justice courses at the police academy and at community colleges.

His passion for military history and research has turned into a second career as the author of *They Also Served: Military Biographies of Uncommon Americans*. Scott resides in Watsonville, California, with his wife Marisela, their two sons Eric and Heath, and two foster sons Anthony and Mitchell.

Appendix

American Medals and Decorations

The Medal of Honor

Created by Congress (Public Resolution 82) and signed into law by President Abraham Lincoln on December 21, 1861, the Bill authorized the Secretary of the Navy to create 200 medals of honor to "be bestowed upon such petty officers, seamen, landsmen and marines as shall distinguish themselves by their gallantry in action, and other seamanlike qualities during the present war."

Designed by Christian Schussel and sculptured by Anthony C. Paquet, it is considered the first Federal decoration. That it was designed originally solely for award during the "war of rebellion" is indicated by the design on the obverse side. In a letter to Secretary of the Navy, Gideon Welles, dated May 9, 1862, the design is described as one in which "the foul spirit of secession and rebellion is represented in a crouching attitude holding in his hands serpents, which with forked tongues are striking at a large figure representing the union or genius of our country, who holds in right hand a shield, and in her left a fasces. Around these figures are thirty-four stars, indicating the number of States composing the Union." The army was authorized its own version on July 12, 1862.

Because the Medal of Honor was the only military decoration, in 1916 a section of the National Defense Act established an army board of review, and 911 of the 2,625 awards were deemed "inappropriate" and recalled, including the one awarded to Mary Edwards Walker, the only female recipient. This also served as an impetus for Congress to create other, lessor decorations. (In 1976 Mary Walker's medal was restored by a special act of Congress.)

An act of Congress on August 7, 1942, established the Medal of Honor as a combat award only for members of the armed forces who distinguish themselves conspicuously by gallantry and intrepidity at the risk of their lives above and beyond the call of duty while engaged in combat against an armed enemy of the United States. There are separate awards for the Army, Navy (including Marines and Coast Guard) and Air Force. It is this nation's highest award.

The Distinguished Service Cross

Authorized on July 9, 1918, as an award for members of the armed forces of the United States who, while serving in any capacity with the United States Army, distinguish themselves by extraordinary heroism not justifying the award of the Medal of Honor. It is the nation's second highest decoration.

The Navy Cross

Authorized on February 4, 1919, and issued to personnel of the Navy and Marine Corps, it is the Navy equivalent of the Distinguished Service Cross. Originally the Navy's third highest award, it was given precedence over the Distinguished Service Medal by an Act of Congress on August 7, 1942, and put on a par with the Distinguished Service Cross. It is awarded for extraordinary heroism in the face of great danger and personal risk during combat.

The Air Force Cross

Authorized on July 6, 1960, it is the equivalent of the Distinguished Service Cross issued to Air Force personnel.

The Distinguished Service Medal

Authorized for the Army in 1918, the Navy in 1919, and the Air Force in 1960, this medal recognizes individuals who "distinguish themselves by exceptionally meritorious service to the government in a duty of great responsibility." It is awarded for both combat and non-combat services.

The Silver Star

Authorized as a Citation Star in July 1918, it was redesignated a medal on August 8, 1932. It is awarded to any "member of the armed forces who, while serving in any capacity, distinguish themselves by gallantry in action against an enemy of the United States, or while serving with friendly forces against an opposing armed enemy force."

Upon its creation in 1932, it was made retroactive to the Spanish American War (1898). It is awarded for combat action only and is the third highest decoration for valor.

The Bronze Star

Authorized on February 4, 1944, this medal is awarded to any member of the military services who, while serving in any capacity on or after December 7, 1941, distinguishes himself (or herself) by heroic or meritorious achievement or service (except in aerial flight).

The Distinguished Flying Cross

Authorized on July 2, 1926, and amended on January 8, 1938, it is awarded to any member of the armed forces who distinguish themselves by heroism or extraordinary achievement while participating in an aerial flight, subsequent to November 11, 1918. The first award was to Capt. Charles A. Lindbergh for his solo flight across the Atlantic. Other recipients include Commander Richard E. Byrd and Amelia Earhart.

The Purple Heart

Authorized in 1932, the modern Purple Heart is a descendant of the original award established by General Washington during the Revolution in 1782. It is awarded for wounds received in combat by any member serving in the United States Armed Forces.

The Air Medal

Established on May 11, 1942, this medal is awarded for meritorious achievement while participating in aerial flight. It is awarded for single acts of heroism in combat or non-combat, or for sustained distinction in the performance of duty involving regular and frequent participation in aerial flight.

The Legion of Merit

Authorized on July 20, 1942, the Legion of Merit is the first American decoration designed to recognize exceptionally meritorious conduct in performing outstanding service to the United States by foreign military personnel and civilians. It can also be awarded to officers of U.S. Armed Forces. Like European awards, it has four degrees: Chief Commander, Commander, Officer and Legionnaire. It is generally awarded to foreign heads of state and high ranking military officers.

The Medal of Merit

Authorized on July 20, 1942, the Medal of Merit is the civilian Legion of Merit and is awarded exclusively to civilians who distinguish themselves in performing outstanding service to the United States. It is awarded to U.S. and foreign civilians of friendly foreign nations waging war under a joint resolution.

The Presidential Unit Citation

Created by Executive Order 9075 on February 26, 1942, Unit Citations recognize the outstanding heroism or achievements of an entire unit, and are not an individual award. It is represented by a ribbon bar, and not by a medal. Originally called the Distinguished Unit Citation, it was redesignated as the Presidential Unit Citation by Executive Order 10694 on January 10, 1957.

The Soldiers Medal

Established by Congress on July 2, 1926, the Soldiers Medal is awarded to members of the U.S. Army, National Guard or reserves who, at risk of life, voluntarily distinguish themselves by "heroism not involving actual conflict with an armed enemy." Congress authorized the Navy and Marine Corps Medal for navy and marine personnel on August 7, 1942, the Airman's Medal on July 6, 1960, for U.S. Air Force personnel or anyone serving in any capacity with the U.S. Air Force, and the Coast Guard Medal for U.S. Coast Guard personnel in 1951. The criteria is essentially the same for all four medals.

Commendation Medals

All of the armed services have their own Commendation Medals which are awarded to individuals who distinguish themselves by heroism, meritorious service or achievement, in combat or non-combat situations. The Navy Commendation Medal was established on January 11, 1944, the Army Commendation Medal in December 1945, the Air Force Commendation Medal on March 28, 1948, and the Coast Guard Commendation Medal on August 26, 1947. Each service may award its Commendation Medal to members of other branches serving with or attached to that service.

The National Security Medal

Established by executive order on January 19, 1953, the National Security Medal is awarded for "distinguished achievement or outstanding contribution in the field of intelligence relating to the national security." It can be awarded to civilians or military personnel, either U.S. citizens or foreign nationals.

The Medal of Freedom

Established at the end of WWII, the Medal of Freedom is a civilian award presented to U.S. and foreign civilians as well as members of allied military units for meritorious acts or service against the enemy. It has four degrees, Chief Commander, Commander, Officer-Legionnaire and the Medal of Freedom. The top three orders are distinguished by gold, silver and bronze palms.

Battle Stars

During WWII, medals were authorized to denote service within one of three campaign areas: American Campaign Medal, Asiatic-Pacific Campaign Medal, and European-African-Middle Eastern Campaign Medal. A bronze battle star was authorized to be worn on the ribbon to denote service in a specific campaign or operation within the area of operations. A silver star was worn to represent five campaigns.

Foreign Medals and Decorations

The following foreign medals are mentioned in the text of this book. See the Index for page numbers.

England—

The Victoria Cross

The Victoria Cross is the highest award given for valor. It was founded by Queen Victoria on January 29, 1856, and is awarded for conspicuous gallantry in battle. It ranks above all other orders and decorations in the British Empire.

The Distinguished Service Cross

Originally called the Conspicuous Service Cross, this medal was established by King Edward VII in 1901 to recognize "meritorious or distinguished services before the enemy" by junior officers of His Majesty's Fleet. King George V changed the title to Distinguished Service Cross in October 1914, and extended the award to all British naval and marine officers below the rank of lieutenant commander/major for "meritorious or distinguished service not sufficient to warrant the Distinguished Service Order." In December 1939, King George VI extended the award up to full commanders in the navy and marine lieutenant colonels. Other service members assigned to the fleet are also eligible.

The Military Cross

This medal was established on December 31, 1914, as an award to junior army officers (captain and below) for distinguished and meritorious service during wartime. Because of the large number of awards during WWI, the qualifications were changed in 1918 to distinguished and meritorious service in action. In 1931 the award was extended to RAF and foreign officers below the rank of major.

The Most Excellent Order of the British Empire

The Order of the British Empire was established on June 4, 1917, by King George V during WWI. It is awarded in six classes:

Knight or Dame Grand Cross, Knight Commander, Dame Commander, Commander, Officer and Member, and is presented for distinguished service other than military, or to military personnel for noncombatant acts of service.

France—

Legion d'Honneur

This is France's highest decoration, established by Napoleon Bonaparte on May 19, 1802, as an award for outstanding service to France, either civilian or military. It has five classes (Grand Cross, Grand Officer, Commander, Officer and Chevalier).

Croix De Guerre

This is awarded to members of the French Armed Forces and foreign nationals for outstanding bravery or ability. The recipient must be mentioned in a dispatch by a high ranking officer. Subsequent awards earn a bronze palm, with a silver palm awarded for the fifth presentation.

Croix de la Liberation

Popularly known as the Croix de Lorraine because the medal is a Cross of Lorraine superimposed over a sword on a rectangular background, the award was instituted by General Charles De Gaulle in November 1940. It had only one class, Compagnons (Companion), and was awarded to persons, French or foreign, civil or military, male or female, for exceptional service aiding in the liberation of France and her colonies. The award was discontinued on January 23, 1946.

Italy—

Ordine Della Corona D'Italia

The Order of the Crown of Italy was founded by King Victor Emanuel II on February 20, 1868, to commemorate the annexation of Venato which completed the unification of Italy. It was awarded to Italians and foreigners who rendered services for the good of Italy. It was awarded in five classes: Cavaliere di Gran

Croce, Grande Ufficiale, Commendatore, Cavaliere Ufficiale and Cavaliere. The award is obsolete.

Vietnam—

National Order of Merit

Many of the awards of the Vietnamese Republic are carry-overs from French Indochina. The National Order of Merit was originally the Order of the Green Dragon of Annam, and the dragon remains on the medal. It is awarded to individuals, civilian or military, Vietnamese or foreigner, who distinguish themselves by outstanding achievement, exceptional service, sacrifice, heroism, or extraordinary talent that benefits the country.

A Brief History of Women in the Military

The military has never been a traditional career choice of most American women, nor until recently have women had the opportunity to fully participate in the U.S. armed forces. Nevertheless, the desire to serve one's country in time of need is not gender specific, and American history is filled with women who answered the call to arms, many concealing their sex to do so.

Molly Pitcher manned her husband's artillery piece during the Revolutionary War. During the War of 1812, Lucy Brewer served as a marine aboard the USS *Constitution*, calling herself George Baker. An estimated 400–500 women disguised their sex and served on both sides during the Civil War. Dr. Mary Walker (who did not disguise herself) earned the Medal of Honor. Women also provided cooking, laundry, intelligence and other noncombative services in pre-20th century armies.

By the middle of the nineteenth century, women were beginning to be accepted as military nurses, but their status was that of civilian volunteers. Their contributions in medicine and health care resulted in advances in patient care, but at the end of the war, primary care returned to enlisted orderlies, and the women went home. It was only the army's inability to raise a needed 6,000 medical orderlies during a typhoid epidemic at the start of the Spanish-American War that prompted Congress to authorize women nurses, but they remained as civilians without military status. Between 1898 and 1901, 1,500 women served stateside, overseas and aboard the hospital ship, *Relief*.

In 1901 Congress authorized an Army Nurses Corps (ANC) as an auxiliary to the army. In this quasi-military status, nurses held no military rank, earned lower pay, and had no veteran's benefits like retirement. On May 12, 1908, the U.S. Navy created its own nurses corps (NNC) under similar conditions.

In 1916, Secretary of the Navy Josephus Daniels, perhaps anticipating America's entry into WWI, gave a liberal interpretation to the term "citizen" in the regulations and authorized women to enroll in the navy reserve. He believed that women would become essential in the operation of stateside installations as manpower was diverted overseas. Experience proved him correct, and on March 19, 1917, women were allowed to enlist in the naval reserve as Yeoman (F). Thus when the U.S. entered the war on April 6, the navy was ready. Although the Marine Corps allowed women into the reserve in 1918, the army and the War Department refused to allow women to serve with the army, except as nurses in the ANC.

During the First World War, 34,000 women served in the U.S. Navy, Marines, Coast Guard and Army/Navy Nurses Corps. Over 10,000 nurses served overseas with the American Expeditionary Force (AEF) in England, Italy, Belgium and France earning three Distinguished Service Crosses and 23 Distinguished Service Medals. In addition to confirming the value of women in the military, the war provided the first opportunity for women to participate in non-traditional skilled and semi-skilled labor. With the Armistice in November 1918, the process of demobilization began despite the proven value of women during the war.

By 1920 the only women remaining in the military were nurses. In 1925 the wording in the 1916 Naval Reserve Act was changed from "citizen" to "male citizen." In the mid-1920s, in recognition of their wartime service, military nurses were granted "relative rank" which allowed them to wear insignia of rank, but pay and benefits were at the next lower grade.

The rise of women's suffrage prompted the War Department to undertake three separate studies regarding the creation of a women's corps of the army (1926, 1928 and 1939). The studies recommended the corps be "with" but not "in" the army. Despite the predisposition of the generals to negate the role of women, some planners with foresight such as Major (later Major General) Everett Hughes saw "the inevitability of large numbers of women participating in the next war."

Once again it was a war that broke the logjam. Shortly after the Japanese attacked the U.S. fleet in Hawaii, steps were taken to mobilize all of the nation's resources. On May 15, 1942, FDR signed legislation creating a Women's Auxiliary Army Corps (WAAC) as an emergency wartime measure. On July 30, Congress authorized all of the services to form their own auxiliaries. The U.S. Navy created the WAVES (Women Accepted for Volunteer Emergency Services), the Coast Guard followed with the SPARS (Semper Paratus—Always Ready) on November 23, 1942, and the Marines created the Women Marines on February 12, 1943, the last service to create an auxiliary.

In 1943 Congress passed a law making the various auxiliaries part of the Regular Services, but only as a wartime emergency measure, and the WAAC became the WAC. In 1947 the Army Nurses Corps was integrated into the Regular Army, but the auxiliaries remained an emergency measure.

In 1948, with the Women's Armed Forces Integration Act, the auxiliaries were integrated into the Regular Services, and the WAC (Women's Army Corps) became a branch of the Regular Army, like the Signal Corps or the Infantry.

In 1976 the women's corps were abolished and women were integrated into all branches of the military except combat related fields (infantry, armor, artillery, warships and warplanes). With the advent of modern warfare, the distinction has become blurred (e.g., women MPs at the front, support pilots in combat areas). At this writing, women are still prohibited by law from participating in combat.

U.S. Army Levels of Command

Unit	Composition	Normally Led By
Squad	8 to 12 men	Sergeant
Platoon	3 or more Squads	Lieutenant
Company	3 or more Platoons	Captain
Battalion	3 or more Companies	Lt. Colonel
Regiment	3 or more Battalions	Colonel
Brigade	3 or more Regiments	Brigadier General
Division	3 or more Brigades	Major General
Corps	3 or more Divisions	Lieutenant General
Army	3 or more Corps	General
Army Group	3 or more Armies	General

WWII Navy Reserve Training Programs

V-1   Accredited College Programs (NROTC)
V-2   Aviation Branch (pre-war aviation)
V-3   Communication Training
V-4   Intelligence
V-5   Aviation Cadet (college flight training)
V-6   General Duties (enlisted and specialists)
V-7   Midshipman Officer Candidate (officers for surface ships)
V-8   Aviation Pilot (enlisted pilots)
V-9   WAVE Officer Candidates
V-10 WAVE Enlisted Training
V-11 Midshipman Officer Candidate (older candidates)
V-12 College Training Program (professional & future officers)

Because the pre-war navy was so small, the rapid expansion of the navy after Pearl Harbor created a critical need for mid-level managers. There were two paths to a reserve commission:

The V-7 program. A four month program, usually at a college, after which the candidate was commissioned a 2nd Lt. in the marines or an ensign in the navy.

The V-11 program. To bring in experienced managers, those with advanced degrees or extensive experience were given direct commissions first, after a two month indoctrination school.

Current American Military Rankings

Officers

Rate	Army, Air Force, Marines	Navy, Coast Guard
O-1	2nd Lieutenant	Ensign
O-2	1st Lieutenant	Lieutenant (j.g.)
O-3	Captain	Lieutenant
O-4	Major	Lieutenant Commander
O-5	Lieutenant Colonel	Commander
O-6	Colonel	Captain
O-7	Brigadier General	Rear Admiral (lower half)
O-8	Major General	Rear Admiral (upper half)
O-9	Lieutenant General	Vice Admiral
O-10	General	Admiral

Enlisted

Rate	Army	Air Force
E-1	Private	Airman Basic
E-2	Private	Airman
E-3	Private 1st Class	Airman 1st Class
E-4	Corporal, Specialist	Senior Airman
E-5	Sergeant	Staff Sergeant
E-6	Staff Sergeant	Technical Sergeant
E-7	Sergeant 1st Class	Master Sergeant
E-8	1st Sgt./Master Sgt.	Senior Master Sergeant
E-9	Sgt. Major/Command Sgt. Maj.	Chief Master Sergeant

Rate	Marines	Navy, Coast Guard
E-1	Private	Seaman Recruit
E-2	Private 1st Class	Seaman Apprentice
E-3	Lance Corporal	Seaman
E-4	Corporal	Petty Officer 3rd Class
E-5	Sergeant	Petty Officer 2nd Class
E-6	Staff Sergeant	Petty Officer 1st Class
E-7	Gunnery Sergeant	Chief Petty Officer
E-8	1st Sergeant/Master Sgt.	Senior Chief P. O.
E-9	Sgt. Major/Master Gunnery Sgt.	Master Chief P. O.

Brief Chronology of Major Military Activities, Revolutionary War to Grenada

1773, December 16. Boston Tea Party at Boston Harbor.

1774, September 5. First Continental Congress convenes in Philadelphia.

1775, April 19. Battle of Lexington and Concord.

1775, June 15. Washington selected as Commander in Chief of the Continental Army.

1776, July 4. Continental Congress adopts Declaration of Independence.

1776, December 26. Battle of Trenton.

1782, August 7. Gen. Washington establishes Order of the Purple Heart.

1783, September 3. Peace Treaty signed in Paris granting the United States all land east of the Mississippi River, south of Canada, and north of the Floridas.

1812, June 18. Congress declares war on England.

1813, October 5. Gen. Harrison defeats British Gen. Proctor at the Battle of Thames in Canada.

1814, March 27. Gen. Andrew Jackson defeats Creek Indian Nation at the Battle of Horseshoe Bend.

1814, August 23. British troops invade Washington DC. The next day they set fire to the White House, Capitol and the Navy Yard.

1814, December 24. Treaty of Ghent signed, ending War of 1812.

1815, January 8. 2,000 British casualties at the Battle of New Orleans.

1836, March 6. After a 13-day siege, Mexican troops overwhelm the Texan defenders at the Alamo at San Antonio, Texas.

1836, April 21. Gen. Sam Houston defeats Gen. Santa Ana at the Battle of San Jacinto, earning independence for Texas.

1846, April 30–May 8. The Mexican Army crosses the Rio Grande, entering the new state of Texas. Battle of Palo Alto fought.

1846, May 13. Congress declares war on Mexico.

1847, February 22. Gen. Zachary Taylor, "Old Rough and Ready," disobeys orders and engages Gen. Santa Ana, winning the Battle of Buena Vista.

1847, September. American troops capture Mexico City.

1848, February 2. Treaty of Guadalupe Hidalgo ends war with Mexico.

1861, April 12. South Carolina troops fire on Ft. Sumter, starting the Civil War.

1861, July 18. First Battle of Bull Run.

1862, April 6–7. Battle of Shiloh.

1862, June 1. Robert E. Lee appointed commander of all Confederate forces.

1862, September 17. Battle of Antietam.

1862, December 13. Battle of Fredericksburg.

1863, May 2. Battle of Chancellorsville.

1863, July 2–4. Battle of Gettysburg.

1863, August 21. Quantrill's raiders invade Lawrence, Kansas killing every man in town and burning the buildings.

1863, September 20. Battle of Chickamauga.

1864, March 10. Ulysses S. Grant assumes command of the Union Army.

1864, July 30. Battle of Petersburg.

1864, November 15. Gen. Sherman begins his march to the sea.

1865, April 9. Lee surrenders Army of Northern Virginia at Appomattox Court House, Virginia.

1865, April 14. Lincoln assassinated by John Wilkes Booth.

1898, February 15. U.S. battleship *Maine* blows up in Havana harbor.

1898, April 11. President McKinley, against war, convinces Congress to issue an ultimatum to Spain to leave Cuba.

1898, April 22. U.S. blockades all Cuban ports.

1898, April 24. Spain declares war on U.S. U.S. retroactively declares war on Spain, effective April 21.

1898, May 1. Admiral Dewey defeats Spanish fleet in Manila Bay.

1898, July 1. Lt. Colonel Theodore Roosevelt leads his "Rough Riders" on a charge up Kettle Hill.

1898, July 17. U.S. forces under Gen. Shafter take Santiago.

1898, August 12. U.S. forces capture Manila. Spain signs an armistice.

1898, December 10. The Spanish American War formally ends with the signing of a treaty in Paris.

1914, June 28. Archduke Ferdinand is assassinated in Sarajevo, beginning the First World War.

1915, May 17. The *Lusitania* is torpedoed by a German U-boat.

1916, March 19. Pancho Villa leads raid into New Mexico, killing nine civilians and eight troopers of the 13th Cavalry. Troops under Gen. Pershing pursue Villa into Mexico.

1917, February 5. Gen. Pershing leaves Mexico, unable to capture Villa.

1917, April. U.S. declares war on Germany and enters war.
1918, July 8–August 6. Aisne-Marne Offensive.
1918, August 10. Gen. Pershing given command of American Expeditionary Force (AEF).
1918, September 26. Battle of Meuse-Argonne begins.
1918, November 11. World War I Armistice.
1921, October 27. Mussolini appointed Premier of Italy.
1933, January 30. Hitler becomes Chancellor of Germany.
1936, July 17. Civil War breaks out in Spain. Hitler and Mussolini send troops to aid Franco.
1938, March 12. Germany invades Austria.
1939, September 1. Germany invades Poland.
1939, September 3. France and England declare war on Germany.
1939, September 17. Soviet Union invades Poland.
1939, November 30. Soviet Union invades Finland.
1940, March 12. Soviet-Finnish war ends. Finland cedes territory.
1940, April 9. Germany invades Denmark and Norway.
1940, May 10. Germany invades Belgium, Holland and Luxembourg. Churchill elected Prime Minister of England.
1940, May 12. Germany invades France.
1940, May 14. Holland surrenders.
1940, May 26–June 4. Evacuation of Allied forces at Dunkirk.
1940, June 28. Belgium surrenders.
1940, June 9. Norway signs armistice with Germany.
1940, June 10. Italy declares war on France and England.
1940, June 11. Italy invades France.
1940, June 14. Fall of Paris.
1940, July 10. Battle of Britain begins.
1941, March 11. Lend Lease becomes law. U.S. begins supplying war materials to Allied forces.
1941, March 24. Field Marshal Rommel begins offensive in Libya.
1941, May 22. Germany, Italy and Rumania declare war on Soviet Union. Germany invades Soviet Union.
1941, October 17. Hedeki Tojo becomes Prime Minister of Japan.
1941, December 7. Japan attacks U.S. fleet at Pearl Harbor.
1941, December 8. Japan declares war on U.S. and Britain, attacks Phillippines, Wake Islands, Guam, invades Thailand, Malaya and Hong Kong.
1941, December 9. Japan invades Gilbert Islands.
1941, December 11. Germany and Italy declare war on U.S. Japan invades Burma.
1941, December 22. Japan begins offensive in Philippines.
1941, December 23. Wake Island falls. U.S. troops surrender.

1942, February 15. Singapore surrenders.
1942, April 9. U.S. troops surrender on Bataan.
1942, April 18. Doolittle leads air raid on Tokyo.
1942, May 6. U.S. fortress of Corregidor surrenders. U.S. forces in Phillippines surrender.
1942, June 4–6. Battle of Midway. End of Japan's eastward thrust.
1942, June 24. Eisenhower assumes command of U.S. forces in Europe.
1942, August 7. U.S. Marines land on Guadalcanal.
1942, November 8. Allies invade Morocco and Algeria.
1943, January 2. U.S. and Australian forces retake Buna, New Guinea.
1943, February 9. U.S. secures Guadalcanal.
1943, July 9. Allied invasion of Sicily.
1943, July 25. Mussolini overthrown and arrested. Marshal Pietro Badoglio assumes command.
1943, August 17. Allies capture Sicily.
1943, September 8. Italy makes peace with Allies.
1943, September 9. Allies land at Salerno, Italy.
1943, October 1. Allies liberate Naples.
1943, October 13. Italy declares war on Germany.
1943, November 1. U.S. invades Bougainville in the Solomon Islands.
1943, November 21. U.S. lands on Makin and Tarawa in Gilbert Islands.
1944, January 16. Eisenhower named Supreme Commander of Allied Forces in Europe.
1944, January 22. Allies land at Anzio.
1944, January 29. U.S. lands in Admiralty Islands.
1944, January 31. U.S. lands on Marshall Islands.
1944, March 22. U.S. forces land in Dutch New Guinea.
1944, June 4. Allies enter Rome.
1944, June 6. D-Day. Allies land at Normandy to invade Europe.
1944, June 15. U.S. bombs Tokyo. U.S. troops land on Saipan.
1944, June 19–20. Japanese fleet defeated at Battle of Philippine Sea.
1944, June 27. Allies liberate Cherbourg, France.
1944, July 25. Allies begin breakout from Normandy.
1944, August 10. Allies land in southern France.
1944, August 25. Paris liberated.
1944, September 1–4. Dieppe, Brussels and Antwerp liberated.
1944, October 20. U.S. forces land at Leyte in the Philippines.

1944, October 23. Gen. Charles De Gaulle recognized as leader of Provisional French Forces.

1944, October 23–26. U.S. naval forces defeats Japan at Battle of Leyte Gulf.

1944, November 7. Roosevelt wins fourth term as President.

1944, December 16. German counter-offensive begins in Ardennes; called Battle of the Bulge.

1945, January 9. U.S. forces invade Luzon, Philippines.

1945, January 16. Battle of Bulge ends with German defeat.

1945, February 3. U.S. forces enter Manila.

1945, February 13–14. Allies firebomb Dresden, Germany.

1945, February 19. U.S. forces land on Iwo Jima.

1945, March 7. Allies seize Remagen Bridge over Rhine.

1945, April 1. U.S. lands on Okinawa.

1945, April 12. Roosevelt dies. Truman becomes President.

1945, April 23. Soviets enter Berlin.

1945, April 29. German forces in Italy surrender. Allies liberate Dachau concentration camp.

1945, April 30. Hitler commits suicide in Berlin.

1945, May 1. Berlin surrenders.

1945, May 7. Germany formally surrenders.

1945, May 8. VE-Day (Victory in Europe Day).

1945, August 6. Atomic bomb dropped on Hiroshima.

1945, August 9. Atomic bomb dropped on Nagasaki.

1945, August 14. Japan surrenders.

1945, September 2. Formal surrender aboard USS *Missouri* in Tokyo Bay. V-J Day (Victory Over Japan Day).

1945, November 20. Nuremberg war crimes trial begins.

1949, April 4. North Atlantic Treaty Organization (NATO) formed.

1950, June 25. North Korea attacks South Korea beginning Korean War.

1950, July 1. U.S. forces land in Korea.

1950, October 7. U.S. forces cross 38th parallel in Korea.

1951, April 11. Gen. MacArthur relieved of command in Korea.

1953, July 27. Armistice ends Korean War.

1960, May 5. U-2 pilot Gary Powers shot down over Soviet Union. Sentenced on August 19 to ten years in prison. Exchanged for Soviet spy in February 1961.

1961, December 11. First U.S. military advisors arrive in South Vietnam (4,000 men, 32 helicopters).

1962, February 20. Marine Lieutenant Colonel John Glenn becomes first American to orbit Earth.

1962, March 9. Pentagon admits that U.S. pilots are flying combat missions in Vietnam.

1964, August 2. North Vietnamese P.T. boats attack U.S. destroyer in Gulf of Tonkin, allegedly in international waters. U.S. warships accompany South Vietnamese boats shelling North Vietnam.

1964, August 4–5. U.S. bombs North Vietnam in retaliation for attack.

1964, August 7. Gulf of Tonkin Resolution passed by Congress permitting the President to take military action to fight aggression in Southeast Asia. The resolution substituted for a declaration of war.

1965, February 7–8. U.S. begins policy of bombing North Vietnam.

1965, June 8. U.S. announces policy of allowing American troops to engage in direct combat if requested by South Vietnam. Twenty days later, first U.S. ground offensive begins.

1966, June. U.S. escalates war by bombing Hanoi. Congressional opposition increases.

1968, January 30. North Vietnam begins Tet Offensive, attacking major cities in South Vietnam.

1968, April 3. North Vietnam agrees to peace talks in Paris. Talks begin in May.

1969, July 20. Astronaut Neil Armstrong becomes first man to walk on the moon.

1969, November 15. Massive march in Washington DC protests U.S. involvement in Vietnam.

1970, April 30. U.S. invades Cambodian territory.

1970, May 4. National Guardsmen kill four students during anti-war protest at Kent State University, Ohio.

1971, June 13. *New York Times* publishes the Pentagon Papers.

1972, October 26. Secretary of State Henry Kissinger announces "peace at hand" in Vietnam.

1973, January 28. The U.S. and North Vietnam sign treaty ending direct U.S. military involvement in Vietnam.

1975, April 30. Last 1,000 Americans leave Saigon. Within hours the South Vietnamese government surrenders to North Vietnam ending a conflict that cost over 55,000 American lives.

1983, October 25–28. Invasion of Grenada.

Brief Chronology of the U.S. Selective Service (Draft), WWI to Vietnam War

1917, May 18. Selective Service Act of 1917 enacted.

1917, June 5. Registration of men ages 21–30.

1939, September 8. President Roosevelt declares a limited national emergency.

1940, August 31. President orders National Guard to active duty.

1940, September 16. Selective Training and Service Act of 1940 enacted.

1940, October 7. First local draft boards appointed.

1940, October 16. Men ages 21–35 must register with Selective Service.

1940, November 18. First inductees sent to army induction centers.

1943, January 1. Voluntary enlistments prohibited for men 18–37; all* must enter armed forces through Selective Service.

1947, March 31. Selective Training and Service Act allowed to expire.

1948, June 24. Selective Service Act of 1948 enacted.

1951, April 23. First call for physicians under the "Doctor Draft" (Public Law 779, September 9, 1950).

1951, June 19. Universal Military Training and Service Act enacted; replaces 1948 Act.

1967, June 30. Military Selective Service Act of 1967 enacted; replaces 1951 Act.

1970, April 23. After this date no new occupational, agricultural or paternity deferments granted.

1971, September 28. Amendments to Military Selective Service Act phase out deferments for students; institute uniform national call based on lottery numbers with youngest men drafted first.

1972, December. Last calls for inductees received from Department of Defense.

July 1, 1973. President's authority to induct expires; armed forces rely solely on volunteers.

*All except 17-year-olds and those over 36. These were allowed to enlist. The navy had an upper age limit of 51 to enlist older men with construction skills for the Seabees.

Bibliography

A Narrative of the Life of David Crockett, by Himself. University of
Nebraska Press, 1987.
A Separate Battle: Women in the Civil War, Ina Chang. Penguin
Books, 1991.
Aaron Burr: Portrait of an Ambitious Man, Herbert Parnet and Marie
Hecht, Macmillan Co.
All My Yesterdays, Edward G. Robinson, Leonard Spigelgass.
Hawthorn Books, 1973.
America at D-Day, Richard Goldstein, Dell Publishing, 1994.
American Medals and Decorations, E. Kerrigan. Mallard Press,
1990.
Biographical Directory of the American Congress, 1774–1971, U.S.
Government Printing Office, 1971.
Black Fighting Men in U.S. History, Edward Wakin. Lothrop, Lee,
and Shepard Co, 1971.
Bob Hope's Own Story: Have Tux Will Travel, Pete Martin. Simon
and Schuster, 1954.
Bogey, Clifford McCarty. Citadel Press, 1965.
The Book of Womens' Firsts, Phyllis Read, Bernard Witlieb. Random
House, 1992.
Bugs Bunny: 50 Years and Only One Grey Hare, Joe Adamson.
Henry Holt and Co, 1990.
Captain Tripps: A Bio of Jerry Garcia, Sandy Troy. Thunder Mouth
Press, 1994.
Cesar Chavez: Autobiography of La Causa, Jacques Levy. W.W.
Norton & Co, 1975.
Citizen Nader, Charles McCarry. Saturday Review Press, 1972.
Conduct Unbecoming, Randy Shilts. St. Martin's Press, 1993.
Confession and Avoidance: A Memoir, Leon Jaworski, Mickey
Herskowitz. Anchor Press (Doubleday), 1979.
Cosby, Ronald L. Smith. Thorndike Press, 1986.
Cosell, Howard Cosell. Playboy Press, 1973.
Crossed Currents: Navy Women, WWI to Tailhook, Jean Ebbert, Marie
Beth Hall. Brasseys, 1993.
David Brinkley: A Memoir, David Brinkley. Alfred Knopf, 1995.
Donovan of O.S.S., Corey Ford. Little, Brown and Co, 1970.
Dr. Suess and Mr. Geisel, J. and N. Morgan. Random House, 1995.
Dr. Spock: Biography of a Conservative Radical, Lynn Z. Bloom.
Bobbs-Merrill Co, 1972.

Earl Warren: A Public Life, G. E. White. Oxford University Press, 1982.
Education of a Wandering Man, L. L'Amour. Bantam Books, 1989.
Facts About the Presidents, Joseph Kane. H.W. Wilson Co, 1993.
The Fairbanks Album, Richard Schickel. Little, Brown Co, 1975.
The Films of Clark Gable, Gabe Essoe. Citadel Press, 1970.
Fiorello La Guardia: A Biography, B. Rodman. Hill and Wang, 1962.
The Fitzgeralds and the Kennedys, Doris Kearns Goodwin. Simon and Schuster, 1987.
Fonda, My Life, Howard Teichmann. New American Library, 1981.
Frank Capra: The Name Above the Title, F. Capra. Macmillan, 1971.
Go for Broke: History of 442nd Regiment, Chester Tanaka. Go for Broke Inc.
Goldwyn: A Biography, A. Scott Berg. Alfred A. Knopf, 1989.
Good Grief: The Story of Charles M. Schulz, Rheta Grimsley Johnson. Pharos Books, 1989.
Great Lives, Nature and the Enviornment, Doris and Harold Faber. Charles Scribner & Sons, 1991.
The Great Stage Stars, Sheridan Morley. Facts on File, 1986.
Great Time Coming: The Life of Jackie Robinson, David Falkner. Simon and Schuster, 1995.
Hefner, Frank Brady. Macmillan Publishing, 1974.
Henry Cabot Lodge, William Miller. James Heineman Inc, 1967.
Heroes of WWII, Edward F. Murphy. Presidio Press, 1990.
The Hustons, Lawrence Grobel. Charles Scribner's Sons, 1989.
In My Own Fashion, Oleg Cassini. Simon and Schuster, 1987.
The Invisible Soldier, Mary Pennick Motley. Walden State University Press, 1975.
It Wasn't All Velvet, Mel Torme. Penguin Books, 1988.
I've Had It: Survival of a Bomber Group Commander, Colonel Beirne Lay. Harpers Brothers, 1945.
Jack Benny, Mary Livingstone Benny. Doubleday and Co, 1978.
James Garner, Raymond Strait. St. Martin's Press, 1985.
James Michener, John P. Hayes. Bobbs Merrill Co, 1984.
James Stewart, Helene McGowan. Crescent Books, 1992.
JFK: Reckless Youth, Nigel Hamilton. Random House, 1992.
Jimi Hendrix: Electric Gypsy, H. Shapiero. St. Martin's Press, 1990.
Jimmy Stewart: A Wonderful Life, J. Coe. Arcade Publications, 1994.
John Fitzgerald Kennedy, Bill Harris. Crescent Books, 1983.
Josephine Baker, Patrick O'Connor. Jonathan Cape (London), 1988.

Joycelyn Elders MD, Joycelyn Elders and David Chanoff. Wm. Morrow Co, 1996.

Justice Oliver Wendell Holmes, G. Edward White. Oxford University Press, 1993.

The Kennedys: An American Dream, Peter Collier, David Horowitz. Summit Books, 1984.

Kerouac: A Biography, Ann Charters. St. Martin's Press, 1973.

King of the Night: The Life of Johnny Carson, Lawrence Leamer, Wm. Morrow and Co, 1989.

Kit Carson's Autobiography, Kit Carson, Milo Quaife. University of Nebraska Press, 1966.

The Landry Legend, Bob St. John. Word Publishing, 1989.

Last of the Great Outlaws, H. Croy. Duell, Sloan and Pierce, 1956.

Leaving Home: A Memoir, Art Buchwald. G.P. Putnam's Sons, 1993.

Legend: The Secret World of Lee Harvey Oswald, Edward Jay Epstein. McGraw-Hill, 1978.

Lincoln Library of Essential Information. Frontier Press Co, 1964.

Lindbergh: A Biography, Leonard Mosley. Doubleday and Co, 1976.

The Lone Star: The Life of John Connally, J. Reston Jr. Harper Row.

Mailer: His Life and Times, Peter Manso. Simon Shuster, 1985.

Margaret Bourke-White: A Biography, Vicki Goldberg. Harper and Row Publishers, 1986.

Mountain, Get Out of My Way, M. Williams. Thorndike Press, 1996.

My Turn at Bat, Ted Williams. Simon and Shuster.

My War, Andy Rooney. Random House, 1995.

The Nine Lives of Mickey Rooney, Arthur Marx. Stein and Day, 1986.

Nixon: Education of a Politician, S. Ambrose. Simon Shuster, 1987.

Once There Was a War, John Steinbeck. Viking Press, 1958.

Orders and Decorations of All Nations, R. Werlich, Quaker Press, 1965.

P.S. Jack Paar, Jack Paar. Doubleday, 1983.

Palimpest: A Memoir, Gore Vidal. Random House, 1995.

Pappy: The Life of John Ford, Dan Ford. Prentice Hall.

Paul Newman, J. C. Landry. McGraw Hill, 1983.

Rendezvous by Submarine, T. Ingham. Doubleday, Doran Co, 1945.

Rewrites: A Memoir, Neil Simon. Simon and Schuster, 1996.

Ribbons of Orders, Decorations and Medals, G. Rosignoli, Arco Publishing, Blanchford Press, 1976.

Rock Hudson: His Story, Rock Hudson, Sara Davidson. Morrow and Co, 1986.

Rod Serling: Dreams and Nightmares, Joel Engel, Contemporary Books, 1989.
The Salad Days, Douglas Fairbanks Jr. Doubleday, 1988.
Say Hey: The Autobiography of Willie Mays, Willie Mays, Lou Sahadi. Simon and Schuster, 1988.
Scott Fitzgerald, Andrew Turnbull. Scribners, 1962.
The Secret Life of Tyrone Power, H. Arce. Morrow and Co, 1979.
Spencer Tracy, Alison King. Crescent Books, 1992.
Spencer Tracy: Illustrated History, Romano Tozzi. Pyramid Publications, 1973.
Stars in Blue, J. Wise, A. Collier Rehill. Naval Institute Press, 1997.
Stone, James Riordan. Hyperion Press, 1995.
The Story of Walt Disney, D. Disney Miller. Curtis Publishing, 1956.
Sugar Ray, Sugar Ray Robinson, Dave Anderson. Viking Press, 1994.
Sword of San Jacinto: A Life of Sam Houston, Marshall de Bruhl. Random House, 1993.
This Life: Sidney Portier, Sidney Portier. Alfred Knopf, 1980.
Time Enough to Win, R. Staubach, F. Lursa. Word Books, 1980.
To Be Loved, Berry Gordy. Warner Books, 1994.
Tom Mix, Paul E. Mix. MacFarland Co, 1995.
Traps, the Drum Wonder: The Life of Buddy Rich, Mel Torme. Oxford University Press, 1991.
Waltzing Matilda: The Life and Times of Senator Robert Kerry, Ivy Harper. St. Martin's Press, 1992.
Webster's American Biographies, Merriam Co.
Webster's American Military Biographies, Robert McHenry, Ed. Miriam-Webster Inc, 1978.
When the Stars Went to War, Roy Hoopes. Random House, 1994.
Why Me?, Sammy Davis Jr, Boyar Farrar. Straus and Giroux, 1989.
William Wyler, Axel Madsen. Thomas Crowell Co.
Winchell, Neal Gabler. Alfred A. Knopf, 1994.
Women in the Military, Maj. Gen. Jeanne Holm. Presidio Press, 1982.
Woody Guthrie: A Life, Joe Klein. Alfred Knopf, 1980.
World Book of America's Presidents. World Book Encyclopedia, 1982.
WWII: Strange and Fascinating Facts, Don McCombs, Fred Worth. Wing Books, 1983.
Zanuck, Leonard Mosley. Little Brown and Co, 1984.
Zero Mostel: A Biography, Jared Brown. Antheneum, 1989.

Index

(Main entries are in **bold**.)

Bookstore

How to Locate Anyone Who Is or Has Been in the Military: Armed Forces Locator Guide (8th Edition) by Lt. Col. Richard S. Johnson (Ret). Learn all conceivable means of locating current and former members of the Air Force, Army, Coast Guard, Marine Corps, Navy, Reserve and National Guard. This new edition is completely updated and expanded. Includes a new chapter on using the Internet to find people. 300 pages, $19.95.

Find Anyone Fast (2nd Edition) by Richard S. Johnson and Debra Johnson Knox. Father-daughter private investigators teach you how easy it is to find anyone using state-of-the-art computer searches. Includes a detailed chapter on using the Internet and comprehensive State resource section. 261 pages, $16.95.

Checking Out Lawyers by Don Ray—the first in the *Check 'Em Out* Series of do-it-yourself investigating books. It helps you decide if you really need a lawyer and how to find the best lawyer out of the crowd. Provides a listing of useable resources including state bar associations, secretary of states, and bankruptcy court information. Know that you're dealing with the best! 188 pages, $15.95.

Secrets of Finding Unclaimed Money by Richard S. Johnson. An experienced heir searcher reveals all the secrets of finding unclaimed money held by state unclaimed property offices, other state agencies and the federal government. He also teaches how to earn money by becoming a professional heir searcher. Includes sample forms and contracts. 182 pages, $11.95.

Please add $4.05 shipping/handling to all orders. Send to:

MIE PUBLISHING
PO Box 17118
Spartanburg, SC 29301
(800) 937-2133, (864) 595-0813 Fax
www.militaryusa.com, E-mail: miepub@aol.com